THE REAL WATERGATE SCANDAL

THE *REAL*
WATERGATE
SCANDAL

COLLUSION, CONSPIRACY, AND THE PLOT THAT BROUGHT NIXON DOWN

GEOFF SHEPARD

REGNERY
HISTORY

Regnery History™ is a trademark of Salem Communications Holding Corporation; Regnery® is a registered trademark of Salem Communications Holding Corporation

Library of Congress Cataloging-in-Publication Data

Shepard, Geoffrey Carroll, 1944-
 The real Watergate scandal : collusion, conspiracy, and the plot that brought Nixon down / Geoff Shepard.
    pages cm
  ISBN 978-1-62157-328-9
  1. Watergate Affair, 1972-1974. 2. Nixon, Richard M. (Richard Milhous), 1913-1994. 3. United States--Politics and government--1969-1974. 4. Conspiracies--United States--History--20th century. I. Title.
  E860.S529 2015
  973.924--dc23

                                            2015012716

Distributed to the trade by
Perseus Distribution
250 West 57th Street
New York, NY 10107

Manufactured in the United States of America

10 9 8 7 6 5 4 3 2 1

Books are available in quantity for promotional or premium use.
For information on discounts and terms, please visit our website: www.Regnery.com.

Published in the United States by
Regnery History
An imprint of Regnery Publishing
A Division of Salem Media Group
300 New Jersey Ave NW
Washington, DC 20001
www.RegneryHistory.com

*To the outstanding group of men and women
who served honorably and with distinction
in the Nixon administration*

Prud'hon's *Justice and Divine Vengeance Pursuing Crime*

CONTENTS

INTRODUCTION

MY ROLE

I was there, in the room, at the very moment Richard Nixon's Watergate defense collapsed. It was a Monday afternoon, July 26, 1974, just hours after the Supreme Court had upheld the special prosecutor's subpoena for sixty-four more White House tape recordings. Fred Buzhardt, special counsel to the president and Nixon's principal defense lawyer, had been directed to review one conversation in particular. It had taken place on June 23, 1972, just six days after the Watergate burglary arrests. Soon known as the "smoking gun," it revealed Nixon concurring with his staff's recommendation that they get the CIA to tell the FBI to limit its Watergate investigation. Nixon could not explain the tape, and Buzhardt had no reason to think it was anything other than confirmation that the president himself had authorized an obstruction of justice within a week of the Watergate arrests.

On that Monday afternoon, Buzhardt telephoned Nixon and his chief of staff, Alexander Haig, and told them what he had heard on the June 23 tape. With no explanation forthcoming and bound by the Court's ruling, the president's lawyers quickly concluded they could no longer support his efforts to avoid impeachment. Left alone and defenseless, the Nixon presidency quickly collapsed.

I was in Buzhardt's office during that conversation and remember it as vividly as if it were yesterday. As soon as it ended, I became the third person to hear that key tape. I was the one who prepared its official transcript and the one who named it the "smoking gun."

One of Watergate's great ironies is that we all misinterpreted that recorded conversation. John Dean, President Nixon's principal accuser, has recently acknowledged that the president and his defense team were totally mistaken about that tape and its significance. If we had known the context in which that conversation had taken place, the president would not have had to resign and, in Dean's own words, "could have lived to fight another day."

But resign he did, just four days following the tape's public release. I was in the East Room of the White House when he bid his staff adieu and on the South Lawn when his helicopter lifted off for the last time. It was the saddest day of my life, but my association with Richard Nixon neither started nor ended with Watergate.

It is as though I have been living in Nixon's shadow since I came of age, and happily so. Readers deserve to know this background, so they can properly appreciate the analysis and disclosures that follow.

I was Nixon's junior by some thirty years. Like him, I was born and raised in Southern California. I know what it is like to have grown up far from the liberal Eastern establishment in what was then the cultural backwater of greater Los Angeles. I first heard Nixon speak in 1960, when he was running for president, at something called the Iowa Picnic in Long Beach. So many people from the Hawkeye state had moved to the area in the 1930s and '40s that it was known as "Iowa by the Sea," and their annual picnic was a huge social affair. A junior at Woodrow Wilson High School, I'd been assigned to write a paper on Nixon's speech. I don't remember much of what he said, but I do recall my disappointment that he talked more about his family's Iowa connections than about the weighty issues of the day. It made it tough to write my report.

Our paths crossed again five years later at a scholarship luncheon given by the Republican Women's Club of Whittier, California. Now a junior at Whittier College, Nixon's alma mater, I had just been elected student body president and had won the Richard Nixon scholarship— worth $250, not an insignificant sum in those days to a struggling student. Since that speech at the Iowa Picnic, Nixon had lost the 1960 presidential race to John Kennedy and the 1962 California gubernatorial race to Pat Brown. He had decided to quit politics for good and relocated to New York City to practice law. He was loyal to Whittier College but hadn't come all that way just to present my award. Having arranged for Bob Hope to be Whittier's commencement speaker that year, Nixon came for the graduation ceremony. To everyone's pleasant surprise, the former vice president also came to the ladies' luncheon, and I was seated next to him. We talked about our respective college experiences, he gave a nice speech about how much Whittier meant to him, and we parted ways. The following week I learned that Nixon, upon returning to New York, had personally doubled my scholarship. Money was tight in those days, and even after fifty years I still consider myself indebted to him for his generosity.

The following year, I was off to Harvard Law School (again on scholarship), and Nixon was off to pursue the presidency. Somewhere in my files, I still have the homemade campaign badge that says "Nixon Shepard," as though I were his running mate. After all, I had made no secret to my Harvard classmates about my hopes to be a part of his administration, should he be victorious.

He was and so was I. A month after Nixon's victory, at the ripe age of twenty-four, I applied to be a White House Fellow. I ended up being among the youngest ever chosen for that outstanding program, which is essentially a year-long seminar on how the federal government functions. I spent my fellowship year working at the Treasury Department for Paul Volcker, then the undersecretary for monetary affairs. At its conclusion, I landed a much coveted position on John Ehrlichman's White House Domestic Council staff, where I stayed for five years and eventually became associate director for general government.

And so this backward kid from Irvine Ranch ended up as the youngest policy-making lawyer on the White House staff. A little like Nixon himself, I had enjoyed a fast rise. I had been student body president and a champion team debater at Whittier. I had also graduated with honors from Harvard Law School, been selected a White House Fellow, and landed a prestigious position on the White House staff. Nixon's rise, however, was through electoral politics; I was ecstatic just to be a member of his staff.

Years later, I learned that Nixon and I had studied under the same English professor at Whittier, although three decades apart. It seems clear that this was why the president liked my policy memos (I prepared hundreds of them over my five years on his staff)—he was unconsciously seeing the same organizational structure and approach that he'd been taught as a Whittier student many years before.

Again, like Nixon, I had had my share of disappointments growing up, but things were really coming up roses for me, at least until the Watergate scandal came along. Having been on Nixon's staff almost from the outset, and my policy responsibilities extending to the Department of Justice, I knew and had worked with virtually every major Watergate figure. I was on John Ehrlichman's staff and had reported to Egil ("Bud") Krogh, later to gain notoriety as the head Plumber. Gordon Liddy was a colleague at Treasury and at the White House. Chuck Colson's office was right across the hall; John Dean's was just down the corridor.

When H. R. Haldeman, Ehrlichman, and Dean left at the end of April 1973, to be replaced by Alexander Haig and Fred Buzhardt, I sought a place on the president's Watergate defense team. I never changed payrolls, but quickly began functioning as Buzhardt's principal deputy. I ran the document rooms that housed the files maintained by Haldeman, Ehrlichman, and Dean. I helped to hire and assimilate the dozen lawyers who assisted James St. Clair, the president's outside defense lawyer. I transcribed all of the White House tapes that were included in the Blue Book released to the public at the end of April 1974. And I was the official White House representative at the Supreme Court oral arguments in the case that ultimately upheld the subpoena for those White House tapes.

As you already know, it was all for naught. We failed in our defense, and the president was forced to resign. My responsibilities, however, did not end with his departure. Because of my legal work, I ended up being a chain-of-custody witness for the government at the Plumbers trial and was subpoenaed to appear in the same capacity in the cover-up trial. Testifying against my former colleagues, even about something as mundane as how a particular document or tape got from their files to the courtroom, was excruciatingly painful.

After so many of my friends and former colleagues had resigned in disgrace and been marched off to jail, I deemed myself a "Nixon hold-over"—one of those who ought to leave government for the good of the country. After helping with the transition to President Ford, I voluntarily left early in 1975.

As close as I was to the tsunami that was Watergate, I was fortunate to have emerged relatively unscathed. The special prosecutor even provided a letter, carefully preserved in my safe deposit box, stating that I was not and had never been the object of any investigation of his office. Mine is one of only two such letters that were written on behalf of former members of the Nixon White House staff.

As does everyone else who was in the Nixon White House, I have strong personal feelings about my former colleagues. Many I hold in the highest esteem. Those whom I believe to have been culpable I studiously avoid. On balance, President Nixon attracted an exceptional group of people to his administration. Having worked on the policy development side, I am particularly proud of Nixon's many accomplishments in both foreign and domestic affairs and have done my best to keep in touch with the people responsible for these successes and to help preserve an accurate record of how they were achieved.

For over thirty-five years, I have arranged and hosted annual reunions of Nixon's White House staff who worked on policy analysis and development. Most of these people served on the staff of the Domestic Council, the Office of Management and Budget, or the National Security Council. The others, who worked elsewhere in the White House on policy implementation, were counselors, speechwriters, and congressional relations staff. But the annual reunions are only part of the story. Long before email, cell phones, and the internet, my office maintained a directory of where and how former staff members could be reached. Real expertise in governance is quite scarce, and I'm proud of my role in holding our team together. Ours is the only former White House staff that gathers every year to discuss issues of governance.

Since 2010, I have helped produce a series of Nixon Legacy Forums highlighting many of the public policy initiatives of our administration. They allow those who helped with a particular policy formulation to explain the background of the documents available to scholars and researchers. Preparing for each forum is something like preparing for a trial. We have to review the initiative, its documentation, and the people involved, and we have to remind ourselves of how it all came about and what results were achieved. There have been more than thirty forums so far, all co-sponsored by the Richard Nixon Foundation and the National Archives. The programs are available on their respective websites, as well as my own (www.geoffshepard.com). Most have been broadcast on C-SPAN's American History channel. Ours is the only administration producing such group oral histories.

———————

That's my background. I believe that Nixon was unfairly hounded from office and that the public has been misled about the Watergate scandal. By 2002, it was apparent that others who were on the inside of Nixon's Watergate defense were not going to write about their experiences, so I resolved to do so myself. I discovered that the records of the Watergate Special Prosecution Force (like those of any governmental agency) are maintained by the National Archives and can be obtained by request under the Freedom of Information Act. I have spent hundreds of hours at Archives II in College Park, Maryland, which houses most executive branch records, and Archives I on the National Mall, which houses congressional and court records. Papers of other Watergate luminaries, including Judge John Sirica and Edward Bennett Williams, are housed at the Library of Congress.

My first Watergate book, *The Secret Plot*, published in 2008, detailed how Nixon's political opponents exploited the scandal with such success. This second book reveals how others, particularly judges and lawyers who should have known better, committed gross violations of legal propriety. By cutting ethical and legal corners in the Watergate prosecution, they made a mockery of the rule of law and inflicted a "cure" on our body politic far worse than the disease.

I have spent fifty years in Nixon's shadow, explaining and defending the actions of a fellow Californian and Whittier alumnus. Much more remains to be done. The American public deserves a better understanding of Watergate, and this book is meant as a down-payment. Before turning to the wrongdoings of the prosecutors and jurists who toppled the Nixon administration, I want to set the stage with a brief account of the accomplishments of the man who supposedly was the worst president of our lifetime.

RICHARD NIXON, A MAN IN FULL

But for Watergate, Richard Nixon would have gone down in history as one of America's greatest presidents.

The only president born and raised in California, Nixon had an unexceptional childhood but one characterized by earnest dedication and hard work, only to be followed by disappointment. He was not handsome, and, like most Americans, he did not come from great family wealth or enjoy the head start of an Ivy League education. Yet this man, his ideas, and the people he attracted to our nation's capital dominated American political debates for the second half of the twentieth century, and their influence is still felt today.

Who was this man and what did America lose when he fell?

COMING OF AGE

Richard Milhous Nixon was born in 1913 in Yorba Linda, an agricultural community of some two hundred people thirty-five miles east of Los Angeles, dominated by acres and acres of citrus groves. When he was still very young, his family moved to nearby Whittier, where his father ran a general store. In later years he would recall lying awake at night listening to the sounds of trains disappearing into the distance and wondering about the faraway places they were headed. He longed for more.

Nixon graduated second in his high school class and won a scholarship to Harvard, but his family couldn't afford the loss of his help with the store. So he went instead to the small Quaker college just four blocks up the street. He lived (and worked) at home—as did about a third of his classmates—commuting to classes and other activities on campus. Still, he worked hard at fitting in: he was champion team debater and student body president. He weighed too little to excel at football, so he mainly warmed the bench, but he never gave up trying to make the first string.

After Whittier College, where he finished second in his class, Nixon attended the newly established Duke University law school in North Carolina. Despite graduating third in his law school class, he was unable to land a job with a New York City firm or even with the FBI. He ended up returning home and joining the two-man firm of Wingert and Bewley in downtown Whittier.

With America's entry into World War II, Nixon joined the navy, served in the South Pacific, and rose to the rank of lieutenant commander. While preparing to muster out, he received an invitation from back home that caused his life to dramatically change course.

RAPID RISE IN POLITICS

The sudden six-year rise to the pinnacle of national politics that followed is the stuff of legend, but Nixon also incurred the life-long enmity of a growing cadre of political opponents and media critics. It was personal, it ran deep, and it eventually evolved into the visceral hatred that continues to this day.

A returning veteran, Nixon was recruited by local Republicans to challenge Whittier's five-term incumbent congressman, Democrat Jerry Voorhis. Though he was a political novice, Nixon devoted himself to his campaign with the same single-minded determination that had set him apart as a student. The nation's mood was changing, and 1946 was not a good year for incumbents anywhere, but Voorhis also was not prepared for the intensity of his challenger. Nixon won 56 percent of the vote in a stunning victory over a popular incumbent. But there was a price to pay. He had knocked off the congressman voted most popular by the Washington press corps—and they were not pleased that he had bested their good friend.

The Republican congressional leadership, who saw Nixon as a hardworking moderate, convinced him to accept an appointment to the House Un-American Activities Committee, which was already displaying some of the tendency to excess that would boil over in the Senate during the McCarthy era, years after Nixon had left that arena. But what Nixon proceeded to do was seen by Democrats as outright sacrilege: He led the committee's investigation into communist penetration of the Truman administration's State Department, which culminated with the exposure of Alger Hiss as traitor and perjurer.

This is not the place to re-hash that much-told story, but two points should be mentioned. First, Hiss was everything that Nixon was not. An honors graduate of Harvard Law School, where he had been a protégé of Felix Frankfurter, Hiss had clerked for Supreme Court Justice Oliver Wendell Holmes. Beginning in 1936, he held a series of prominent positions within the State Department, including serving as the executive secretary of the Dumbarton Oaks Conference, which led to the creation of the United Nations, and being a part of the department's delegation to the Yalta Conference, where Roosevelt, Churchill, and Stalin decided how to divide Europe following Hitler's defeat. The Un-American Activities Committee's investigation was dismissed by many as amateurish, and Hiss demeaned Nixon for his non-Ivy academic background, but Nixon pursued his prey with the same determination he displayed throughout his life.

Second, and perhaps more importantly, Nixon never saw the Hiss case as just a *mano a mano* contest. Years later, as the Watergate scandal unfolded, even his closest aides would misunderstand Nixon's constant references to Hiss—there were dozens of them in the White House tapes. Nixon was not referring to the man himself but was voicing his twin convictions that the truth eventually will emerge and that the real damage from the Hiss scandal was not to Hiss, but to the Truman presidency itself.

Nixon came to national prominence as a result of this investigation, and Hiss was convicted of perjury in 1950. The liberal Eastern establishment, particularly its many Harvard-educated members, never forgave Nixon for his leadership in bringing down one of their own.

The next step in Nixon's rise to political prominence was his 1950 run for the Senate. His eventual opponent was Helen Gahagan Douglas, a graduate of Barnard College and a Broadway star in the 1920s. Barnard is the sister college to Columbia University in New York City and one of the Seven Sisters (the female counterpart to the Ivy League). Douglas had also starred in a successful movie, *She*, before running for Congress in 1944. Once there, she had a rather public affair with Congressman Lyndon Johnson of Texas. Douglas was the first congresswoman from California and had served three terms representing the San Francisco Bay area before deciding that her real place was in the Senate. To get there, she had to challenge California's three-term Democratic incumbent, Sheridan Downey.

Downey withdrew from the primary in the face of Douglas's aggressive challenge, so it technically became an open seat. Regardless, her contest against Nixon was by all accounts a vicious campaign. Douglas was liberal, moneyed, and a movie star. Nixon was unglamorous but doggedly competent. When the smoke cleared, Nixon won by almost 20 percentage points, handing a devastating loss to the liberal establishment. Two epithets that came to prominence during their contest were "the Pink Lady" (first used by another of Douglas's Democratic primary opponents) and "Tricky Dick."

Oscar Wilde observed "You can always judge a man by the quality of his enemies." By that standard, Dick Nixon was quite a success, since he had incurred the life-long hatred of the entire liberal establishment, whether they lived in the Northeast, the San Francisco Bay area, or in Hollywood.

Nixon's star continued its ascendency. In 1952, Dwight Eisenhower chose him as his running mate. His six-year rise from novice and unknown congressman to vice president of the United States was as spectacular as any in American political history. And Nixon had done it all by himself—without family money or connections and without being someone's protégé. He had also earned a reputation for hardball campaigning, which he maintained in his new position. Eisenhower, a military hero who could have run on either ticket, did not have to stoop to partisan politics; he had a vice president ready and willing to undertake those difficult tasks for him.

PRESIDENTIAL CANDIDATE

When Nixon finally won the presidency in 1968, he was perhaps the best prepared victor in modern times: Not only was he a former congressman, senator, and vice president, but he had lost an exceptionally close race in 1960 and had had eight years to think about what he would do if he ever got to the Oval Office.

Those eight wilderness years had seen some bitter moments, too. The loss to Kennedy must have galled him to no end, for JFK (like Alger Hiss and Helen Douglas) was everything that Nixon wasn't. He was movie-star handsome, with an equally beautiful wife. He was the son of one of the richest men in America and had been raised in the lap of luxury. And he was Eastern establishment and Harvard through and through. Nixon said that writing his first memoir, *Six Crises*, was the hardest thing he had ever attempted. Kennedy's *Profiles in Courage*, which was awarded a Pulitzer Prize, was ghost-written by Ted Sorensen. When the PT boat Kennedy commanded was run over by a Japanese destroyer in World War II (an unthinkable blunder to any navy veteran, including Lt. Commander Nixon), he was decorated for valor instead of being court martialed. Dubbed the playboy senator, he had no important legislation to his name, but the media adored him. Courageous and scrappy but drab, Nixon could not compete with Kennedy's glamour and lost one of the closest elections in history.

Nixon had come of age at the dawn of television, but that medium was never his friend. Though he saved his place on Eisenhower's ticket with his famous Checkers speech in 1952, he convincingly lost the first televised presidential debate with Kennedy in 1960, and his campaign never really recovered. In today's era of Botox and blow-dried hair, of the sound bite and the photo-op, it is not clear that Nixon could ever have been successful. He was small-bore, rural America. In addition, Nixon was, as he freely admitted to his staff, an introvert in an extrovert's game.

Nixon was accustomed to the rough and tumble of politics, both local and national, but he was often on the receiving end. For example, Nixon believed he had been bugged in each of his three previous campaigns. As the Watergate scandal grew in intensity, the Republican National Committee released sworn affidavits showing that the hotel suite in which Nixon prepared for the opening debate with John Kennedy in 1960 had been bugged. His opponent's ability to anticipate every point he made in their first encounter, Nixon believed, had cost him the debate, and losing that first debate had cost him the presidency.

Nixon's grand jury testimony from July 1975, which was released in 2010, revealed his barely controlled anger at having been bugged again in 1962 during his California gubernatorial campaign against Edmund G. "Pat" Brown. No one in authority had cared or done anything about it. He also pointed out, with equal bitterness, that his tax returns had somehow been leaked from the IRS in that same race.

Finally, J. Edgar Hoover himself told Nixon that he had been ordered by President Johnson to bug Nixon's plane during the final two weeks of the 1968 campaign, to monitor Nixon's possible response to Johnson's announced bombing halt, and telephone numbers dialed during the campaign by Nixon's running mate, Spiro Agnew, were reconstructed. Scholars disagree about the nature of the surveillance that was actually carried out, but Nixon was nevertheless personally assured by the head of the FBI that President Johnson had ordered such bugging. Nor was the harassment of Nixon by his enemies limited to spying. The IRS had audited his income tax returns every year of the Kennedy and Johnson administrations.

THE 1968 CAMPAIGN

Nixon's election in 1968 was seen by many, especially Democrats and the liberal media, as an electoral fluke—one which would be corrected four years hence. Johnson's unpopular war, the assassinations of Robert Kennedy and Martin Luther King Jr., and the chaos of the Democratic National Convention in Chicago had combined into the perfect storm to allow the hated Nixon to slip undeservedly into the Oval Office. What they failed to appreciate was that Nixon had been elected precisely in response to those same events.

People who did not live through it have difficulty understanding the political unrest of the 1960s. It began with the civil rights marches, grew to include the massive and violent opposition to the Vietnam War, and culminated, many think, in Nixon's resignation in 1974. By 1968, as the nation swirled toward anarchy, the Kennedy brother and King had been assassinated, there had been violent riots in at least nineteen cities, and great universities had been brought to their knees by student sit-ins and protests.

Nixon's election did not alleviate the anti-war sentiments that had driven Johnson from office—it only served to increase them. Democrats had held their displeasure in check when one of their own occupied the Oval Office, but now they turned with vehemence on Richard Nixon, and they encouraged the protests, which grew in frequency and intensity.

Nixon's basic campaign promise was twofold: He would end the war and he would restore law and order. It was enough to win the popular vote over Hubert Humphrey by a single percentage point (43.42 percent to Humphrey's 42.72 percent, with third-party candidate, George Wallace, siphoning off 13.53 percent).

1968 is now seen as a realigning election, marking the end of the New Deal coalition first assembled by Franklin Roosevelt, but this realignment was not recognized at the time. Nixon's election was seen as an aberration. He was the first president to take office since Zachary Taylor whose party did not control either house of Congress. The

Goldwater debacle, in which down-ballot Republicans had lost in droves, had taken place only four years earlier, and the Democrats' congressional majorities approached the two-thirds mark. Further, there was no institutional support in Washington for the incoming thirty-seventh president. Congressional staffs, the city's law and lobbying firms, its few think tanks, the federal career civil service employees, whose numbers had expanded so rapidly under Johnson's Great Society initiatives, and the national media themselves all leaned heavily Democratic.

NIXON'S PEOPLE

President Nixon was sufficiently confident of his own views and abilities to surround himself with strong and accomplished advisors, several of whom had not supported his campaign. Among them were Henry Kissinger, Nelson Rockefeller's long-time foreign affairs advisor, and Daniel Patrick Moynihan, a liberal Democrat who had served in the Kennedy administration. Both were professors at Harvard, the cradle of so much opposition to Nixon throughout his political career. Senior advisors also included Arthur Burns, of Columbia University, and George Shultz, of the University of Chicago. But from the time of the '68 campaign, his three closest aides were the ones who figure so prominently in Watergate: John Mitchell, Bob Haldeman, and John Ehrlichman.

John Mitchell was a preeminent municipal bond lawyer and Nixon's law partner at Nixon, Mudge, Rose, Guthrie, Alexander, and Mitchell. Born the same year as the president, he had that aura of self-confidence that comes from being a senior partner in a big city law firm. Because municipal bond work is frequently entwined with local politics, Mitchell had excellent and long-standing contacts in cities and counties throughout the country. While hardly an accomplished politician, he was treated as an equal by the president, which was why he was an excellent choice to head Nixon's 1968 campaign. He then did an outstanding job as Nixon's attorney general, ruling with a soft touch but an iron hand. Career officials in the Department of Justice, who had chafed under his predecessor, the nebbish Ramsey Clark, welcomed Mitchell with open arms. I worked with dozens of DOJ officials during my Domestic Council years, and, to a man, they were in awe of John Mitchell, believing him to be an eminently fair and impartial enforcer of the law. One assistant attorney general observed to me that he was struck by Mitchell's self-control—never saying a single word more than he felt necessary.

The criticism you hear of Mitchell's tenure as AG reflects the partisan bitterness of the opposition party. His later problems, and they were considerable, stemmed not from his work at Justice but from his role as head of the Committee to Re-Elect the President and from his wife, Martha, whose alcohol-fueled late-night phone calls with eager reporters brought an end to his time in Washington.

Harold Robbins ("Bob") Haldeman, a California native like Nixon, graduated from UCLA and joined the J. Walter Thompson advertising agency. Thirteen years Nixon's junior, he took time off to work in Nixon's campaigns. He was an advance man in 1956 and 1960, and ran Nixon's 1962 gubernatorial campaign. Crew-cut, intensely loyal, and unafraid of personal confrontations, he was Nixon's chief of staff for the first four years. He is known for his observation that every president needs an SOB and he was Nixon's. Haldeman ran a tight ship and tolerated no fooling around or lackadaisical staff attitudes.

I freely admit that I was scared to death of him, convinced that nothing good could result from coming to his attention. I worked for Ehrlichman, and the only way I might be noticed by Haldeman would be as a result of a screw-up. On my first trip on Air Force One, having put together a presidential visit to Laredo to showcase drug interdiction programs, I noticed Haldeman chatting with Ehrlichman, while looking my way. Uh-oh, I thought, he's asking just who let this kid on the plane—when John brought him over and introduced me as the one who staffed the president on narcotics interdiction initiatives. To my surprise and great relief, Haldeman was complimentary and as nice as he could be.

I later came to realize, when spending hundreds of hours transcribing the White House tapes, that Haldeman—in the privacy of the Oval Office—was the president's most candid critic. Far from being a "yes man," Haldeman was the voice of reason and restraint. In a very real sense, he was an ideal chief of staff, possessing absolute power over whom and what Nixon would see, but entirely without a political agenda of his own. His only goal was to be sure the president heard all points of view before making a decision.

Haldeman's associate in this effort was his UCLA roommate, John Ehrlichman, who had graduated from Stanford Law School and then practiced law in Seattle. Initially counsel to the president, Ehrlichman became assistant to the president for domestic affairs and head of the Domestic Council staff in July 1970—essentially Kissinger's counterpart on the domestic side. Ehrlichman was popular with virtually everyone on the staff, even taking flowers to the White House operators, whose ability to locate recipients of White House phone calls was renowned.

Ehrlichman is largely responsible for President Nixon's innovative record on domestic policy initiatives, and he was not the least bit hesitant about sharing credit for good ideas. He encouraged his Domestic Council staff, including me, to be sure that the president received all points of view on policy issues. We counted ourselves the most fortunate members of the White House staff, responsible for addressing policy and governance issues of national importance in an atmosphere that encouraged the full and free exchange of ideas.

The Haldeman-Ehrlichman "Berlin Wall" so decried by their many critics was really an accommodation to President Nixon's approach to governance. A deep thinker who was put off by personal salesmanship, Nixon demanded that ideas, proposals, and issues be presented in written form—not unlike legal opinions—which he would then think through in the privacy of his hideaway in the Old Executive Office Building. Oval Office and Cabinet Room sessions were mainly ceremonial or information-gathering events; the real decisions were made on the basis of written analyses, candidly and thoroughly discussed with only a handful of trusted aides. It was not that Nixon was uninformed of differing points of view, it was that he preferred to receive those views in written form rather than in face-to-face meetings.

Mitchell, Haldeman, and Ehrlichman were dedicated, talented public officials, who produced outstanding work. Their reputation as thoroughly corrupt evil-doers, unfit for public service, is utterly undeserved.

ACCOMPLISHMENTS AS PRESIDENT

It took Nixon until June 1969 just to get the last of his cabinet secretaries through confirmation—and the sub-cabinet appointments for a department could not even be formally submitted until the secretary had been confirmed. Given these challenges, it is astonishing how much Nixon actually accomplished. But he had thought long and hard about what he wanted to do if he should ever return to power. Far from being content to sit and wait for issues to be presented for decision (to "preside," in the literal sense), Nixon arose each day filled with ideas and an urgency to get them accomplished. He was, in the truest sense, leading as president, every day and every step of the way.

There were many initiatives and many disappointments, but Nixon's major accomplishments can be grouped into three categories: foreign affairs, domestic policy, and the institution of the presidency.

No president since Nixon has entered office with a background and expertise in foreign policy comparable to what he brought to the presidency in 1969. With Henry Kissinger as his assistant for foreign affairs, he scored a string of victories in a very difficult era. He saw himself as a peacemaker and spoke of achieving a full generation of peace. He ended the most controversial foreign war in American history. He engineered the opening to China after twenty-five years of isolation, something only a strong anti-communist like Nixon could do. He achieved détente with the Soviet Union and laid the groundwork for the strategic arms limitation treaties. In the challenging arena of the Middle East, Nixon befriended Anwar Sadat and wooed Egypt from the Soviet orbit, making it a strong U.S. ally. He strengthened our ties with other critical allies in the region, including Jordan and Saudi Arabia, and he almost single-handedly saved Israel through his forceful intervention in the 1973 Yom Kippur War. But Nixon's greatest foreign policy triumph might have been his revitalization of the National Security Council under Henry Kissinger. Together they developed an approach to planning and analysis and trained a cadre of professionals that began America's golden era of diplomacy. They and their progeny continue to serve and advise Republican leaders to this day.

Nixon was elected to the presidency in a time of domestic turmoil. He ran on a strong law and order platform but exercised a surprising degree of compassion toward his political adversaries. Sir Robert Thompson, the noted counter-insurgency expert, has astutely observed that unless a government can address the legitimate concerns of its citizens, particularly perceived injustices, it can never be successful against an insurgency. Though Nixon receives little credit for it, he addressed an astonishing number of injustices. His agenda had no catchy moniker like the "New Deal" or "Great Society," but we might fairly call it the "Pursuit of the Just Society." Here's why.

The Nixon administration extended a helping hand to a surprisingly large group of oppressed minorities, never expecting and rarely receiving any acknowledgment or gratitude in return. He achieved the peaceful desegregation of Southern schools in the fall of 1971, he continued the integration of Northern unions under the Philadelphia plan, and he brought home rule to the District of Columbia. He restored the right of self-determination to Native Americans, ending the previous policy of assimilation, which paid Indians to give up their treaty rights and relocate to inner cities. He quadrupled the number of women appointed to senior government positions and signed Title IX, which ended funding discrimination in college sports. He established the National Institutes of Mental Health, ended the draft, and gave eighteen-year-olds the vote. He created the Environmental Protection Agency, the National Oceanic and Atmospheric Administration, and proposed both the Clean Air and Clean Water acts. He restored respect for law and order in a nation swirling toward anarchy. He initiated a program of block grants to states and localities that not only assured fair allocations of federal funds, but removed the heavy hand of federal bureaucrats in determining how such money was spent. He launched the War on Drugs and broke the inner-city heroin epidemic through a methadone maintenance program that was coupled with stronger law enforcement. It is a record of enviable domestic accomplishments and was achieved by working in partnership with a Congress totally controlled by the opposition party.

Besides these foreign and domestic accomplishments, President Nixon instituted a series of enduring organizational reforms that laid the foundation for the modern presidency. In addition to revitalizing the National Security Council under Henry Kissinger, he established its counterpart, the Domestic Council, under John Ehrlichman and transformed the old Bureau of the Budget into the Office of Management and Budget under George Shultz and Roy Ash. He professionalized the presidential appointment process under Fred Malek, recruiting hundreds of highly qualified persons into the executive branch. Each of these organizational initiatives has withstood the test of time, helping each new president to establish his hold on the levers of power and influence to manage the executive branch.

Richard Nixon compiled an enviable record of presidential accomplishment. As the world burns in the absence of U.S. leadership, partisan gridlock ties up Washington, and the economy languishes, we should pine for a leader with Nixon's vision, expertise, and ability to work across party lines.

NOW, ABOUT WATERGATE

I began my assessment of Richard Nixon by asserting that, but for Watergate, he would have gone down in history as one of America's great presidents. But Watergate did happen, and it vastly diminished Americans' appreciation of all of the good just detailed.

I know, I was there—on the White House staff from Watergate's beginning to its dramatic conclusion. I knew and worked with virtually everyone involved—in the scandal and in Nixon's defense. It was like watching a slow-motion train wreck, with the crew and passengers alike caught in the crushing of the cars.

PART I

A BASIC WATERGATE BACKGROUND

CHAPTER 1

IDENTIFYING THE REAL WRONGDOING

OPENING SALVO

Even serious students of Watergate are not aware that the "smoking gun" tape that drove Nixon from office has been misinterpreted and had nothing to do with the crimes of Watergate. Most people don't realize that John Dean, who was sentenced to a prison term of one to four years for his role in the Watergate scandal, never spent a day behind bars, or that the prosecutors' contention that Nixon himself had authorized the final "hush money" payment (the core of their case against him at the time) proved to be totally erroneous.

Something that Carl Sagan wrote about the popular understanding of science applies equally as well the public's understanding of Watergate:

One of the saddest lessons of history is this: If we've been bamboozled long enough, we tend to reject any evidence of the bamboozle. We're no longer interested in finding out the truth. The bamboozle has captured us. It's simply too painful to acknowledge, even to ourselves, that we've been taken. Once you give a charlatan power over you, you almost never get it back.[1]

In politics, as in war, truth is usually the first casualty. It certainly was in the Watergate scandal. This book is my attempt to set the record straight. I intend to expose some of the charlatans who bamboozled the American people, and you'll be surprised to find out who they were.

Historians may eventually conclude that Nixon was done in by his political enemies, but they'll continue to insist that, as Nixon put it himself, he "gave them the sword." Surprisingly, that's not what happened. Oh, Nixon had political enemies, boatloads of them. But politicians will always act like politicians. They have danced on their opponents' graves since time immemorial. But his many political enemies are not the ones who did Nixon in.

No, Nixon was done in by officers of the court, the very people sworn to uphold the law and the Constitution—federal judges and federal prosecutors, who met in secret and reached back-room deals on how best to take him down and secure convictions of his senior aides. That is the *real* Watergate scandal, a story told for the first time in this book.

I have recently uncovered documents at the National Archives that make it clear that as the Watergate scandal unfolded, federal judges hearing the Watergate cases held secret meetings with persons whose interests were adverse to President Nixon's and his top aides'. The most outrageous of these confidential gatherings were the *ex parte* meetings between judges and Watergate prosecutors. I have been able to document ten of them, but it's likely there were many more. As Leon Jaworski, the second Watergate special prosecutor, later confided to the reporter Bob Woodward, "there were a lot of one-on-one conversations that nobody knows about except [me] and the other party."

Secret meetings, secret documents, secret collusion between judges and prosecutors, culminating in the reversal of the will of the people expressed in President Nixon's re-election—that's the part of the Watergate scandal that has remained hidden until now. The subversion of the right to due process guaranteed by the Fifth and Sixth Amendments to the Constitution was part of a conscious plan to engineer the downfall of the president and the conviction of his senior aides. The principles that were violated are basic. You don't need a law degree to understand and appreciate them, and they go to the very heart of our constitutional form of governance.

In his landslide re-election, Nixon received every vote in the Electoral College except those of the Commonwealth of Massachusetts and the District of Columbia. The effort to un-elect him was led, fittingly enough, by people from those two political jurisdictions.

I will elaborate on these charges in the chapters that follow, and I have reproduced in full the most damning documentation in the appendices. But before proceeding to the details of the judicially assisted coup that brought down Nixon, it is important to explain the context in which it occurred.

PUTTING WATERGATE INTO CONTEXT

In 1808, Pierre Paul Prud'hon painted the allegorical *Justice and Divine Vengeance Pursuing Crime* for the criminal tribunal hall in the Palace of Justice in Paris.[2] The painting, which now hangs in the Louvre, captures the universal aspiration that criminals be brought to account, in this world or the next. As Prud'hon himself described it,

> Divine Justice is forever pursuing crime; and crime never gets away. Wrapped in the veil of night, in a remote and wild place, voracious Crime has killed a victim, taken his gold and is turning to see whether any remains of life might give him away. Fool! He does not see that Nemesis, that terrible agent of Justice, like a vulture descending upon his prey, is pursuing him, will catch him and hand him over to his unbending companion.

Americans share these deep-seated feelings about justice. They are expressed less colorfully but majestically in the words carved into the west pediment of the Supreme Court building in our nation's capital: EQUAL JUSTICE UNDER LAW. Though this phrase appears in none of our founding documents—it was suggested in 1935 by the building's architect, Cass Gilbert—it nonetheless reflects our nation's faith in the pursuit of justice under the rule of law.[3]

A corollary of this maxim—"No man is above the law"—became a leitmotif of the Watergate scandal. And the "man" in question was the president of the United States, since he and senior members of his staff stood accused of having covered up the identities of those responsible for planning and authorizing the break-in at the offices of the Democratic National Committee in the Watergate office building on June 17, 1972.

The ensuing investigations and disclosures culminated in Nixon's resignation and the conviction and incarceration of over twenty of his former associates.[4] The most notable of those associates were John Mitchell, Bob Haldeman, and John Ehrlichman, who were found guilty in the Watergate cover-up trial, which ended on January 1, 1975, some two and a half years after the break-in.

While justice, symbolized by the fearsome companion of Vengeance in Prud'hon's painting, means the pursuit and punishment of wrongdoers, Americans also believe that it entails the right to a fair trial. Lady Justice, therefore, is more commonly depicted as blindfolded, to represent impartiality, and serenely holding a set of balancing scales in one hand and a double-edged sword in the other. Indeed, virtually all Americans would agree that the more heinous the crime or notorious the accused, the more essential it is that the trial is fair.

The public was assured that justice had prevailed in the aftermath of the Watergate scandal, that Haldeman, Ehrlichman, and Mitchell had been tried and convicted by a jury of their peers, and that their convictions had been duly reviewed and upheld on appeal. After a full and fair process, each was sentenced to a prison term of two and half to eight years.

And there things have stood for the past four decades.

Documents recently uncovered, however, show that these men—regardless of their conviction in the court of public opinion—did not receive anything close to the fair trial guaranteed by our Constitution. Without a fair trial, of course, a jury could not have rendered a valid verdict.

The internal records generated by the Watergate Special Prosecution Force are still being released by the National Archives, but only in response to requests under the Freedom of Information Act. Recently released records provide many of the missing pieces to the Watergate puzzle, pieces that have never before been available to researchers or to the general public.

Those documents and other disclosures that form the heart of this book reveal how, at a time of intense and highly politicized partisan combat, the constitutional rights of criminal defendants were intentionally trampled. They show that the judges and prosecutors involved in the Watergate trials met and reached agreements designed to assure convictions. These people cheated justice and then they lied to the appellate courts about having done so.

When judges conspire with prosecutors, any pretense of a fair trial is lost. There were at least a dozen secret meetings between Watergate judges and prosecutors or other interested parties, summarized in the chart on pp. 6–7.

Prominent and distinguished public officials, all members of the bar, violated their oaths of office in order to obtain convictions they believed were richly deserved. It is a sordid tale of meetings, memos, and collusion. These men undermined our Constitution's guarantees of due process and the even-handed application of justice.

The consequences of these prosecutorial and judicial misdeeds have extended far beyond injustices to individuals. These convictions were the capstone of the Watergate scandal. President Ford's pardon may have allowed Nixon himself to escape criminal prosecution, but the conviction of his senior aides on all counts was intended to extinguish any doubt that they and the president they served were as guilty and as evil as the public had been led to believe.

Ex Parte Meetings

	Date	Participants	Purpose	Source
1	12/72 Series of Meetings	Federal District Court Chief Judge John Sirica and former White House Special Counsel Clark Mollenhoff	To convince Sirica that senior Nixon aides must have been involved in Watergate	Mollenhoff's two books: *Game Plan for Disaster* (1978) and *Investigative Reporting* (1981)
2	12/72 Two Known Meetings	Judge Sirica and Counsel for the Democratic National Committee and the *Washington Post*, Edward Bennett Williams	To convince Sirica to go easy on Bob Woodward and Carl Bernstein, who had approached Watergate grand jurors	Evan Thomas's biography of Williams, *The Man to See* (1991)
3	1/73	Judge Sirica and Principal Ass't U.S. Attorney Earl Silbert	To tell Silbert how Sirica felt they should conduct the break-in prosecutions	Sirica's book, *To Set the Record Straight* (1979)
4	3/73	Judge Sirica and Ervin Committee Chief Counsel Samuel Dash	To convince Sirica to impose harsh temporary sentences, with possible reduction dependent upon cooperation with the Ervin Committee's investigations	Dash's book, *Chief Counsel* (1976)
5	6/19/73	Judge Sirica and Special Prosecutor Archibald Cox	Unknown	Newspaper reports cited in defendants' appeal brief
6	7/18/73	Judge Sirica and Special Prosecutor Cox	Unknown	Associated Press report cited in defendants' appeal brief
7	9/73	Special Prosecutor Cox and DC Circuit Chief Judge David Bazelon	To urge Bazelon to stack the appellate panels on appeals from Judge Sirica's trials	Bazelon's law clerk, Ronald Carr
8	11/5/73	Judge Sirica and newly appointed Special Prosecutor Leon Jaworski	Courtesy call on first day in office	Jaworski's handwritten "to do" list (in his papers at National Archives)

	Date	Participants	Purpose	Source
		Ex Parte Meetings		
	Date	**Participants**	**Purpose**	**Source**
9	12/14/73	Judges Sirica and Gesell, along with Special Prosecutors Leon Jaworski, Henry Ruth (Deputy), Philip Lacovara (Counsel to the Special Prosecutor) and Richard Ben-Veniste (Deputy Director of the Watergate Task Force)	To discuss status of Watergate investigations and possible creation of an additional grand jury	Jaworski's 12/27/73 letter to Sirica (Appendix C)
10	1/2/74	Judge Sirica, along with Special Prosecutors Lacovara and Peter Kreindler (Executive Assistant to the Special Prosecutor)	To follow up on rumor about Silbert that Sirica had heard at a New Year's Eve Party	Lacovara's 1/2/74 memo to Richard Ben-Veniste (in Jaworski's papers at National Archives)
11	2/11/74	Judge Sirica and Special Prosecutor Jaworski	To inform Judge Sirica of the prosecutors' intent to have the grand jury issue a special sealed report about President Nixon to the House Judiciary Committee.	Lacovara's 1/23/74 memo to Jaworski proposes such a meeting. (Appendix D) Jaworski's 2/12/74 memo confirms its occurrence (Appendix E)
12	3/1/74 Pre-Hearing	Judge Sirica and Special Prosecutor Jaworski	To coordinate conduct of indictment presentation, such that Sirica could appoint himself to preside over the cover-up trial	Jaworski's 3/1/74 memo to file (Appendix H)
13	3/1/74 Post-Hearing	Judge Sirica and Special Prosecutor Jaworski	To review the hearing and coordinate any further actions	Jaworski's 3/1/74 memo to file (Appendix H)

If the validity of those convictions is undermined, then the lid is removed from the Watergate scandal and all sorts of issues resurface: Do we really know who authorized and directed the original break-ins? Are we certain of who actually was running the subsequent cover-up? Is it possible that President Nixon was unfairly run out of town by an overly aggressive and highly partisan team of prosecutors, who were secretly sharing their mistaken conclusions with the House Judiciary Committee's impeachment inquiry?

Had due process prevailed, the Watergate prosecutions would have been handled far differently:

- The trials would have been held outside of the District of Columbia, most likely in Baltimore or Richmond, and far away from the taint and bias of Judge Sirica and a Washington jury.
- The cases would have been presented by career federal prosecutors, bound by rules and procedures applicable to all federal criminal prosecutions.
- Prior inconsistent statements by John Dean and Jeb Magruder would have been shared with defense counsel, as required by law, allowing their credibility as the government's principal accusatory witnesses to be aggressively challenged.
- Appeals from any convictions would have been heard by three-judge panels of the Fourth Circuit Court of Appeals, a dramatically more conservative appellate court than the D.C. Circuit.

The issues I raise in this book could well have led an unbiased jury to acquit one or more of the principal defendants. Such an acquittal would have raised questions about the forces that culminated in President Nixon's resignation. We might today have a far different view of the Watergate scandal and of Richard Nixon and his three top aides, Mitchell, Haldeman, and Ehrlichman.

CHAPTER 2

UNDERSTANDING WATERGATE

To understand Watergate, it is important to know the key figures and the basic chronology of the scandal.

KEY WATERGATE FIGURES

WHITE HOUSE STAFF

Before April 30, 1974:

H. R. "Bob" Haldeman (1926–1993), Chief of Staff. Convicted on all counts in the cover-up trial.

John Ehrlichman (1925–1999), Assistant to the President for Domestic Affairs. Convicted on all counts in the cover-up trial.

Charles "Chuck" Colson (1931–2012), Special Counsel to the President. Prominent political operative; indicted in the cover-up case, but pleaded guilty in the Plumbers case instead. Became a government witness in the cover-up trial.

John Dean (1938–), Counsel to the President. Coordinator of the cover-up, who switched sides to become the government's principal witness in the cover-up trial.

Gordon Strachan (pronounced "strawn") (1943–), Haldeman's liaison to the Committee to Re-Elect the President. A young lawyer from Nixon's law firm, he was indicted in the cover-up case but never brought to trial because of a grant of immunity from the Ervin Committee.

After April 30, 1974:

Alexander Haig (1924–2010), Chief of Staff. Career military officer, former National Security Council deputy director under Kissinger and later secretary of state under President Reagan.

Fred Buzhardt (1924–1978), Special Counsel to the President. Lead Watergate defense counsel. Former legislative aide to Senator Strom Thurmond and general counsel for the Defense Department.

Charles Alan Wright (1927–2000), outside counsel retained to defend the president in the White House tape litigation. Distinguished law professor at the University of Texas and the leading authority on federal procedure.

James St. Clair (1920–2001), Special Counsel to the President. Outside counsel retained for Watergate defense. Top litigator at the Boston firm of Hale and Dorr.

COMMITTEE TO RE-ELECT THE PRESIDENT (CRP)

Coming from the Department of Justice (DOJ):

John Mitchell (1913–1988), Director. Nixon's first attorney general. Convicted on all counts in the cover-up trial.

Robert Mardian (1923–2006), Special Counsel. Former assistant attorney general. Helped CRP respond to the civil suit brought by the Democratic National Committee. His conviction in the cover-up case was reversed and remanded on appeal but never re-tried.

Fred LaRue (1928–2004), Special Assistant. Former Mitchell aide at DOJ. Pleaded guilty to a single count of obstruction of justice and became a government witness in the cover-up trial.

Coming from the White House:

Jeb Magruder (1934–2014), Chief of Staff. Former White House deputy director of communications. Liddy's supervisor at CRP and active in the cover-up. Pleaded guilty to a single count of obstruction of justice and became a government witness in the cover-up trial.

Gordon Liddy (1930–), Counsel to the Finance Committee. A former FBI agent, he orchestrated break-ins at the office of Daniel Ellsberg's psychiatrist on behalf of the White House Plumbers unit, as well as DNC offices in the Watergate office building. Convicted in the break-in trial and served the longest prison term of any defendant (over five years).

Coming from the Central Intelligence Agency:

Howard Hunt (1919–2007), Consultant. Partner in crime with Gordon Liddy on both break-ins. Pleaded guilty to all six counts in the break-in trial and granted immunity from further prosecution. Became a government witness in the cover-up trial.

James McCord (1924–), Outside consultant retained to oversee CRP security. The wiretap expert on the Watergate break-ins, he was one of the five burglars arrested on June 17, 1972. Convicted in the break-in trial. His letter to Judge Sirica is credited with triggering the cover-up's collapse.

FEDERAL PROSECUTORS

Career prosecutors in the U.S. attorney's office:

Earl Silbert (1936–), Principal Assistant U.S. Attorney for the District of Columbia. Became U.S. attorney in 1974.

Assistant U.S. Attorneys *Seymour Glanzer* and *Donald Campbell*
Watergate Special Prosecution Force (WSPF):
Special Prosecutors:

Archibald Cox (1912–2004). First Watergate Special Prosecutor, May 19–October 20, 1973. Harvard law professor and confidant of the Kennedy family.

Leon Jaworski (1905–1982). Second Watergate Special Prosecutor, November 1, 1973–October 25, 1974. Managing partner of Fulbright & Jaworski in Houston.

Staff Prosecutors:

Henry Ruth (1932–2012), Deputy (and third Watergate Special Prosecutor, October 25, 1974–October 6, 1975); Philip Lacovara, Counsel; Peter Kreindler, Executive Assistant.

Watergate Task Force:

James Neal (1929–2010), Lead Counsel; Richard Ben-Veniste, Deputy; Other Counsel: George Frampton, Peter Rient, Judith Denny.

FEDERAL JUDGES

John Sirica (1904–1992), Chief Judge of the U.S. District Court for the District of Columbia. A biased and publicity-seeking judge who appointed himself to preside over both the break-in and cover-up trials.

Gerhard Gesell (1910–1993). Judge of the U.S. District Court for the District of Columbia. Presided over other Watergate trials, including the Plumbers case.

David Bazelon (1909–1993), Chief Judge of the U.S. Court of Appeals for the District of Columbia, which heard all appeals from the Watergate trials. Deeply biased, he stacked the appeals court panels to assure that Judge Sirica was not reversed.

CRIMINAL DEFENSE COUNSEL

Charles Shaffer (1932–2015), counsel for John Dean. A former DOJ prosecutor and a brilliant and resourceful lawyer who obtained far more lenient treatment for Dean than he deserved.

William Bittman (1931–2001), counsel for Howard Hunt. A former DOJ prosecutor who was heavily involved in the cover-up payoffs. It is all but impossible to explain why he was not indicted in the cover-up case, as was recommended by the entire Watergate Task Force.

THE FALSE HEROES OF WATERGATE

The focus of this book is not the three famous defendants convicted in the cover-up trial—John Mitchell, Bob Haldeman and John Ehrlichman—but five other men—two judges, two special prosecutors, and the government's principal accusatory witness—whose collusion in undermining the rule of law in the Watergate prosecution has only recently come to light. Though these men have been lionized by the press, no one who dispassionately examines their misdeeds can regard any of them as a "hero" of Watergate.

Before his role in the Watergate prosecution propelled him to national fame and *Time* magazine's selection as its Man of the Year for 1973, John Sirica[1] had had what is charitably characterized as an undistinguished legal career. He never attended college and twice dropped out of law school before finally graduating in 1925. He admitted in his memoir that he seldom understood the legal concepts being taught. Small of stature but arrogant and stubborn to a fault, he had moved to Miami after graduation to pursue his boxing career and was as surprised as anyone when notified that he had passed the bar exam.

Working as an assistant U.S. attorney in the District of Columbia during the Prohibition, Sirica lost each of his first seventeen prosecutions. It has been suggested that this may have been intentional, since his father (with whom he lived) was secretly peddling liquor from his barber shop. With the repeal of Prohibition, Sirica returned to private practice, later recalling it as his "period of starvation." His situation improved dramatically after he joined the Washington law firm of Hogan & Hartson at the behest of his career mentor, the prominent Democrat and trial lawyer Edward Bennett Williams.

President Eisenhower appointed Sirica to the federal District Court in 1957. Feisty and argumentative on the bench, Sirica earned the nickname "Maximum John" because of his harsh sentencing, and his lack of respect for defendants' rights made him one of the most frequently reversed judges in the D.C. Circuit. By operation of seniority he became chief judge in 1971, a position he would have to relinquish on his seventieth birthday—less than three years away—on March 19, 1974.

Sirica became convinced that he alone could thwart the cover-up and bring Nixon and his top aides to justice—*his* justice and in *his* courtroom. He assumed for himself the combined roles of Prud'hon's Vengeance and Divine Justice, rather than that of blindfolded Lady

Justice, impartially presiding over trials in which it was the jury's job to weigh the evidence. The actions and initiatives of this arrogant jurist are the key to understanding how the defendants' constitutional rights were so thoroughly disregarded throughout the scandal.

When President Truman appointed forty-year-old David Bazelon[2] to the court of appeals for the D.C. Circuit in 1949, he became the youngest judge ever to sit on that powerful bench. Bazelon had been an assistant U.S. attorney in Illinois and then an assistant attorney general at the Department of Justice at the very time that Congressman Nixon was ravaging Truman and his administration over the Alger Hiss scandal. Bazelon became chief judge of his court—like Sirica, merely by operation of seniority—in 1962.

Bazelon was a relentlessly liberal and highly influential judge on the second-most important court in the country. He was also the best friend of Justice William Brennan, who had replaced Earl Warren as the leader of the Supreme Court's liberal bloc. The two judges socialized two or three times each week and invested together in real estate ventures. Aspiring liberal lawyers knew that the ideal career path began with a clerkship for Judge Bazelon, followed by a clerkship with Justice Brennan, culminating with a position on the Senate staff of Edward Kennedy.

Bazelon improperly conspired with Watergate prosecutors to stack the appellate panels to assure that Sirica's bizarre judicial conduct did not result in any reversals on appeal.

Professor Archibald Cox,[3] the original special prosecutor, came from an exceptionally distinguished legal background. After graduating from Harvard College in 1934 and from Harvard Law School in 1937, he clerked for Judge Learned Hand of the Second Circuit and joined the Harvard Law School faculty shortly after World War II. A lifelong Democrat and a friend of John Kennedy since the 1950s, Cox traveled with the candidate and served as his speechwriter and advisor during the 1960 presidential campaign. Cox went on to serve as solicitor general at the Department of Justice under Robert Kennedy. After his return to Harvard, he acted as an informal advisor to Edward Kennedy as the senator emerged from his Chappaquiddick scandal to lead the opposition to President Nixon's first-term Supreme Court nominations.

Distinguished, erudite, and professorial, Cox was the ideal figure to preside over the legal assault on the Nixon presidency, though at sixty-one he was already losing his hearing and showing his age. After only six months as special prosecutor, he was fired in what is known as the "Saturday Night Massacre" of October 20, 1973. But six months was enough time for him to staff the WSPF with equally ardent liberal Democrats. Indeed, six of his seven top assistants had served with him in Robert Kennedy's Department of Justice, and after Cox's departure the Watergate prosecution continued along the lines he had established.

In targeting specific Nixon aides for investigation and prosecution, Cox allowed partisan politics to undermine equal protection of the laws. He also became so worried that Sirica's judicial antics constituted reversible error that he secretly approached Judge Bazelon with a remedial plan.

Leon Jaworski was appointed as Cox's successor as special prosecutor in November 1973. He had undertaken special assignments for the Kennedy Department of Justice but was really a Southern Democrat and a confidant of Lyndon Johnson. A graduate of Baylor Law School in Waco, Texas, Jaworski had served as a prosecutor at the Nuremberg trials following World War II. He later joined the firm that became Fulbright & Jaworski in Houston, which he led to national prominence, and served as president of the American Bar Association.

There are indications of considerable tension and mistrust between Jaworski and the attorneys recruited by his predecessor, who prided themselves as "Cox's Army" and were intent on retaliating for their leader's abrupt removal. Jaworski, it seemed, had a tiger by the tail. Unable to gain control over the intense partisanship of the special prosecutor's office, he exercised only minimal influence—and certainly not leadership—over the investigations already well underway when he arrived. Jaworski's one-year tenure included the successful litigation over access to the White House tape recordings, the indictment of the president's senior aides for the Watergate cover-up, and the resignation and subsequent pardon of Nixon.

When Jaworski resigned and returned to Texas in October 1974, shortly after the beginning of the cover-up trial, he took all of his confidential Watergate files with him, effectively preventing any scholarly access to them for almost four decades.[4] Those files, recently opened at my behest, reveal a series of secret meetings with Judge Sirica and raise troubling questions about how the subjects of the comprehensive indictment for the Watergate cover-up were selected. In hindsight, Jaworski's indictments look like a preview of the prosecutorial abuse that has become a tradition in Texas, where the political weapon of a baseless but highly publicized indictment has been turned on three prominent Republicans—Senator Kay Bailey Hutchison, House Majority Leader Tom DeLay, and Governor Rick Perry.

John Dean,[5] the principal government witness in the cover-up trial, had become counsel to the president despite his thin experience as a lawyer, an undistinguished academic record, and a surprising number of false starts early in his career. For reasons that remain unclear, Dean repeatedly transferred (and at somewhat odd times) from one school to another; he did not graduate from the high school, college, or graduate school in which he had originally enrolled. Dean also had been summarily fired after only six months from his first and only job in private practice—at a boutique law firm specializing in broadcast licensing—for what was described as unethical conduct.

After this inauspicious beginning, however, Dean had enjoyed a meteoric rise as a young Washington lawyer, beginning with a post as a minority counsel for the House Judiciary Committee. In the new Nixon administration, Dean was appointed associate deputy attorney general for legislation at the Department of Justice and then named counsel to the president in June 1970. In the latter capacity he became involved in domestic intelligence issues and recruited Gordon Liddy to prepare a campaign intelligence plan for CRP.

In the course of his work with Liddy, Dean had attended two meetings in the attorney general's office in which Liddy's illegal campaign proposals were described and discussed. When the Watergate burglars were caught, therefore, Dean found himself in serious risk of prosecution. He quickly became, in his own words, "chief desk officer" for the ensuing cover-up, coordinating efforts to thwart the FBI and grand jury investigations that followed. He instigated and oversaw payments of money to the burglary defendants and their lawyers, sat in on all FBI interviews of White House personnel, and coordinated the administration's overall Watergate defense.

In addition to obstruction of justice, Dean committed a series of other distinctly criminal acts. He twice helped to rehearse Magruder for his perjured testimony before the grand jury, he obtained and improperly shared government investigatory information with the Watergate defense counsel, he destroyed evidence that had been removed from Howard Hunt's White House safe, and he embezzled campaign funds stored in his office safe, supposedly to pay for his honeymoon.

When the cover-up collapsed, Dean was the first to approach prosecutors to seek immunity for testimony against his former colleagues—a course of action that worked out well for him. Dean's testimony that he had undertaken these and other criminal acts at the direction and under the control of Nixon's principal aides—Mitchell, Haldeman, and Ehrlichman—resulted in their convictions. Recently uncovered documents show, however, that Dean's recollections changed over the course of his meetings with prosecutors and that clearly exculpatory information about what he had shared with prosecutors was kept from Watergate defense counsel.

Now a successful author and television commentator and inevitably introduced as the former counsel to the president, Dean is a convicted felon, having been sentenced to a prison term of one to four years and disbarred from the practice of law for his role in Watergate.

Let's see how these key players fit into the overall Watergate picture.

WATERGATE: THE CONVENTIONAL VIEW

After more than four decades of repetition in the media, the view of Richard Nixon and his administration as uniquely wicked and corrupt has hardened into unassailable orthodoxy, making it difficult to understand how a third-rate burglary, in which five culprits were caught red-handed, culminated in the only presidential resignation in American history and the imprisonment of twenty of his associates. This disastrous scandal has been the subject of dozens, if not hundreds, of books, but our understanding of Watergate has evolved considerably since Carl Bernstein and Bob Woodward launched the genre with *All the President's Men* in 1974.

Sometimes the scandal seems like a kaleidoscope. What seemed like a settled image is suddenly changed into an entirely new picture by new information or events. Howard Hunt was excoriated for drafting false cables suggesting President Kennedy was complicit in the 1963 coup against Vietnam president Ngo Dinh Diem, but a 2009 book by John Prados documents this complicity.[6] The eighteen-and-a-half-minute gap was a cause célèbre when first disclosed but was recently dismissed by John Dean as "historically insignificant."[7] Virtually all of the abuse of power allegations against the Nixon administration turn out to be little different from those of prior administrations stretching back to 1936.[8] The release of the "smoking gun" tape led directly to President Nixon's resignation, but that conversation, misinterpreted by Nixon and his defense lawyers, is now understood to have had no connection to Watergate.[9]

What follows is an overview of the conventional wisdom, which is the necessary background for the new and rather exciting developments in Watergate scholarship.

THE AMBIGUITIES OF "COVERT" AND "CONTAIN"

At the core of Watergate is the essential ambiguity of just two words, *covert* and *contain*. We will see how different meanings given to these words in conversations between White House colleagues led to dramatically different perceptions of what was authorized and intended.

First, "covert": Is a covert operation necessarily an illegal one? Apparently not. The *Defense Dictionary of Military and Associated Terms*, published by the Department of Defense, defines a covert operation as "an operation that is so planned and executed as to conceal the identity of or permit plausible denial by the sponsor." Unless an exception is made by the president, only the CIA is authorized under U.S. law to carry out international covert operations. A covert operation is intended to have a desirable political effect but without anyone knowing who was behind it.

Following the publication in 1972 of the classified Pentagon Papers in the *New York Times*, a Special Investigations unit was formed within the White House to ferret out and prevent further leaks. Soon known as the Plumbers, it proposed a covert operation to find out if Daniel Ellsberg, the leaker of the Pentagon Papers, had informed his psychiatrist, Dr. Lewis Fielding, of his intentions regarding the fifty-four thousand other pages of classified materials to which he had access. Ehrlichman approved a covert operation (without further definition) before the Plumbers even knew that Cubans, who previously had worked with Hunt on the Bay of Pigs fiasco, would be retained to carry it out. Did that mean he was criminally responsible for their subsequent break-in at Fielding's office, which was orchestrated by Howard Hunt and Gordon Liddy? According to the WSPF, keeping the Fielding break-in, which was undertaken for national security purposes, a secret was a primary motive of the Watergate cover-up.

As for "contain," did the White House initiative to contain the political fallout from the Watergate burglary of the DNC offices countenance the multitude of criminal acts committed in the course of the cover-up?

Every day, lawyers defend people accused of criminal acts without themselves violating the law. Was it reasonable for Dean's supervisors to assume that he was simply fulfilling that lawyerly function as he worked full-time on containing the Watergate problem to the CRP staff, who were seen as the only ones at risk?

Even Archibald Cox mused about what he might have done under similar circumstances, confiding to the head of the Plumbers task force, "I know I would not have done anything which I knew or felt was questionable, but I wonder how I would have reacted if I had known others were involved in such conduct."[10]

WATERGATE'S THREE CRITICAL PERIODS

Keeping these two terms in mind, let us review the key periods of the Watergate scandal. There are but three of them, each lasting only a week or two. A more complete timeline is provided in Appendix A for ease of reference. It also is important to remember that everyone admits that there was a cover-up and that it was run on a day-to-day basis by Dean and Magruder. The key question, then and now, is whether these two were operating under the direction and control of the president's more senior aides (as they later told prosecutors).

1. The Die Is Cast (June 17–July 1, 1972)

In classical Greek tragedy, the hero commits a seemingly insignificant act early in the play, an act that seals his doom. The remainder of the play portrays his struggle against his inevitable and tragic destruction. Until recently, Watergate seemed to be such a tragedy. Here are the key events that occurred in the critical first two weeks.

On Saturday, June 17, 1972, five burglars were caught in the offices of the Democratic National Committee on the seventh floor of the Watergate office building in Washington, D.C. Four of the men were Cuban. The fifth, James McCord, turned out to be a former CIA wireman, then employed as head of security for the Committee to Re-Elect the President. The group was operating under the direction and control of two other CRP officials, Liddy and Hunt. Virtually no one today alleges that anyone at the White House (particularly Nixon, Haldeman, or Ehrlichman) was aware of this break-in in advance.

The president was in Key Biscayne, Florida, on the day of the arrests and did not return to Washington until Monday, the 19th. He met for the first time with Haldeman, his chief of staff, the next day. Haldeman's notes from that meeting contain the word "Watergate," but the tape of that conversation turned out to have an eighteen-and-a-half-minute gap, which appeared to be a deliberate erasure. Much was made of this gap, and the attempted explanations by White House officials only undermined their credibility. John Dean, however, has recently asserted that whatever was on that tape is "historically insignificant," mainly because the substance of their discussion can be reconstructed by their contemporaneous diary entries.

On Friday, June 23, Nixon concurred with Haldeman's suggestion that they get the CIA to ask the FBI to limit its investigation of funds found on the Watergate burglars. When the recording of this conversation was released in early August 1974 as a result of a Supreme Court decision, it appeared to reveal a clear obstruction of justice and led to Nixon's resignation three days later. It is easy to see why this tape was called the "smoking gun," for it seemed to be "proof positive" that Nixon had been in on the Watergate cover-up from the very outset. This interpretation of the conversation between Nixon and Haldeman was openly challenged for the first time in 2014 when John Dean declared that the conversation concerned their effort to prevent disclosure of the names of notable Democratic donors (whose contributions had inadvertently been paid to the Cubans) and had been totally misunderstood from the outset.

John Mitchell announced his resignation as head of Nixon's re-election campaign on Saturday, July 1, ostensibly to tend to his wife, Martha, whose alcoholic outbursts had become a distraction and an embarrassment to the campaign. At the time, everyone accepted his explanation at face value. We now know that Nixon and his people had been told that responsibility for the Watergate break-in might, if followed carefully, end up at Mitchell's doorstep (because of his alleged approval of Liddy's campaign intelligence plan), and he was strongly encouraged to resign. The president took action. He fired his best friend but refused to publicly throw him to the wolves. This apparent act of kindness would cost him his presidency.

Thus the apparent Greek tragedy: Nixon's concurrence with a recommendation made only six days after a burglary he knew nothing about would come back more than two years later to end his presidency.

2. Collapse of the Cover-Up (March 19–March 28, 1973)

The second set of critical events occurred nine months later, when the cover-up collapsed and Dean switched sides.

The first response of every bureaucracy is to cover-up, to protect itself and its people from outside attack. The guilty declare their innocence, usually twisting the facts of their involvement to minimize their culpability. Their friends and colleagues want to believe them. It's "us against them."

This is what happened at the outset of Watergate. The initial reports to the White House were that the Watergate break-in originated at CRP, and the White House goal from the outset was to contain it there. CRP people might ultimately go to jail, but no one on the White House staff was thought to be at risk. Dean, the president's lawyer, was sent to CRP to help contain the problem and, above all, make sure it stayed at CRP.

Unfortunately, Dean was a bad choice for this assignment, since he had recruited Liddy to develop a campaign intelligence plan and had attended the two critical meetings in Mitchell's office where Liddy's plans were detailed. Since Mitchell was still attorney general at the time, these were highly suspect meetings. Following the burglars' arrests, Dean must have realized that he was at risk of prosecution for the break-in and appears to have cast his lot with others at CRP who were equally at risk.

So there was certainly a cover-up. The essential and lingering question is just who was running it? Was Dean operating under the direction and control of Haldeman and Ehrlichman, as he has maintained, or did they believe he was acting as their lawyer, doing his best to "contain" the problem in a lawful manner? Regardless, the cover-up eventually collapsed (as it should have).

Sentencing for the Watergate burglars was scheduled for Friday, March 23. Howard Hunt, who had pleaded guilty to all six counts at the beginning of the trial, knew that he would immediately be taken into custody to begin serving an exceedingly stiff sentence. On Monday, March 19, wanting to pay his lawyer and to put his financial affairs in order before his incarceration, Hunt requested payment of $135,000 from his former friends at CRP, who had been subsidizing him and the other burglars almost since the time of their arrests. Perhaps understandably, they viewed a request for money over and above his actual legal expenses as a form of blackmail. Dean informed Haldeman and Ehrlichman of Hunt's request and asked that LaRue inform Mitchell.

Having decided that it was long past time to inform Nixon of the specifics of the Watergate problem, including Hunt's new monetary demand, Dean met with the president at ten o'clock on the morning of Wednesday, March 21. He began by telling Nixon that there was a "cancer on the presidency," which was spreading, and he told him about Hunt's "blackmail" demand. Dean managed to omit the details of his own criminal acts, but it was not Nixon's finest moment, either. The president clearly played with the idea of meeting Hunt's demands, if only to buy time to get out ahead of Hunt's threatened disclosures. Haldeman joined the meeting toward the end, and all agreed that they needed to bring Mitchell down from New York to decide how to respond.

At about five o'clock that afternoon, Haldeman, Ehrlichman, and Dean again met with the president. They knew that Mitchell was to join them the next day, but they were still worried about Hunt's demands. Nixon seemed to suggest that the only way out would be for staff members to appear before the Ervin Committee, in private session, in exchange for forgoing any claim of executive privilege. Later that night, at about ten o'clock, seventy-five thousand dollars was delivered to Hunt's lawyer.

The next day, Thursday, March 22, this same group met again, joined by John Mitchell. This seems to have been the first time that the president had met in person with Mitchell since his resignation from CRP some nine months earlier. The distance Nixon maintained from his old friend probably indicates how radioactive Mitchell was thought to be. The conclusion of the meeting was that Dean would go to Camp David and write a report about what he had learned in his investigation on behalf of the president. On the basis of that report, the president, in turn, would send his staff to testify before the Ervin Committee. The unspoken assumption was that any such appearance by Mitchell would require him either to commit perjury or to take responsibility for authorizing the Watergate break-in. At the meeting's conclusion, Nixon lingered alone with Mitchell and, according to the House Judiciary Committee's transcription of the tape recording, instructed him to "stonewall," invoke the Fifth Amendment, cover up, or do anything else necessary to save the plan. I maintain, however, that this is a mis-transcription of this key recording.[11]

At the sentencing of the Watergate burglars on Friday, March 23, Judge Sirica shocked the courtroom by dramatically reading a letter from James McCord alleging a cover-up and then proceeded to hand down surprisingly harsh sentences—up to thirty-five years—to each of the defendants, with the provision that the sentences might be reduced in exchange for cooperation with prosecutors and the Ervin Committee.

That weekend, Dean dutifully journeyed to Camp David to draft the promised report, but he found himself unable to produce it, perhaps because anything he wrote, if remotely true, would have been self-incriminating. On Wednesday, March 28, Dean retained criminal defense counsel Charles Shaffer, a Democrat who had served in Robert Kennedy's Department of Justice. It turned out to be a most astute choice. A brilliant and resourceful lawyer, Shaffer's adroit initiatives and defense tactics got Dean off almost scot-free.

3. Nixon's Fall (July 24–August 9, 1974)

The third and final stage of the Watergate scandal began on Wednesday, July 24, 1974, with an eight-to-zero decision of the Supreme Court in *United States v. Nixon*, ordering the president to turn over some sixty-four subpoenaed tape recordings to Judge Sirica for review for relevancy to the Watergate prosecutions. The "smoking gun" tape would not become public for two more weeks, but the fuse had been lit.

The Supreme Court decision was followed almost immediately by extensive and dramatic debate on the House Judiciary Committee over articles of impeachment against the president. On Monday, July 29, the committee recommended adoption of three articles of impeachment for (1) obstructing the investigation of the Watergate burglary inquiry, (2) misusing law enforcement and intelligence agencies for political purposes, and (3) refusing to comply with the Judiciary Committee's subpoenas for White House tapes.

Late on the afternoon of Monday, August 5, the White House released the transcript of the meeting on June 23, 1972—the "smoking gun"—in which Nixon agreed with a recommendation to get the CIA to ask the FBI to limit its Watergate investigation. This was seen as a clear instance of obstruction of justice and was thought to show that the president had been in on the cover-up from its very outset.

His remaining political support having evaporated, Nixon announced to the nation on the evening of Thursday, August 8, that he would resign the presidency at noon the next day. After a farewell to his staff in the East Room on Friday morning, a helicopter lifted President and Mrs. Nixon from the White House lawn for the journey home to San Clemente, and Gerald Ford took the oath of office as the thirty-eighth president.

It is important to appreciate that the Watergate scandal was a *political* battle. It was waged mainly in the public media and in televised congressional hearings. But the Watergate Special Prosecution Force led the attack on the Nixon White House with grand jury and court proceedings conducted under the federal criminal code. They provided the substantive back-up for what was being debated. But they also became politicized themselves and cut too many corners in their efforts to oust Nixon and secure convictions of his senior aides. The result was the criminalization of politics. That is the *real* Watergate scandal.

CHAPTER 3

WHAT WENT WRONG

The *Washington Post*'s Carl Bernstein delivered the most famous assessment of the Watergate scandal: "What happened is that the system worked, the American system worked." But Bernstein was badly mistaken. Virtually nothing worked as intended.

A "NEWTONIAN" SCANDAL

Newton's third law of motion—for every action, there is an equal and opposite reaction—applies to Watergate. The unacceptable actions of the Nixon campaign and White House provoked equally unacceptable reactions by Nixon's many political opponents, though the nature and extent of those reactions have remained undisclosed these many years. The responses of Congress, the courts, and the press were marred by excesses at every stage, some of which have come to light only recently.

Ervin Committee:[1] The Senate Select Committee on Presidential Campaign Activities, chaired by Sam Ervin of North Carolina, was really a continuation of an investigation originated some six months before by Senator Edward Kennedy. A partisan undertaking that employed Kennedy's lead investigator, the Ervin Committee conducted a legislative trial of the Watergate defendants, leaking adverse information with abandon and ending any hope of seating untainted juries for the eventual trials. Half of the Senate's Republicans declined to support the creation of the committee, which was established by a vote of seventy-seven to nothing, because of earlier votes giving Democrats a clear majority of members, thereby assuring a partisan investigation, and limiting the inquiry to the 1972 presidential election, thereby precluding the investigation of extensive Democratic abuses in previous campaigns.

Watergate Special Prosecution Force:[2] Even more partisan than the Ervin Committee, the WSPF included no active Republicans at all. Exempted from normal departmental hiring procedures, its staff numbered about one hundred and were hand-picked for their prior service in the Kennedy and Johnson administrations (seven of the eight top officers had all worked together in the Kennedy-Johnson Department of Justice) or for their Eastern establishment, liberal bias. The prosecutors themselves admitted that "On paper, Cox's army was predominantly Eastern-oriented and heavily Ivy League."[3] Calling on their "old boy network," they hired only people already known to them, usually friends or former students.

Five task forces were soon created, each designed to target specific Nixon administration officials. Without the burden of other crimes to investigate or other laws to enforce and freed from effective restraints on their budget, the prosecutors could be single-minded in the pursuit of their quarry, calling upon three grand juries and much of the FBI and IRS for assistance. Operating with total independence from the Department of Justice, they reported, if at all, only to the Democratic majority on the Senate Judiciary Committee.

Proving once again that power corrupts, the WSPF launched investigations far afield from the Watergate cover-up itself, the collapse of which had been triggered by McCord's letter to Judge Sirica. The prosecutors postponed the key Watergate indictments for ten months while they investigated twenty-five agency and department decisions without finding any hint that regulatory decisions had been influenced by campaign contributions (later characterized as "pay to play.") They sent IRS and FBI agents to interview some 150 substantial contributors to the 1970 mid-term election campaigns (having nothing to do with Watergate but certainly scaring off future GOP contributions). They launched extensive investigations, entirely unrelated to Watergate, into likely Republican candidates for the 1976 presidential election, including President Gerald Ford, Vice President Nelson Rockefeller, the vice presidential candidate Senator Robert Dole, former Secretary of the Treasury John Connally, and even California Governor Ronald Reagan. It is an astonishing record of abuses of prosecutorial discretion.

House Judiciary Committee:[4] In establishing the checks and balances of three separate but equal branches, the framers of the Constitution envisioned that the House would conduct its own investigations of impeachable offenses. But the HJC undertook virtually no independent investigation at all. Instead, it relied on grand jury information and faulty prosecutorial representations secretly transmitted through the connivance of Watergate prosecutors and Judge Sirica. Further, the HJC effectively denied the Republican minority any representation through the adoption of a unified staff (the nominal Republican leader of which dramatically switched sides and agreed to recommend impeachment as the committee prepared to vote). The committee did institute a study led by the Yale historian C. Vann Woodward but suppressed the findings, which showed that the accusations of abuse of power lodged against Nixon were not much different from accusations lodged against prior presidents going all the way back to Thomas Jefferson.[5] Renata Adler, one of HJC's key staff members, has even suggested that the committee was more successful at covering up past government wrongdoing than at producing a defensible case against President Nixon:

In view of the Church Committee's accounts of the conduct of previous administrations, including violations of law and abuses of power since at least 1936, the first two Articles [of Impeachment] seemed to dissolve; as to [the third Article], there had been a disagreement about it from the start. The problem with all three Articles, and with their accompanying Summary of Information and Final Report, and with the thirty-odd volumes of Statements of Information ... is that ... all those volumes never quite made their case or any case.[6]

The Media: The news media acted as irresponsibly as they customarily do in national scandals, breathlessly reporting rumors as established fact and inflaming the public with rank speculation. It's great sport as long as you're not the target, but it is hardly the proper role for an independent press that is accorded such special status by the First Amendment.

For many years one of the most famous Watergate figures was, paradoxically, unknown—Bob Woodward's secret inside source known as "Deep Throat." While the public was encouraged to believe that "Deep Throat" was a member of Nixon's White House staff who was appalled at the wrongdoing of his colleagues, we learned in 2007 that he was really Mark Felt (1913–2008), the ambitious associate director of the FBI, who was angling for the top job.[7] Now we can better appreciate prosecutor Earl Silbert's assertion that nothing in Woodward's and Bernstein's stories was helpful in building their case: What Felt was leaking was already known to federal prosecutors. One might ask whether merely reporting what prosecutors already know and are actively pursuing really constitutes the sort of ground-breaking investigative reporting for which Woodward and Bernstein have received national acclaim. More troubling, it was revealed in 2013 that this duo had, in fact, successfully interviewed at least one Watergate grand juror, seemingly more than once—a flagrant breach of law that they had piously denied for decades.[8]

The Courts: As we shall see, judges too were caught up in the partisan excitement of the process. The conduct of the trial judge was exceptionally egregious. Sirica became so enthralled by attention from the adoring media that playing to the galleries became more important than assuring that trials were fairly conducted.

A Crippling Legacy for Divided Governments: Perhaps the most disturbing result of Watergate is the pattern of devastating scandals whenever a lame duck president has faced a Congress in which both houses are controlled by the opposing party, scandals made all the worse by special prosecutors.[9] President Nixon was forced to resign by prosecutors Cox and Jaworski. President Reagan was humbled by prosecutor Lawrence Walsh, who investigated the Iran-Contra affair (and whose indictment of Secretary of Defense Casper Weinberger the week before the 1992 election probably contributed to President Bush's loss to Bill Clinton). President Clinton was impeached as a result of investigations by prosecutor Kenneth Starr, who exposed the Whitewater and Monica Lewinsky affairs. That experience convinced Democrats to allow the Independent Prosecutor statute to expire, but departmentally appointed special prosecutors can still do great political harm. Most recently, George W. Bush's presidency was crippled by the special prosecutor Patrick Fitzgerald's investigations of the outing of Valerie Plame and the politically motivated firings of eight U.S. attorneys. One can only wonder what lies ahead, given the outcome of the 2014 mid-term elections.

This pattern suggests an institutional weakness—exacerbated by the twenty-four-hour news cycle—in a constitutional system in which the executive's term does not end when the opposing party gains control of Congress. In a parliamentary form of government, as in the United Kingdom, the executive cannot govern without the support of the legislature. Under our system, however, the president is expected to finish out his term surrounded by the opposition. This constitutional weakness was responsible for the only other presidential impeachment, that of Andrew Johnson, a Southern Democrat who ran on a national-unity ticket with Lincoln late in the Civil War and who faced a hostile Republican Congress. The same weakness was

The Wages of Divided Government

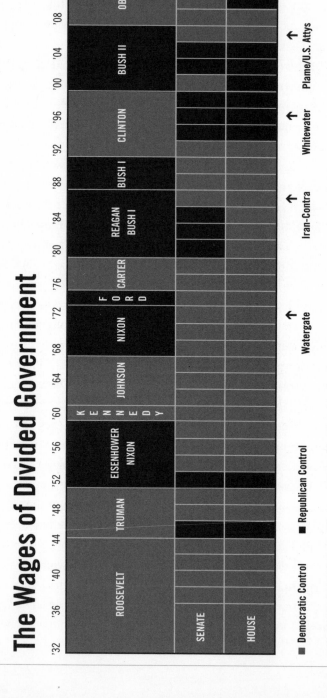

■ Democratic Control   ■ Republican Control

■ Our only major political scandals in modern times have occurred each and every time a lame duck president was faced with a totally hostile Congress.

exploited a hundred years later to reverse Nixon's re-election, but the phenomenon has grown more disturbing with each subsequent recurrence.

JOHN DEAN'S RECENT DISCLOSURES

The most recent disturbing revelations about the Watergate prosecutions have come, surprisingly enough, in John Dean's book *The Nixon Defense: What He Knew and When He Knew It* (2014). The book has been said to pound the final nails into Nixon's Watergate coffin, but a careful reading reveals some startling admissions by the president's principal accuser that call into question certain conclusions about Nixon's involvement in the scandal.

For example, Dean clearly agrees that no one on the White House staff had any advance knowledge of the Watergate break-in.[10] He also believes that, contrary to Magruder's testimony, Gordon Strachan never received information from wiretaps and therefore could not have passed such information along to Haldeman or to Nixon.[11] He repeatedly affirms that there was no express intent by President Nixon or his advisors to break the law[12] and that Nixon had little idea of Watergate's implications prior to their meeting of March 21, 1973.[13] In fact, Dean asserts that members of the president's staff did not inform one another or Nixon of their own involvement or of what had happened as the scandal unfolded.[14]

Dean even portrays Nixon as constantly alluding to his experience in the Alger Hiss case as the reason for his belief that any cover-up would be worse than the actual facts:

> "But the worst thing a guy can do, there are two things, each is bad: One is to lie, and the other is to cover up." Ehrlichman agreed, and Nixon continued, "If you cover up, you're going to get caught. And if you lie, you're going to be guilty of perjury. Now, basically, that was the whole story of the Hiss case."[15]

It is important to understand that Nixon did not see the Hiss case as merely exposing a Soviet spy in the State Department. He remembered it as a devastating scandal for President Truman, whose administration had made the scandal much worse by trying to cover it up. There are some two dozen references to Hiss on tape segments that Dean cites. It is clear that if the president had been asked directly, he would have responded with the advice not to lie or cover up because the truth will come out in any event.

Dean also denies that Watergate was part of a larger espionage or sabotage operation, as Deep Throat had so dramatically asserted in one of his meetings with Woodward:

> Woodward and Bernstein had been focused on who was responsible for the break-in and on portraying it as part of a larger espionage and sabotage effort. If that operation existed in any organized fashion, I did not (and do not) know who was behind it, and even four decades later I have never found evidence for its existence; it seems, instead, to have been a fantasy scenario apparently advanced by their Deep Throat source, Mark Felt.[16]

A critique by the journalist Max Holland of the Nixon Library's oral history project shows why this statement of Dean's is important. Referring to an interview with Bob Woodward and Carl Bernstein by the library's former director Tim Naftali, Holland writes:

> One of the critical questions that should have been put to them, as any Watergate scholar would know, has to do with the *Post*'s centerpiece story of 10 October 1972. Occupying the prestigious upper-right quadrant of the front page, it was boldly headlined "FBI Finds Nixon Aides Sabotaged Democrats." The story was and still is regarded as the "centerpiece" of the newspaper's pre-election coverage. It seemingly tied together the scandal's disparate strands and

tried to put the break-in into a context, as one element in a far-flung program to subvert the Democrats if not the democratic process—which included greasing the way so that Nixon faced the one candidate he wanted to run against the most, George McGovern.[17]

Without this "centerpiece," Watergate is nothing more than a case of excessive zeal that crossed the line into criminality, not part of a larger coordinated attempt to subvert the democratic process.

UPENDING CONVENTIONAL WISDOM REGARDING TWO KEY TAPES

Perhaps the most important of Dean's revelations are his new conclusions about two key Watergate tapes that were discussed in chapter two, those of June 20 and June 23, 1972. These conversations occurred in the week immediately following the June 17 burglary arrests and have been cited again and again as "proof positive" of Nixon's cover-up involvement.

The tape of June 20, 1972, contains the famous eighteen-and-a-half-minute gap in a conversation between Haldeman and Nixon, which caused such a furor when first disclosed. Haldeman's own notes from the conversation contain the word "Watergate," leading to the assumption that the break-in was the subject of the erased discussion. That's a mistake, Dean maintains:

> Haldeman's note-taking procedures have been misunderstood; he did not make a record of or even cite the highlights of what was said at any given session but instead recorded only matters that called for further attention and follow up.[18]

What was erased and who erased it? The answers to these questions, says Dean, "have virtually no historic significance whatsoever as they provide no information about or insight into Watergate that cannot already be found in abundance elsewhere."[19]

Even more startling is Dean's acknowledgment that the "smoking gun" tape of June 23, 1972, has been totally misunderstood from the outset:

> When revealed by order of the U.S. Supreme Court in late July 1974, this became known as the "smoking gun" conversation, because it was viewed as hard evidence, demonstrating beyond question that Nixon's final defense about the Watergate break-in in his April 30, 1973, speech, followed by his May 22nd statement, was bogus, which doomed the Nixon presidency. Ironically, this conversation has been mistakenly understood as an effort by Nixon and Haldeman to shut down the FBI's entire Watergate investigation. This appears to be the case only when viewed out of context. In August 1974, when the conversation was revealed, and Nixon and his lawyers had to focus on this conversation, he had long forgotten what was actually involved; they assumed it had the same meaning as everyone else. In reality, it was only an effort by Haldeman to stop the FBI from investigating an anonymous campaign contribution from Mexico [by Democratic donors who wanted to keep their support confidential] that the Justice Department prosecutors had already agreed was outside the scope of the Watergate investigation. In approving this action, however, Nixon slightly expanded the request, saying that the FBI should also stay out of Howard Hunt's CIA-related activities. In fact, this conversation did not put the lie to Nixon's April 30 and May 22, 1973, statements, and had Nixon known that he might have survived its disclosure to fight another day. In short, the smoking gun was only firing blanks.[20]

Dean is correct. It was a misunderstanding by Nixon's own lawyers that forced his resignation. I know that for a fact, because I was there when the lawyers reported their understanding of the substance of that tape.

To keep certain large campaign contributions by key Democrats from becoming public, the CRP converted those contributions into cash. Weeks later, this same cash ended up in the pockets of the Watergate burglars, even though the two events were not connected in any way. The White House effort to get the CIA to ask the FBI to not interview the two persons who had been conduits for the Democratic donors was motivated solely by the desire to keep their identities from becoming public.[21]

The acknowledgment by Nixon's principal accuser, forty years later, that the president's forced resignation was the result of a mistake is stunning. The revelation leaves us searching for any serious presidential wrongdoing in Watergate. No less an opponent of Nixon than Ben Bradlee, the *Washington Post*'s executive editor at the time of the scandal, has admitted as much:

> I mean the crime itself was really not a great deal. Had it not been for the Nixon resignation it would be really a blip in history. The Iran-Contra hearing was a much more significant violation of the democratic ethic than anything in Watergate.[22]

President Nixon's alleged abuses of power seem trivial today, particularly in light of other presidential transgressions before and since. The Church Committee's disclosures of governmental abuses of privacy stretching back to 1936, discussed in a subsequent chapter, show that the Nixon administration's actions were hardly unique. And the epithet of "imperial presidency" that Nixon's detractors attached to his administration seems laughable after the brazen executive overreach of the Obama administration.

FLAGRANT VIOLATIONS OF DUE PROCESS

From the perspective of the defendants, the greatest abuse in the Watergate prosecution was the systematic denial of their constitutionally guaranteed rights to due process of law. For these accused men, the hope of a fair trial evaporated as the government's prosecution became a mockery of justice.

Should federal criminal charges be brought against you—never a good thing—the case would be styled *United States v. [Your Name Here]*. Against the awesome power and authority of the federal government, with its legions of lawyers, seemingly unlimited funds, and inherent credibility, all a defendant has is his own lawyer—and the Fifth and Sixth Amendments.

The Fifth Amendment provides, in pertinent part, "No person's life, liberty or property shall be taken without due process of law." The Sixth Amendment, addressing criminal prosecutions, provides that "the accused shall enjoy the right to a speedy and public trial, by an impartial jury…and to be informed of the nature and cause of the accusation; to be confronted with the witnesses against him; [and] to have compulsory process for obtaining witnesses in his favor."

The right to a full and fair trial—derived from English common law and the product of countless procedural refinements—is at the very center of our judicial system. Indeed, the Supreme Court has described the right to a fair trial as "the most fundamental of all freedoms," which "must be maintained at all costs."[23]

Justice Robert Jackson made a telling point in 1953 when he observed:

> Let it not be overlooked that due process of law is not for the sole benefit of an accused. It is the best insurance for the Government itself against those blunders which leave lasting stains on a system of justice but which are bound to occur on ex parte consideration.[24]

Fundamental requirements designed to assure a fair trial have also been enshrined in applicable codes of professional conduct, for judges and lawyers alike.

For purposes of our review of the Watergate trials, the constitutional guarantees envision, at a minimum: (1) a public trial with the right to confront and cross-examine one's accusers, (2) presided over by a fair and impartial trial judge, (3) with the government's case presented by nonpartisan prosecutors, subject to uniformly applied rules of conduct, (4) whose verdict is rendered by an untainted and unbiased jury of one's peers, followed by (5) the right to a fair and impartial appellate review. These are not esoteric concepts requiring careful scrutiny to understand or appreciate. They are fundamental rights that most Americans understand and take for granted. Let us examine each of them in more detail.

(1) *A public trial with the right to confront and cross-examine one's accusers.* This is one of the very foundations of our concept of justice—assuring that we are not tried outside of public view or on charges brought by secret accusers. It also is an acknowledgment of the vital importance to be played by a free and vigorous press. This right assures the public that justice is being done and ensures that defendants are fully informed of the source and rationale of the accusations raised against them—and that a proper record is kept for an appeal.

The right to confront one's accusers is absolute—and the ability to cross-examine them under oath has been characterized as the greatest engine of truth-finding in our adversarial system of justice.

> In the Anglo-American adversary system, the parties to a dispute, or their advocates, square off against each other and assume roles that are strictly separate and distinct from that of the decision maker, usually a judge or jury. The decision maker is expected to be objective and free from bias. Rooted in the ideals of the American Revolution, the modern adversary system reflects the conviction that everyone is entitled to a day in court before a free, impartial, and independent judge. Adversary theory holds that requiring each side to develop and to present its own proofs and arguments is the surest way to uncover the information that will enable the judge or jury to resolve the conflict.

In an adversary system, the judge or jury is a neutral and passive fact finder, dispassionately examining the evidence presented by the parties with the objective of resolving the dispute between them. The fact finder must remain uninvolved in the presentation of arguments so as to avoid reaching a premature decision.[25]

The Sixth Amendment's express requirement that the defendant "be confronted with the witnesses against him" is the basis for excluding hearsay testimony, that is, testimony in which the witness repeats what another person, not testifying himself, has said. For example, to prove that the defendant was in town, Jack may not testify, "Jill told me that the defendant was in town." The defendant's lawyer cannot cross-examine Jill, who is not a witness under oath. If the prosecution wants to get Jill's statement into evidence, it must put Jill herself on the stand. There are at least sixty-four exceptions to the rule banning hearsay testimony, one of which is for statements made by co-conspirators. As we will see later, prosecutors in important cases frequently include co-conspiracy charges so that they can take advantage of this exception to the hearsay rule.

(2) *Presided over by a fair and impartial trial judge.* The judge is not a participant in the trial, favoring one side or the other, and should have no personal stake in the trial's outcome. The Code of Conduct for Federal Judges states, "A judge should be faithful to, and maintain professional competence in, the law and should not be swayed by partisan interests, public clamor, or fear of criticism."[26] An important part of maintaining his impartiality is the way a judge communicates with parties to the case before him. The code of conduct forbids "ex parte" meetings—that is, meetings with interested parties outside the presence of counsel for both sides: "A judge should accord to every person who has a legal interest in a proceeding, and that person's lawyer, the full right to be heard according to law. [A] judge should not initiate, permit, or consider ex parte communications or consider other communications concerning a pending or impending matter that are made outside the presence of the parties or their lawyers."[27]

The code admonishes judges not to become public figures: "A judge should not make public comment on the merits of a matter pending or impending in any court."[28]

To protect judges from undue temptation, the District of Columbia Code of Professional Ethics states, "It is professional misconduct for a lawyer to...[k]nowingly assist a judge or judicial officer in conduct that is a violation of applicable Rules of Judicial Conduct or other law."[29]

(3) *With the government's case presented by nonpartisan prosecutors, subject to uniformly applied rules of conduct.* At stake here is the even-handed enforcement of the laws and the avoidance of selective prosecution—in other words, "equal justice under law." Prosecutors are not supposed to dust off laws which haven't been enforced for decades or bring charges under entirely novel interpretations in order to "get" particular parties they don't like.

(4) *Whose verdict is decided by an untainted and unbiased jury of one's peers.* The right to a jury trial is also one of the hallmarks of our system of justice and specifically enshrined in the Sixth Amendment. Historically, a jury of one's peers at common law was composed of the defendant's neighbors, people who had known him all his life. This safeguard was seen as a protection from being unjustly accused by the king's distant enforcers. Today, jurors are still expected to represent the community's interest in resisting overzealous prosecutions, but they will be promptly excused if they actually know anyone involved in the trial. Their impartiality must not have been tainted by pretrial publicity, and they must be free of racial, political, and other prejudices against the defendant. They must learn the facts of the case from evidence presented in court and not from outside sources.

(5) *The right to a fair and impartial appellate review.* Every defendant convicted of a federal crime has an automatic and guaranteed right to an appeal, to a full and fair review of all aspects of his trial. These appeals are typically heard before a panel of three circuit court judges. An accurate record of all of the proceedings below is required to be kept for this purpose.

The right to due process of law is guaranteed to every defendant, no matter how hated or infamous he might be. In fact, the more despised a defendant is, the more critical it is that he be accorded his right to due process. Yet all five elements of the defendants' right to due process were violated in the Watergate trials:

(1) The trials themselves were media circuses, like show trials of political prisoners in a banana republic. At least one of the principal accusers was not even present in court to be confronted or cross-examined.

(2) Chief Judge Sirica, who appointed himself to preside over both Watergate trials, acted as an arm of the prosecution, held a series of highly improper secret meetings with parties whose interests were adverse to the defendants, and defrauded the jury with his temporary sentencing of the government's principal accusatory witnesses.

(3) The defendants faced an extraordinarily hostile and unaccountable prosecution. The Watergate Special Prosecution Force was staffed almost exclusively by partisan Democrats. It operated without oversight and was unconstrained by the rules and procedures applicable to all other prosecutions brought by the Department of Justice, including the rules and constraints imposed by the Manual for U.S. Attorneys. The WSPF wielded all the prosecutorial powers of the Department of Justice but in a totally independent and unreviewed manner.

(4) The District of Columbia voter pool from which the Watergate juries were drawn was hopelessly tainted by the ubiquitous and adverse pretrial publicity that accompanied the unfolding of the Watergate scandal and was intensely biased politically, consistently delivering 80 percent of its votes to the Democratic Party.

(5) The Court of Appeals for the D.C. Circuit, which heard all appeals from Judge Sirica's two Watergate trials, was corrupted by a

secret ex parte meeting between its chief judge and the original special prosecutor.

PART II

COLLUSION

In his extraordinarily perceptive "Reflections" column in the June 10, 1974, issue of the *New Yorker*, the legal commentator Richard Harris mused about the unfairness of the Watergate prosecutions. The only way to punish corruption in the Nixon administration, he wrote,

> was by bringing the Watergate criminals to justice. This is being done—to an extent. But to restore public confidence in our democratic system fully, it was also essential that the prosecutions be conducted fairly. That has not been done. In fact, many legal practices employed by the prosecutors to re-establish the primacy of the law in this nation appear at this stage to have perilously subverted it. In the end, history may conclude that the way in which those guilty of crimes in the Watergate affair were brought to justice did more lasting

damage to the highest purpose of American law than did the crimes themselves.

Harris went on to detail the legal abuses of the Watergate prosecutors:

> The use of generally discredited and unenforced laws in order to "get" someone who has probably, or even certainly, broken other laws but cannot be successfully prosecuted for those crimes; the use of grand juries, which were originally set up to protect the innocent, as investigative aids to the prosecution rather than accusatory bodies; the use of plea bargaining, in which a prosecutor offers a defendant a lesser charge in exchange for either a guilty plea or information about crimes committed by others; the use of partial or total immunity from prosecution in exchange for information; the use of selective prosecution, in which one person is tried for a crime although others who are equally guilty of the same crime are ignored; the use of conspiracy charges when evidence of the crime that is believed to have been committed is flimsy; the use of perjury charges for the same purpose; the use of criminal sanctions that can be applied against ordinary citizens but not against government officials; and the unequal application of the law in general.

Finally, he talked about how public perceptions and expectations were the driving force behind these prosecutions:

> Once a large majority finally became convinced that serious wrongs had indeed been intentionally committed by some of the nation's highest officials, probably including the President, public demand for cleaning up the wreckage and punishing those who had caused it grew irresistibly. Pressed by this demand and persuaded that there was an urgent need to meet

it swiftly, the prosecutors—with an astonishing disregard for fairness—fell back on all the means that could reasonably be justified by the end, including use of some of the same legal practices that had been so freely and perniciously employed by the Nixon Administration and so roundly condemned by its critics.

But Harris's concerns—expressed mid-way through 1974, after the cover-up indictments but before the actual trial—fell on deaf ears, and prosecutors proceeded to put on the greatest political show trial in American history.

As alarmed as Harris was in the summer of 1974 by the prosecutorial abuse he perceived, he was unaware of the secret collusion between judges and prosecutors, an abuse of due process that was far worse than he could have imagined.

CHAPTER 4

THE SECRET MEETINGS BETWEEN JUDGES AND WATERGATE PROSECUTORS

Many of the due process questions explored in subsequent chapters involve issues and rulings whose significance will need to be re-evaluated in light of the collusion between judges and prosecutors that I have uncovered after years of research and that are disclosed here for the first time. This collusion occurred in a series of secret meetings, the most important of which are outlined below.

COX'S SECRET MEETING WITH BAZELON

In the fall of 1973, the special prosecutor, Archibald Cox, met secretly with Chief Judge David Bazelon of the D.C. Circuit Court, a meeting that tainted all of that court's subsequent decisions on Watergate criminal appeals.

While Cox had no experience as a prosecutor, he was an expert in the federal appellate process and knew how to anticipate votes on appeal.

He had clerked for Judge Learned Hand on the U.S. Court of Appeals for the Second Circuit in 1938 and, as solicitor general (January 1961–July 1965), had headed the office that determined whether and on what basis to argue the government's position on appeals of any and all federal cases. As a result, Cox knew all about the political predilections of the judges on the D.C. Circuit.

The liberal bloc, which included Chief Judge Bazelon, controlled the court with a narrow five-to-four majority, but it could exercise that control only when the court sat en banc—that is, with all of its nine judges hearing a case. Ordinarily, however, a randomly selected three-judge panel heard each appeal to the circuit court, making liberal control on any particular case unpredictable.

As Cox saw it, Sirica's overwhelming indulgence of the prosecution, his tendency to turn the Watergate prosecution into a one-man search for truth, and his penchant for playing up to the suddenly adoring media could well boomerang. The more he thought about it, the more concerned he became that the Watergate criminal cases, where convictions were a near certainty before Judge Sirica, stood in substantial peril of being reversed on appeal, especially since they would be heard before a circuit court known for its interest in preserving defendants' rights.

A worried Cox finally took matters into his own hands, meeting personally with his friend Chief Judge Bazelon. Cox unburdened himself of his concerns about Sirica and then explained how he thought the problem could be finessed—an idea that had already worked on Nixon's own lawyers. Professor Charles Alan Wright, the president's outside counsel in the litigation over the White House tapes, had been euchred into requesting the court of appeals to take the unusual step of hearing the earlier tapes case en banc from the outset (no doubt convinced that the full court would ultimately hear the appeal in any event). The country's leading authority on the federal courts, Professor Wright apparently was unaware that Democratic appointees still controlled the D.C. Circuit Court and that he stood a better chance of prevailing with a randomly selected three-judge panel. Whatever his reasons, Wright's maneuver ultimately put Nixon's fate in the hands of the court's liberal majority.

It dawned on Cox that if Bazelon could convince his liberal colleagues to hear all of the other appeals from Sirica's trial court en banc, Sirica's decisions were more likely to be upheld. For his own part, Bazelon immediately grasped the significance of Cox's recommendation and the benefits to be gained from adopting it. The important thing was not to get hung up over legal technicalities, but to be certain that the Nixon people got precisely what they had coming to them. These were extraordinary times and called for extraordinary measures.

The only way we know about this secret—and highly improper—meeting is that there was a third person in the room, Bazelon's law clerk, Ronald Carr, who had just graduated from the University of Chicago Law School. Perhaps this was how things were done in Washington, but the lead prosecutor's meeting with the chief appellate judge seemed wrong to him. He found himself unable even to look at the other two men as their discussion became more specific. He kept his head down and his mouth shut.[1]

We will see in a later chapter how Bazelon went about putting Cox's suggestion into practice. For now it is enough to appreciate that a totally unethical discussion took place between the special prosecutor and the chief judge of the very court that would hear any appeals from cases brought by his office. Regardless of what they discussed, it was improper for such a meeting to take place at all. That Bazelon ultimately followed Cox's recommendation only made the due process violations even worse.

JAWORSKI'S SECRET MEETINGS WITH SIRICA

Archibald Cox was fired as special prosecutor in the Saturday Night Massacre of October 20, 1973, and replaced by Leon Jaworski some three weeks later.

Cox's firing must have changed attitudes considerably, since WSPF prosecutors proceeded to hold a series of private meetings with Sirica that culminated in the comprehensive cover-up indictment. We don't know the full extent of those off-the-record, secret meetings, but what we do know raises serious questions as to whether the defendants received the fair trial envisioned by the Fifth and Sixth Amendments.

Jaworski was well aware of the sensitivity of these meetings but also rather proud of what they accomplished. He appeared to allude to them, for example, in his first detailed interview after resigning as special prosecutor. Bob Woodward conducted that interview in Jaworski's office in his Houston law firm on the afternoon of December 5, 1974. The second sentence of Woodward's typed notes contains the cryptic notation, "Says there were a lot of one-on-one conversations that nobody knows about except him and the other party."[2]

The unidentified "other party" was clearly Judge Sirica. The only other possibility would have been Alexander Haig, but Jaworski's meetings with Haig were well-known and well documented. Sirica is by far the better reference, since we now know of at least six such meetings, even if we don't know the full content of their conversations. Regardless, Woodward does not seem to have picked up on the significance of Jaworski's comment, at least not sufficiently to have followed up on it.

NOVEMBER 5, 1973

At the top of Jaworski's hand-written "to do" list for his first day in office is the word "oath." On the next line is the notation, "Courtesy call on Sirica." Neither party mentions this first meeting in his book, but it must have been an interesting one—especially in light of what followed.

DECEMBER 14, 1973

At Sirica's specific request, four top WSPF officials participated in a private, ex parte meeting with him and Judge Gerhard Gesell. In addition to Jaworski, the prosecutors present were Henry Ruth, deputy special prosecutor; Philip Lacovara, special counsel; and Richard Ben-Veniste, acting head of the Watergate Task Force. Because no record was kept, we do not know the extent of the meeting or the topics that were covered. None of the participants ever even mentioned this meeting in their three subsequent books.

Jaworski had assumed office just the month before, so the meeting is likely to have been a full-blown review of the ongoing and anticipated WSPF criminal investigations. It simply strains credulity to believe that there was no discussion of potential defendants or of the evidence that had been gathered against them. This conclusion is all the more likely in light of the presence of Ben-Veniste, the acting head of the Watergate Task Force. The omission of all four other task force heads suggests the meeting's focus was on his group's investigations.

One topic most likely to have been discussed was the significance and effect of the tape of March 21, 1973, especially because it had only been a matter of days since Sirica had turned the first set of subpoenaed White House tapes over to WSPF prosecutors. Indeed, the prosecutors had listened to the March 21, 1973, meeting only two days before this session with Sirica and Gesell. It thus seems clear that a primary purpose for the meeting was for Sirica to get the prosecutors' reactions to those tape recordings—the ones he had just finished reviewing himself. It is unlikely that the prosecutors concealed their horror at hearing that particular conversation, which they dwell on rather extensively in their respective books.[3] Of course, *any* discussion of actual evidence to be introduced in the coming cover-up trial was clearly and strictly forbidden by the canons of professional and judicial ethics.

It is not clear why Judge Gesell alone was invited to the December 14th meeting, but Sirica assigned to him all of the Watergate-related cases that Sirica did not take for himself. Indeed, Gesell was already involved in several Watergate-related matters. He had recently accepted Donald Segretti's guilty plea, on October 1, for political sabotage of campaign opponents, Sirica had assigned him the related trial of Dwight Chapin, who had been indicted for perjury on November 29, and Gesell had accepted, on November 30, Egil Krogh's guilty plea for his role in the Plumbers break-in of Daniel Ellsberg's psychiatrist's office.

With these six participants in attendance, the meeting of December 14 could not have been a brief or casual encounter. The only reason that we now know anything about it, however, is a copy of a letter that Jaworski sent to Sirica on December 27. It is interesting that in the intervening forty years, no other copy has come to light. Jaworski's letter predicts the timing and nature of forthcoming indictments, should the respective grand juries follow the recommendations of his five WSPF task forces (see Appendix C).

Two observations are in order. First, obtaining some idea of the anticipated indictments would be a perfectly legitimate concern for the chief judge responsible for management of the court's docket and its grand juries. But this could not have been the sole basis for the meeting of these six men. If this were all that Sirica wanted to know, he could have had his law clerk convey such a request to WSPF officials.

Second, if Jaworski had wanted to protect Sirica from subsequent questions about the nature and extent of this highly unusual get-together, he could have supplied the requested information without specifically describing their ex parte meeting. Instead, his letter opened with the following sentence:

> When Messrs. Ruth, Lacovara, Ben-Veniste and I met with you and Judge Gesell at your request on Friday, December 14, you suggested that it would be helpful if we could provide you with some sense of the caseload that we would be generating for the Court over the next several months.

We don't know if Jaworski was protecting himself in the event their meeting became public or was somehow trying to alert Sirica to the idea that such meetings could not go unnoticed.

There also is a separate item of interest in Jaworski's letter—his prediction that the comprehensive cover-up indictments would be handed down by the grand jury "by the end of January or the beginning of February." This was information that Sirica very much welcomed, because grand jury action within this time frame—before Sirica's seventieth birthday—would allow him to appoint himself to preside over that trial.

JANUARY 21, 1974

The next instance of prosecutorial coordination with Sirica origi-nated within Jaworski's own staff. WSPF prosecutors had concluded that it was vitally important to share information they had gathered concerning President Nixon, including grand jury materials, as soon as possible with the House Judiciary Committee's Impeachment Inquiry. Their method for doing so—an interim grand jury report—is explored in a subsequent chapter. What matters now, however, is the proposal in Lacovara's memo of another private meeting with Sirica, the purpose of which was to make sure that the judge fully appreciated that a grand jury presentment was in the works and that he would be prepared to order its sealed report to be forwarded to the House of Representatives in the manner that WSPF attorneys desired (see Appendix D). As Laco-vara explained in his memo, "It would be most unfortunate, for exam-ple, for the grand jury to return a presentment without forewarning and then have the judge summarily refuse to receive it because of his lack of awareness of the basis for such a submission."

The goal of this meeting, then, was to lobby Sirica in advance of the forthcoming grand jury report and to gain his concurrence on how it should be handled, but without tipping off the other side. This meeting was particularly important because the grand jury interim report would contain a copy of the March 21st tape, which the D.C. Circuit Court had ruled could be made available only to the grand jury for the purpose of determining whether a crime had been committed. There was simply no legal basis for transferring this tape to the House. In fact, in every instance where the Congress attempted to enforce its own subpoena for these tapes, both the district court and the court of appeals would uni-formly rule that they were not subject to judicial enforcement because of the constitutional separation of powers.[4]

Had the White House or any of the Watergate defendants learned of the intended grand jury interim report in advance—and particularly that it would include the March 21st tape—they could have been expected to challenge such a report as being beyond the grand jury's authority. After all, no grand jury in the history of the D.C. Circuit had ever issued such a report, let alone on an interim basis while it continued with its investigations.

Such a challenge would have addressed the grand jury's authority to act in this manner in the first place, not what should be done with its report after it was issued. By keeping their initiative secret but obtaining Sirica's advance concurrence on how it would be handled, WSPF prosecutors could obtain a significant procedural advantage over their White House adversaries.

Such a meeting, if it were to occur, would constitute outright collusion and, if it were to become known, would certainly have resulted in removal of both parties from the Watergate cases, as well as disciplinary action up to and including disbarment. This sort of communication between prosecutors and judges, including ex parte meetings and submission of undisclosed—and therefore uncontestable—memoranda, would raise serious questions about Sirica's impartiality and about whether the Watergate defendants were being accorded the fundamentals of due process of law.

FEBRUARY 11, 1974

The meeting that Lacovera had recommended actually took place on February 11, 1974, even though it was Sirica who occasioned it. Sirica was a worried man. Jaworski's prediction of cover-up indictments by the "end of January or the beginning of February" had proved inaccurate, and the end of his tenure as chief judge, on March 19, was but a few weeks away. So Sirica sought yet another ex parte meeting with Jaworski. Like their earlier meeting, this one was unmentioned in subsequent books by the parties involved. It was not even acknowledged in subsequent WSPF appellate briefs responding to allegations that such meetings may have occurred.

Here is what Jaworski's memo of the following day said about this meeting (see Appendix E):

> On Monday, February 11, I met with the Judge at which time several matters were covered as we sat alone in the jury room.

He again indicated that provided the indictments came down in time, he would take the Watergate Case, stating that he had been urged to do so by any number of judges from across the nation the most recent of them being those who were in attendance with him at a meeting in Atlanta. He expressed the opinion that these indictments should be returned as soon as possible. He also stated that henceforth all guilty pleas would be taken by him. We talked about the Vesco case and he merely expressed the thought that perhaps a sealed indictment would be of some help.

Again, a secret meeting of the special prosecutor with the trial judge would have been bad enough, but we now also know that the topics of their discussions were way out of bounds. As Jaworski's memo makes clear, they were alone in the jury room. His wording also indicates that this was not the first time that the judge had informed him of his desire to appoint himself to the cover-up trial. Jaworski knew—because Sirica had told him so—that Sirica wanted to run this trial too. It is quite clear that Sirica was urging that the indictments be hurried along so that he could do so, a point mentioned twice in Jaworski's memo.

It is a significant procedural advantage for the prosecution to know in advance which judge is to preside over the trial of the indictments they have under consideration and that he will hear all guilty pleas. They can garner their evidence, tailor their indictments, and consider any plea bargains aided by their knowledge of the peculiarities of that particular judge.

Sirica's discussion of the Vesco case with Jaworski is troubling in and of itself. John Mitchell was about to go on trial in New York City for improperly helping Robert Vesco to resolve an SEC investigation in exchange for a two-hundred-thousand-dollar political donation. When Sirica pressed Jaworski to hurry the cover-up indictments, the prosecutor would have explained (as he detailed in his book) that he didn't want these indictments to be announced until *after* the Vesco jury had been sequestered, lest Mitchell argue that the attendant publicity had poisoned potential jurors' minds for the Vesco case. Sirica's apparent response was to suggest that the cover-up indictments could be brought in time for him to appoint himself to the trial but kept under seal so as not to influence the New York jurors. It is difficult to imagine a more egregious example of a judge's secretly working with the prosecution toward a common goal.

Jaworski's memorandum summarizes his discussion with Sirica of the prosecutors' expected grand jury report about President Nixon:

> The Judge commented upon the status of matters before the grand jury which led into further comments on the possibility of the grand jury considering some type of special report or presentment. He considered this a very touchy problem and cautioned as to what the public's reaction would be to a grand jury stepping out with something that was beyond its normal bounds. He cautioned that the whole effort could be tainted by something irresponsibly being done by the grand jury. He stated that the public would rightfully conclude that the entire proceeding had not been judicious but simply one of wanting to hurt the President. He further said that it was not the function of the grand jury but that of the House Impeachment Committee to express itself on that point. He then told me that in the event that I observed anything along that line being considered by the grand jury that he thought it would be appropriate for him to meet with the grand jury *in camera*. I expressed the belief that it was appropriate for the grand jury to refer to having in its possession evidence that it believed to be material and relevant to the impeachment proceedings and to suggest to the Court that it be referred to the House Committee for that purpose. He countered by stating that he believed he should be informed of the discretion that he could exercise in matters of that kind and further requested that I have a memorandum prepared for him that covers this subject. I agreed to have this done.

This memo confirms that the ex parte discussion that Lacovara had urged in his February 21st memo did, in fact, occur. Yet it is more than a record of Sirica's being informed of an anticipated grand jury report. It is also a record of Sirica's reactions upon learning of the proposed report, along with details of the give and take that followed, as Jaworski sought to bring him to the prosecutors' point of view. In short, Jaworski's memo describes a prosecutor seeking advance concurrence on matters that are certain to come soon before that very judge for rulings—conduct that is indefensible as a matter of law. It is equally disturbing that Sirica's initial reactions—that such a grand jury report was improper—were somehow overcome between this particular meeting and the time the grand jury report (later called the "Road Map") was presented for his disposal.

We should jump ahead for a moment, since Sirica would later dismiss their discussion of the grand jury as but a minor allusion to a possible action. John Wilson, Haldeman's criminal defense attorney, was so incensed at the surprise (and sealed) grand jury report that he submitted a formal letter to Sirica demanding to know if the judge had met with WSPF prosecutors in advance of the report's submission (see Appendix F). This letter, which is to be found among Sirica's papers in the Library of Congress, was never answered directly. Indeed, Jaworski's memo reveals why any honest answer would have been difficult to write.

What Sirica did do, in his order approving of the grand jury transmittal, was simply to state, "The Special Prosecutor notified the Court shortly before delivery of the Report that the Grand Jury intended to take such action." Readers can judge for themselves whether this was a full and fair description of the February 11th ex parte meeting that Leon Jaworski memorialized, whether Sirica's allusion was intentionally misleading, or whether this could refer to a separate ex parte communication between them.

FEBRUARY 19, 1974

In response to a one-page memo from his deputy regarding the Vesco case in New York, Jaworski hand-wrote a response that included the following sentence (emphasis in original): "We *know* that barring unforeseen circumstances the indictment will be in Wed or Thurs of next week & Judge S *expects that*" (see Appendix G).

This simple and forthright assertion of what Sirica expects is further evidence of the explicit agreement that had been reached between Sirica and Jaworski as to when the indictments would be handed down. As events unfolded, Jaworski was off by a single day.

MARCH 1, 1974

The comprehensive cover-up indictments were announced on a Friday in Sirica's courtroom, apparently with the grand jurors actually present to lend additional credence and drama to the festivities. The WSPF prosecution force had met Judge Sirica's birthday deadline with less than three weeks to spare. After announcing the indictment, Jaworski moved for special treatment of the cover-up case, so that Sirica, the chief judge, could assign someone out of the usual rotation to preside over it. Indeed, Sirica signed the order naming himself as trial judge later that same day.

The hearing was beautifully orchestrated, everything coming off precisely as Jaworski and Sirica had discussed. Only the defendants were caught by surprise by the dramatic presentation of a sealed briefcase, containing the grand jury report designed for transmittal to the House of Representatives.

Documents recently coming to light detail how Jaworski slipped into Sirica's chambers a half hour before the hearing for yet another private, off-the-record meeting to go over the judge's and the prosecutor's respective roles. They also met again after the hearing to discuss how smoothly things had gone and to be sure that nothing further needed to be done at that time. While neither of these ex parte meetings is mentioned in subsequent appellate briefs or in Jaworski's or Sirica's book (except for the briefest and almost misleading allusion by Jaworski),[5] we now know about the meetings because of a second secret memorandum that Jaworski wrote for his confidential files, recording the agenda on which they agreed (see Appendix H).

Jaworski's memo must be read in full to be believed. Here is a portion, which confirms the worst fears of prosecutorial and judicial collusion:

> On the morning of March 1, I met with Judge Sirica in chambers at 10:30am. We reviewed the agenda consisting of (1) presentation of indictments and sealed special report of the grand jury; (2) unsealing of the special report and reading by Judge Sirica, and the acceptance of the report and its resealing. I told Judge Sirica that I would ask the Court to specially assign the case in view of its length and protracted nature....
>
> After [the 11:00 a.m. hearing's] opening, Judge Sirica looked at me, asked if I had anything to take up with the Court. I then rose, went to the lectern, and said, "May it please Your Honor, the grand jury has an indictment to return. It also has a sealed report to deliver to the Court." The rest of the agenda was then followed including delivery of a briefcase of material, along with the special report to the Court—also a key to the briefcase. The Judge indicated that he would have an order on the special report on Monday (he told me he would transmit to the counsel for the House Judiciary Committee under rules that would not interfere with the trial of the accused). The Judge in open court asked if I had any further comments, and I stated: "Due to the length of the trial, conceivably three to four months, it is the Prosecution's view that under Rule 3-3(c), this case should be specially assigned, and we so recommend." This meant that Judge Sirica could assign the case to himself, which he did do by order later entered that day.

If such a documented agreement between the prosecutor and the judge—that Jaworski would move for special handling so that Sirica could appoint himself to preside over the trial—had become public, it would have been enough *on its own* to have Sirica removed from the case before the trial or to have any resulting convictions overturned on appeal.

MARCH 7, 1974

A second key indictment also occurred by the deadline imposed by Sirica's birthday. Ehrlichman, among others, was indicted for his role in authorizing the Plumbers' break-in at the offices of Dr. Lewis Fielding, psychiatrist to Daniel Ellsberg, who was responsible for leaking the Pentagon Papers to the *New York Times* and perhaps to the Soviet embassy. This indictment was brought by a separate grand jury, Watergate Grand Jury II, but was presented to Sirica as chief judge. The timing allowed him again to go outside of the normal procedures and specially to assign this case to Judge Gesell, who was the prosecutor's own choice for that case. William Merrill, the WSPF prosecutor who headed the Plumbers Task Force, specifically wanted Gesell as trial judge, because he had already ruled that there was no national security defense to the charges they expected to bring against Ehrlichman. As Merrill later wrote, he had asked Jaworski to ask Sirica to assign the case to Gesell, and their secret request had been granted.[6] Had this advance arrangement between prosecutors and judges been known at the time, it too would have raised important questions about the abuse of due process in the Plumbers' prosecution.

MARCH 19, 1974

Judge Sirica turned seventy and stepped down as chief judge of the District Court for the District of Columbia, as required. He had already assigned himself to the cover-up trial and Gesell to the Plumbers' trial, assignments that the expiration of his term as chief judge did not change. He was replaced by George Hart, a decidedly less media-friendly and activist judge than Sirica had become.

CONCLUSIONS AND IMPLICATIONS

Documents uncovered to date confirm at least nine secret face-to-face meetings between Judge Sirica and Watergate prosecutors. There may have been many more such communications—in person or by telephone. There are certainly more implied in Jaworski's cryptic comment to Woodward, mentioned before: "Says there were a lot of one-on-one conversations that nobody knows about except him and the other party."

It is unfortunate, indeed, that Woodward did not pick up on Jaworski's observation and, as one might expect of a true investigative reporter, vigorously pursue its tantalizing trail. Perhaps he didn't recognize the observation for what it was worth or perhaps he didn't want to spoil an otherwise good interview.

In any event, there are still a few people around who were close to Jaworski or to Sirica, who participated in one or more of the ex parte meetings described above and who might know more specifics about their ongoing conversations. Perhaps they would be willing to share their knowledge of this wrongdoing, even at this late date.

In his 1981 book, *Crossroads*, Jaworski piously concluded, "From Watergate we learned what generations of Americans before us have known: our Constitution works. And during the ordeal it was interpreted again to reaffirm the truth that no one—absolutely no one—is above the law."[7] And yet, Jaworski's own actions made a mockery of the due process guarantees of our Bill of Rights, guarantees that apply to every American—absolutely every American—no matter how disgraced he may be in public opinion. Jaworski and the federal judges with whom he colluded placed themselves above the very laws they were sworn to uphold and enforce.

The extent of collusion between Judges Bazelon and Sirica and Special Prosecutors Cox and Jaworski is simply breathtaking. The judges and prosecutors together took the part of Nemesis in Prud'hon's painting—eager for vengeance, with any concept of justice removed from the picture entirely.

Had any one of the incidents described above come to light at the time, it would have necessitated resignations, removals, and possibly disbarments. Emerging as they have some four decades later, they completely taint the Watergate verdicts and render them indefensible as a matter of law.

PART III

GETTING NIXON "AT ALL COST"

To fully appreciate the abuses of power that forced President Nixon to resign, it is helpful to separate the judicial and prosecutorial collusion aimed at getting the president out of office from the denials of due process that tainted the convictions of his senior aides in the Watergate trials, which are addressed in subsequent chapters.

CHAPTER 5

STAFFING THE NIXON IMPEACHMENT

While internal WSPF documents show that from the very outset prosecutors dreamed of bringing Nixon into the criminal justice system, both Cox and Jaworski felt the proper venue for dealing with the president himself was the House of Representatives, in which the Constitution vests the power of impeachment. That said, Cox's own files contain an analysis prepared by a fellow professor shortly after Cox's appointment concluding that a sitting president can be indicted. This same issue was briefed within the Department of Justice by both the U.S. attorney's office and the Office of Legal Counsel. In the month after Nixon had resigned but before he was pardoned, over a dozen individuals or groups of WSPF prosecutors submitted internal memos to Jaworski urging that the former president be indicted for his alleged Watergate crimes.

A BACKWARD LOOK AT NIXON'S RESIGNATION

With the perspective of forty years, let's look again at how and why Nixon was forced to resign.

There is little question but that his resignation was triggered by his loss of all political support following the release on August 5, 1974, of the "smoking gun" tape of June 23, 1972—a tape, as we have seen, that everyone erroneously took as evidence of the president's obstruction of justice.

Knowing as we now do that the "smoking gun" conversation provided no grounds for impeachment, we can examine the other alleged wrongdoings that might have made it necessary for Nixon to resign. After all, the House Judiciary Committee had voted to recommend three articles of impeachment to the full House at the end of July, some two weeks before the "smoking gun" tape's public release. These articles were grounded in obstruction of justice, abuse of power, and failure to comply with a House subpoena. Let's review them in reverse order and see how they hold up today.

SUBPOENAS FOR WHITE HOUSE TAPES

The Judiciary Committee charged that Nixon's failure to comply with the House subpoena for the tapes was an unconstitutional act. Yet the president's position that he was not obliged to comply with the congressional subpoena because of the constitutional separation of powers was not extraordinary. Presidents as far back as Thomas Jefferson had declined to provide Congress with internal documents of the executive branch, and these presidents had been consistently upheld by the courts. Indeed, both the House and the Senate had sued to obtain judicial enforcement of their subpoenas for the tapes, failing each time.

As a proposed accommodation, the White House had turned over to the Judiciary Committee on April 30, 1974, transcripts of some four dozen conversations, along with the offer that the chairman and ranking member could verify their correctness by listening to the tapes themselves.

The executive and legislative branches carry on this sort of tug of war almost every day. Most recently, the House has refused to turn over to the Securities and Exchange Commission internal documents relating to an investigation of insider trading, and the Obama administration has declined many times to make documents available to House committee investigations. While the House does have the ultimate power of impeachment, that remedy is a "nuclear option" that is never used in practice. The Watergate scandal is the only occasion in history when the House Judiciary Committee has recommended impeachment of the president for refusing to comply with a congressional subpoena.

ABUSES OF POWER

Nixon's alleged abuses of power, which seemed outrageous at the time, pale in comparison with both past and current practices.

Beginning the year after Nixon's resignation, the Church Committee revealed a pattern of abuses in the name of national security stretching back to 1936.[1] During that period (and without court authority), the CIA opened at least 130,000 first-class letters to or from American citizens, the FBI conducted an annual average of 125 surreptitious entries ("black bag jobs") to plant bugs or to review personal files, and various military intelligence agencies routinely violated the privacy rights of American citizens. The Kennedy administration's Ideological Organization Audit Program triggered IRS audits of hundreds of donors to conservative charities. Robert Kennedy approved more wiretaps on Martin Luther King than Nixon, trying to plug leaks, had on his National Security Council staff. The FBI kept its own "enemies list" of some thirty thousand "subversives" to be rounded up in the event of widespread domestic unrest.

During the Obama administration, there have been disclosures of warrantless collection of data by the National Security Agency, as well as specifically targeted drone killings, with at least one American citizen among the targets. The White House has misled the American public about the terrorist attack in Benghazi. The IRS has systematically harassed the president's political opponents. The president has violated the legislative authority of Congress with regard to Obamacare and immigration law and has subverted the process of congressional confirmation of presidential appointments. When it comes to presidential abuses of power, Obama makes Nixon look like an amateur.

OBSTRUCTION OF JUSTICE

The most important article of impeachment that Nixon faced was the one charging him with obstruction of justice. It was the first article to be voted on and was by far the most serious—then and now. What is so interesting in retrospect is that the House Judiciary Committee conducted virtually no investigation of its own, relying instead on the work of the WSPF. Relentlessly focused on removing Nixon from office, those prosecutors took the unprecedented step of secretly conveying to the House Judiciary Committee the results of their investigation—an investigation whose primary factual assertions turned out to be entirely wrong.

Here, I submit, is a tale of prosecutorial and judicial corruption that has never before been disclosed to the American public.

WHAT DID THE PROSECUTORS KNOW AND WHEN DID THEY KNOW IT?

The Watergate Special Prosecution Force was established principally to investigate and prosecute the crimes of Watergate. This mandate meant starting at the bottom with the known crimes and then, in typical prosecutorial fashion, working their way up in the Nixon White House. They might get to the president eventually, but no one expected them to start there. But something intervened in this process of nailing President Nixon's aides. Suddenly, the big prosecutorial guns were no longer aimed just at them. As nearly as can be determined, this dramatic change of prosecutorial focus occurred in December 1973, just after the release of the first set of White House tapes.

Alexander Butterfield, a deputy assistant to the president, revealed the existence of the White House taping system in testimony before the Senate Watergate Committee on July 16, 1973. A week later, relying on Dean's testimony, prosecutors obtained a grand jury subpoena for recordings of eight (later clarified to be nine) presidential conversations. Judge Sirica upheld the grand jury subpoena at the end of August, announcing that he would first review the recordings for relevance to the grand jury's criminal investigations. The court of appeals, sitting en banc, upheld the subpoena on October 12 and ordered the tapes turned over for Sirica's review.

The White House offered a compromise in which it would turn over transcripts, rather than the tapes themselves, which Senator John Stennis, a conservative Democrat from Mississippi, would authenticate by listening to the actual tapes. When Archibald Cox refused the compromise, Nixon had him removed as Watergate Special Prosecutor in the "Saturday Night Massacre" of October 19, 1973.

In the days that followed, the White House agreed to turn over the subpoenaed tapes themselves but soon informed the court that two of the conversations at issue had not been recorded and that the tape of June 20, 1972, contained an unexplained eighteen-and-a-half-minute gap. In late November and early December 1973, Sirica reviewed the seven surrendered tapes himself and arranged for copies to be turned over to WSPF prosecutors. On December 12, according to Richard Ben-Veniste, the prosecutors first listened to the tape of March 21, 1973—Dean's "cancer on the presidency" meeting with Nixon—in which the president was informed of Howard Hunt's blackmail demands. The prosecutors' reaction was immediate and unambiguous: this was evidence that President Nixon had committed a series of criminal offenses.

In his Watergate memoir, Leon Jaworski, who had taken over as special prosecutor on November 5, described his own reaction to hearing that tape:

> I was badly shaken, so shaken that I didn't want anyone to notice it. I left Carl Feldbaum's office that mid-December morning and made my way back to my own. I closed the door behind me. I needed to be alone.
>
> My brain was acting like a ticker-tape. My thoughts were clear, but they ran through my mind without break, one becoming another and then quickly another. But one thought

kept coming back, hammering its way through the others: The President of the United States had without doubt engaged in highly improper practices, in what appeared to be criminal practices. I had heard the evidence. I had listened to that voice…as the President plotted with his aides to defeat the ends of justice.[2]

The White House would argue four months later, when they made this recording available to the House Judiciary Committee and released transcripts to the public, that while the president did toy with the idea of meeting Hunt's blackmail demands, it was only for the purpose of buying time so that the White House could get its story out ahead of his. The president's aim was, in essence, to defeat Hunt's ability to blackmail them by disclosing that information themselves. In any event, the White House would assert, no decision was made during that meeting with Dean to take any such action. Instead, the president had announced to his aides that same day that he had decided to require his staff to appear before the Ervin Committee without claim of executive privilege in exchange for closed, non-public hearings. Besides, the White House argued, the question of Hunt's blackmail demand became moot the following day, when Mitchell indicated that he thought that the matter already had been addressed.

But to Jaworski and his staff the March 21st tape was damning, in and of itself, simply because the payment of blackmail was given serious consideration. Of course, this tape was at the time the only evidence of any presidential involvement that they had, so it should come as no surprise that they chose to view it in its worst possible light.

The second development that re-focused the WSPF prosecutors' sights on the president occurred on or about December 27, when they concluded that they had circumstantial evidence that President Nixon himself had ordered that Hunt's blackmail demands be met.

This was the date when they were first able to pinpoint the time at which the last "hush money" payment was made to Hunt's attorney, William Bittman. It was already known that this payment had occurred sometime during the week ending on Friday, March 23, when Hunt was scheduled to be sentenced and taken into custody. While none of the government's witnesses—including Fred LaRue, who had made the payment, and Bittman, who had received it—had kept detailed records, they all seemed to think that this last delivery had occurred on the evening of Tuesday, March 20.

When WSPF prosecutors determined that the delivery had actually occurred on Wednesday evening, March 21, however, everything changed—at least from their perspective. Wednesday was the very day that Dean had first informed Nixon of Hunt's blackmail demand. If the money had been delivered that very evening, it might be possible to show that President Nixon himself had authorized and directed that final payment.

This possibility, which I call the "Frampton Supposition" (after George Frampton, who authored the memorandum that laid this all out),[3] allowed the prosecutors to think they could show Nixon's active involvement in the payoff scheme—an unambiguous and overt obstruction of justice. You can see why they found this idea so enticing.

The following facts, which supported the Frampton Supposition, were already established:

- Dean had learned of Hunt's monetary demands—seventy-five thousand dollars for legal fees and sixty thousand dollars for future financial needs—from CRP attorney Paul O'Brien on Monday morning, March 19.
- Dean had informed LaRue of Hunt's demands on either Tuesday evening or Wednesday morning and had suggested he might seek John Mitchell's approval before making payment.
- LaRue had spoken to Mitchell by phone and obtained approval for payment of the legal fees. The timing of this call, however, would be crucial to the prosecutors' theory.
- Dean's March 21st meeting with Nixon ran from about 10:00 a.m. until noon. Haldeman joined them for the last half hour.

- Shortly after that meeting concluded, Haldeman called Mitchell. There was no recording of their conversation, and the White House maintained that the sole purpose was to invite Mitchell to a meeting the following day, but it was uncontroverted that such a call had occurred.
- Haldeman, Ehrlichman, Dean, and the president met at 5:00 that Wednesday afternoon to continue their discussions of how to respond to Hunt and how to handle the next day's meeting with Mitchell.
- At 10:00 that same Wednesday evening, LaRue made a seventy-five-thousand-dollar payment to William Bittman, Hunt's attorney.

All that was necessary for the Frampton Supposition to work was for the phone call between LaRue and Mitchell to have occurred *after* Haldeman's call to Mitchell. If that were the case, the prosecution could argue that, after Dean had departed from his morning meeting with the president, Nixon (who in the tape had clearly displayed an inclination to meet Hunt's demands) must have directed Haldeman to contact Mitchell and tell him to instruct LaRue to make the payment to Bittman, as LaRue had done that very evening.

It mattered little that Haldeman and Mitchell (and even Nixon, if it ever came to that) would stoutly deny that this was Nixon's instruction or that the purpose of Haldeman's phone call to Mitchell was to arrange the payment to Hunt. After all, they were soon going to be indicted, and the House Judiciary Committee and the cover-up trial jury could be expected to disregard their denials.

WHAT DID THE PROSECUTORS DO AND WHEN DID THEY DO IT?

The beginning of the WSPF's focus on this beguiling possibility is best illustrated by two internal memoranda. The first is the 128-page draft Prosecutive Report on President Nixon prepared by George

Frampton of the Watergate Task Force and dated January 7, 1974. It details, in the midst of a much longer analysis of possible presidential culpability, the facts summarized above. That section of the report was probably inserted into a draft already under preparation. The second illustrative memo is from Philip Lacovara to Jaworski, bearing the same date (see Appendix I) and accompanying a more detailed analysis by a staff member, explaining how a defendant joining an ongoing conspiracy (which they were now certain that Nixon had done on March 21) could be held equally culpable for that conspiracy. It concluded:

> Thus, D [for Defendant] could expect that failure of the con-
> spiracy to continue successfully would jeopardize his ability
> to continue in office and to discharge his obligations effec-
> tively. The course of action he advised and which was, in fact,
> followed was plainly intended to ensure that the conspiracy
> did not fall apart. Accordingly, it is only fair to conclude that
> D knowingly, deliberately, and for his own benefit adopted
> and promoted the unlawful venture, thereby making it his
> own.[4]

As we will see, WSPF efforts to prove President Nixon's involvement in the last Hunt payoff quickly merged with their work on the comprehensive cover-up indictment. I will address this convergence in the remainder of this chapter but break it into several separate topics for ease of explaining the significance of each: the internal battles within the WSPF, their secret consultations with Sirica, the decision to transmit a sealed grand jury report to the House Judiciary Committee, and the secret naming of President Nixon as an unindicted co-conspirator in the cover-up indictment.

WSPF'S INTERNAL BATTLES: JAWORSKI VS. COX'S ARMY

When Jaworski was appointed special prosecutor on November 5, 1973, his first challenge was to gain the confidence of the staff he had been appointed to lead. He never gained actual control, of course, because their investigatory work was well under way when he arrived. All he could hope to achieve was an uneasy truce in the tug of war over how to handle their intended prosecutions.

It seems clear that the Frampton Supposition occasioned any number of battles within the WSPF, primarily because the staff prosecutors were unsure how best to exploit evidence of their new-found belief in Nixon's personal involvement. Jaworski decided to consult secretly with Sirica—at least that is the logical conclusion from a fascinating section of the book by James S. Doyle, WSPF's communications director. After several pages describing the WSPF lawyers' certainty that Nixon had become an active participant in the cover-up conspiracy and the obligation they felt to so inform the House of Representatives, Doyle writes:

> Toward the end of January a consensus began to emerge from the non-stop discussions and arguments. From the beginning one option had been clear. The grand jury could make a presentment to the judge which would lay out the case against Nixon and note that the grand jury was not issuing a formal indictment only because he was a sitting President. It seemed to carry with it all of the problems and disadvantages of an indictment and none of the legal virtues.[5]

Not happy with this approach, Doyle then describes how Jaworski had been discussing their options and various approaches with Sirica:

> Jaworski met with Judge Sirica privately during this period, and while he never disclosed any discussions he might have had with the judge on this subject, his final, irrefutable argument against an indictment or other accusation against Nixon was, "Judge Sirica will not allow this. He will condemn the grand jury for overreaching, and he will condemn us for condoning or inspiring it. And he will dismiss the action out of hand."[6]

The objections that Jaworski here attributes to Sirica are materially different from the judge's concerns about a grand jury report that were detailed in Jaworski's February 12th memo discussed earlier. It seems clear that Sirica's two sets of concerns were conveyed to Jaworski in different discussions with the judge.

It is possible that Doyle, who is not a lawyer, did not appreciate the significance of his casual disclosure of the meetings between Jaworski and Sirica. In any case, his is the only book that mentions such a series of consultations between these two supposedly independent figures.

These same internal WSPF discussions also triggered a most interesting exchange of memos between Jaworski and Henry Ruth, the deputy special prosecutor. Originally hired by Cox, Ruth was now having second thoughts about the staff's initial conclusions concerning how to handle President Nixon. These memos are also a part of the materials that have only recently come to light as a result of the author's FOIA requests.

Ruth wrote to Jaworski on January 2, 1974, to reiterate his view that, even if criminal charges might be brought against the president, he and Cox had concluded that the proper avenue was the impeachment process, not indictment or naming the president as an unindicted co-conspirator. Ruth urged, however, that WSPF prosecutors immediately share with the House Judiciary Committee all of the evidence and findings of their grand jury with regard to the president. He believed that the committee staff were in substantial need of the WSPF's assistance and, without the WSPF's help, would fail in their high purpose of building a strong case against the president. If that cooperation did not achieve the desired result (i.e., Nixon's impeachment), Ruth continued, then WSPF prosecutors should reconsider the idea of naming Nixon in a subsequent indictment.

In his response, dated January 8, Jaworski agreed that the proper path regarding Nixon was that of impeachment and not indictment (even if the facts were supportive) but disagreed that it was their responsibility to come to the immediate aid of the Judiciary Committee.

Archibald Cox, as well as you, has wisely concluded, it tentatively occurs to me, that the President should not be indicted
nor should he be named as a co-conspirator, assuming that
the proof warrants either of these courses. As to the naming
of the President as a co-conspirator Cox was quoted as opposing it because it was "just a back-handed way of sticking the
knife in." If these are sound conclusions they remain sound
whether the impeachment process falters or flourishes. In my
present view, I can find no justification for violating our other
responsibilities [to bring charges against Nixon's aides]...sim-
ply because we find it unsupportable to indict the President
or to name him as co-conspirator.

Let me add these further thoughts. There are numerous
situations that justify naming as an unindicted co-conspirator,
but the President does not belong in this category. The very
fact that such an act would brand him indelibly without an
opportunity to defend himself, rules out such a procedure, in
my estimation.

One cannot help but be struck by how firmly Jaworski rejected
Ruth's suggestions about assisting the House Judiciary Committee and
naming the president in their cover-up indictment. Replying on January
14, Ruth pointed out that he had argued that it might become crucial to
name the president in the indictment *only* if the House's impeachment
process were to founder, perhaps as a result of some lack of cooperation
from the White House and the special prosecutor. Besides, he emphasized, Cox had "always believed that cooperation with the impeachment
process was proper."

On January 21, Jaworski drafted a response to Ruth, properly char-
acterizing the situation in which he found himself (see Appendix J):

I said before and emphasize again that the mere conclusion
that the President is not indictable or should not be named as
an unindicted co-conspirator furnishes no basis for our

pursuing still another course beset with restraints that should not be violated. I mean this: If it is not sound in law or policy to indict the President; if it is not sound in law or policy to name him as an unindicted co-conspirator—it cannot become so simply because the efforts of the House to impeach are frustrated. Differently stated, if the House bogs down in impeachment because of lack of evidence that cannot be properly and legally released to it or because of its own failures, the unindictable President does not, perforce these shortcomings, become indictable.

Although our mandate authorizes us to proceed against the President, it nowhere suggests that we are to do so regardless of fairness or just procedure. More specifically it does not authorize us to violate grand jury procedures, something I observed your memorandum avoids dealing with.

This direct and candid clarification from the special prosecutor to his deputy—firmly insisting that the president would not be indicted or named an unindicted co-conspirator and that grand jury information would not be shared with the House—is all the more instructive since he felt that he had to put it in into writing. One cannot help but wonder what caused Jaworski to change such a firmly stated position.

In later paragraphs of that same response, Jaworski's description of the WSPF office undermines any claim that they were simply professional prosecutors going about their business without prejudice or political agenda:

Now let me address myself to the general tenor of your memorandum which reflects an attitude I discussed with you before—the subjective conviction that *the President must be reached at all cost* [emphasis added].

What is of some concern to me are the discussions, plans and understandings had and reached between staff members prior to any discussions with me. This results in convictions already formed and frankly, under such circumstances, the meetings are of no help to me.

Perhaps I should not consider it such a lonely task, but inasmuch as I have the final responsibility, henceforward the discussions I seek will be with those I designate. The stubborn fact remains that we must be alert not to give support to the White House charges that have been leveled against the staff. Perhaps it is too late to get objective opinions from others so I will do the best I can in the making of decisions for which I—and not the staff—will be held responsible. It is a simple thing for you and others to discuss views and convictions you formed along the way because you do not have the ultimate responsibility.

These are exceptionally strong words of concern—WSPF prosecutors have lost all objectivity, they are out to get President Nixon "at all cost," and are ironing out internal dissent prior to any meetings with Jaworski. There can be little doubt that the stampede that the special prosecutor denounces was occasioned by the enticing opportunities presented by the Frampton Supposition.

Curiously enough, Richard Ben-Veniste, the head of the Watergate Task Force, recalled Jaworski's attitude at that time quite differently in the Watergate memoir he wrote with George Frampton:

From what little the Special Prosecutor said to us in December and early January about President Nixon it appeared to the task force that his central concern was to see President Nixon removed from office. In the first place, Jaworski had obviously concluded on the basis of the evidence that such a person should not in the national interest continue to lead the country. Moreover, Jaworski calculated that the President probably would not be able to cling to his office for long after the tapes were made public. In Jaworski's mind, seeing Richard Nixon out of the White House was the most important achievement he could render the country as Special Prosecutor.[7]

The WSPF eventually pursued a course at odds with the more cautious approach Jaworski was insisting on in his January memoranda. The indictments in the cover-up case were handed down on March 1, 1974, but were kept sealed from the public at the recommendation of the prosecutors and upon the order of the judge to allow them (one suspects) to control the timing and context of their dramatic disclosure. The grand jury, at Jaworski's urging, named the president as an unindicted co-conspirator, and WSPF prosecutors worked closely with Judiciary Committee staff, in secret, to share grand jury information and their own prosecutorial theories to assist in the committee's investigations of President Nixon and in the writing of its impeachment report. It remains unclear how Sirica's and Jaworski's opposition to one or both of these approaches was overcome, but the "get Nixon at all cost" culture of Cox's zealous army seems to have prevailed.

WSPF EX PARTE MEETINGS WITH JUDGE SIRICA

We have already discussed details that have come to light regarding the series of private meetings that WSPF prosecutors held with Sirica, at least those that we now know of. It appears they discussed the meaning and importance of the March 21st tape in their meeting with Judges Sirica and Gesell on December 14, 1973. Lacovara's January 21st memorandum urged another such meeting to persuade Sirica with regard to the proposed grand jury report to the House, the discussion of which occurred when Jaworski met privately with Sirica on February 11. Doyle seems to describe other discussions between Jaworski and Sirica concerning Nixon's being named in the indictment.

DRAFTING THE GRAND JURY'S ROAD MAP

One of the real public surprises at the March 1st hearing in Judge Sirica's courtroom when the Watergate grand jury's cover-up indictments were handed down was the dramatic presentation of a brown, government-issue satchel containing a sealed envelope addressed to Sirica requesting that he transmit its contents to the House of Representatives. That report, known as the "Road Map" and ultimately transmitted as requested, has remained sealed to this day.

The Watergate Task Force was growing impatient with the House Judiciary Committee's investigations and felt compelled to push them along. Ben-Veniste and Frampton write:

> John Doar, the House Judiciary Committee's chief counsel, had launched an exhaustive staff effort to gather and cross-index every fact, however insignificant, that related to the committee's inquiry. In an ideal world and with infinite time this endeavor could have proved useful. Under the circumstances, however, it precluded immediate action to what was most urgently needed: an attempt to summarize the most *important* evidence against the President in a meaningful way, so that it could be readily understood and assessed by Congress and the public.
>
> The Judiciary Committee's plight convinced some of us that members of Congress from both sides of the aisle were going to have to have the significance of the evidence spelled out for them in neon letters before they would act. The Watergate Task Force believed that the grand jury should be told it could make a report to the Judiciary Committee that not only transmitted evidence but summarized and commented upon it. The summary, we thought, could articulate the "theory of the case" against the President. It could show how the tapes and other evidence fit together and demonstrate that the President had been trying to hold the cover-up together in March and April of 1973.[8]

This is an excellent example of the arrogance displayed by members of the Watergate Task Force. They were supremely confident that they and they alone were in the best position to arbitrate what the House

Judiciary Committee should know and act upon. It also turns out, not insignificantly, that the members of the Watergate Task Force had absolutely no idea of the internal battles and considerations going on between Jaworski and Ruth at the staff level of the special prosecutor's office.

Nor did the task force prosecutors know in 1974, or even when Ben-Veniste's and Frampton's book was published in 1977, that Doar, according to the chief counsel of the House Judiciary Committee, Jerry Zeifman, was intentionally slowing down the committee's impeachment inquiry by occupying the vast majority of its staff with busy work in order to allow public pressure to continue to build against President Nixon and the Republican Party.[9] The prosecutors must have been disappointed in the extreme when the committee did not act immediately on their Road Map or leak any of its contents to the press.

It is not clear whether and to what extent anyone other than WSPF prosecutors and Sirica knew that the satchel also contained copies of White House tape recordings. Indeed, it appears that everyone had been assured that this would not happen, as Ben-Veniste and Frampton write:

> Jaworski had already tried to calm White House fears that we were going to ship our Presidential documents and tapes to the Congress wholesale. In early January the Special Prosecutor gave an interview in which he stated that Presidential material gathered in the Watergate investigation would *not* be turned over by the prosecutor's staff to the House Judiciary Committee. This would violate legal rules of grand-jury secrecy, Jaworski was quoted as saying, and would be contrary to the Court of Appeals tapes decision by which we obtained the tapes explicitly for grand jury use.[10]

In addition, Jaworski's recollection of his phone call with Haig the evening before the indictments were announced suggests another misunderstanding, whether deliberately intended or not:

On the evening of February 28, just as I was preparing to leave my office, General Haig called. Rumors were afloat, he said, about a possible indictment and a sealed report. "Is there anything you can properly disclose to me, Leon?" he asked.

"Nothing about the indictment or the report," I said. "If the grand jury does make a report, you should expect Judge Sirica to accept it and act on it."

"Let me ask you this," he said. "Is there any indictment involving present White House aides? I'd need to make arrangements to meet the situation."

"Don't worry about those arrangements," I said.

He seemed relieved. "You're a great American, Leon."[11]

Haig's own memoir is silent about this phone call, but it is likely that he took Jaworski's disclaimer as all-inclusive—indicating that no action was forthcoming with regard to President Nixon. And indeed, none seemed to be, since Nixon's being named as an unindicted co-conspirator was kept secret when the indictment was announced.

Fooled into believing that Nixon was not implicated in the grand jury actions and that the grand jury report was little more than a rationale for the indictment of the seven Watergate cover-up defendants, the White House took the position that it did not object to its transmittal or even to its public disclosure.

But two of the cover-up defendants, Haldeman and Ehrlichman, did object to the proposed transmittal of the Road Map to the House. They pointed out that never in the history of the D.C. Circuit had a regular grand jury issued such a report—let alone while its investigation was still ongoing. They also asserted that the resulting publicity when this material was inevitably leaked would prejudice their defense.

Amazingly, Sirica had the audacity at his March 6th hearing on this matter to raise the possibility that the Judiciary Committee ought to postpone its impeachment investigation until the conclusion of the cover-up trial over which he would soon preside. "What harm would be done by waiting for this trial, which will begin September 9th?" he asked.

Somehow none of the lawyers present, particularly those representing the Judiciary Committee and the president, felt that halting the committee's own investigation during the pendency of Sirica's show trial was prudent or even feasible.

On March 18, Sirica ruled in favor of transmitting the Road Map. His opinion did not mention the inclusion of any tapes, but it did indicate that he knew what would be transmitted: "After having had an opportunity to familiarize itself with the contents of the Report, the Court invited all counsel who might conceivably have an interest in the matter, without regard to standing, to state their positions concerning its disposition."

Haldeman and Ehrlichman appealed to the D.C. Circuit two days later, and the appellate hearing was held and decided the very next day—a harbinger of the quick affirmations of Sirica's rulings that were to dog them throughout their defense. Sitting en banc, the five members of the circuit court's liberal block issued an unsigned order upholding Sirica's ruling.[12]

In its brief order, the court relied heavily on the judgment of the special prosecutor in instituting the report and on that of Sirica in upholding its transmittal, saying that their determination that the defendants could still receive a fair trial was more persuasive than the "slender reed" raised regarding possible prejudicial pretrial publicity. Nowhere in the court's opinion, including in Judge MacKinnon's dissent, was it acknowledged that some of the "selected evidence" being transmitted included actual tape recordings and WSPF transcripts.

The White House had consistently resisted court enforcement of congressional subpoenas of tape recordings and had prevailed in suits before Sirica, Gesell, and the D.C. Circuit. It seems clear in retrospect that if the White House had known of the inclusion of tape recordings, they would have objected to their transmittal in this manner because of the precedent that would be set. It further appears that had the court of appeals been formally informed of the tapes' inclusion, it too would have been hard pressed to uphold the transmittal's propriety. Both the WSPF prosecutors and Sirica must have realized this, which is why they took great pains to avoid any specific mention of the inclusion of the tapes themselves.

So, what did the much-heralded Road Map say? While it remains sealed, the best source as to its contents is James Doyle, who wrote:

> It was a simple document, fifty-five pages long, with only a sentence or two on each of the pages. Each page was a reference to a piece of evidence—sentences from one of the tape recordings, quotations from grand jury testimony.
>
> Someday the archives will be opened and what the prosecutors referred to as "the road map" will be made public. When that happens it will prove a simple and unimpressive document, for it is narrow, declaratory, without conclusions.
>
> This is how the road map worked: One page might say, "On March 16, 1973, E. Howard Hunt demanded $120,000." Then it would list page references to grand jury testimony from witnesses who saw Hunt's blackmail note and references to tapes where Hunt's demand was discussed. The grand jury transcripts and the tape transcripts would be included. The next page might say, "On March 21, 1973, John Dean told President Nixon that Hunt had demanded $120,000, and that he estimated Hunt and the other Watergate defendants would 'cost' a million dollars in the next two years." More grand jury and tape transcript page references. The next page would say, "President Nixon responded, 'For Christ's sake, get it'"; and there would be further references to the tapes.
>
> The strength of the document was its simplicity. An inexorable logic marched through its pages. The conclusion that the President of the United States took part in a criminal conspiracy became inescapable.[13]

Doyle's example of "how the road map worked" suggests that it made the same unsupported leap that Frampton made in his draft prosecutorial report, namely, that since the March 21st payment to Hunt's lawyer followed Dean's meeting with President Nixon, the payment must have been made as a result of that meeting.

The Frampton Supposition is a classic example of the logical fallacy *post hoc, ergo propter hoc*—literally, "after this, therefore because of this." The Watergate Task Force built its case on this fallacy because it had to—it had nothing else. Charging ahead, the prosecutors privately informed the grand jury and the House Judiciary Committee of their conclusion that President Nixon had personally ordered actions in furtherance of a criminal conspiracy, hoping that everyone would ignore or fail to notice the missing causal link.

NAMING NIXON AS AN UNINDICTED CO-CONSPIRATOR

In addition to transmitting a report to the congressmen contemplating the impeachment of the president, the grand jury followed the WSPF prosecutors' counsel and named Nixon as an unindicted co-conspirator in the Watergate cover-up.

As a part of their comprehensive cover-up indictment, the grand jurors had voted nineteen to zero on February 25, 1974, to take this unprecedented action following a personal appeal by Special Prosecutor Leon Jaworski. When the grand jury had taken an earlier straw poll on whether to indict the president, Ben-Veniste had been in the room, at least according to the grand juror George Gross.[14] Grand jury votes are not supposed to be taken in the presence of prosecutors, and aside from whether straw votes should be taken at all, the episode indicates how closely involved with the jurors the WSPF prosecutors had become.

Naming President Nixon as a co-conspirator was the very action that Archibald Cox had publicly announced he wouldn't allow, but Cox was long gone. Jaworski's own initial, adamant refusal also had been overcome—no doubt as a result of the confidence that the Frampton Supposition had inspired in the prosecution.

Naming the president as an unindicted co-conspirator was deceptively simple and diabolically clever. It put him into an impossible position, both legally and politically—accused of criminal conduct by the grand jury, but unable to come into a court of law to defend himself. But there was an added benefit: the simple expedient of naming Nixon as a co-conspirator made all the White House tape recordings admissible at trial through an exception to the hearsay rule that will be discussed in the following chapter. One wonders whether the advantage in trial tactics was the real reason in overcoming the lead prosecutors' prior objections to including the president among the conspirators.

HELP FOR THE HOUSE JUDICIARY COMMITTEE

Apparently, the Road Map was not clear enough for the House Judiciary Committee, and WSPF prosecutors felt obliged to hold secret meetings with its staff to assure that they appreciated what the prosecutors believed they had uncovered. These secret contacts with the impeachment staff began in May, Ben-Veniste and Frampton write, going out of their way to insist that they and his colleagues were "sensitive" to the rules of grand jury secrecy.[15]

To provide a sharper focus for these meetings, Henry Ruth suggested that Frampton's 128-page Prosecutive Report on President Nixon should be revised so that prosecutors would have "in hand a comprehensive, up-to-date prosecutive memorandum laying out all of the evidence against the President."[16] Frampton's sixty-four-page revision, dated June 28, 1974,[17] reflects a single-minded focus on the events of March 21, as is evident from its opening paragraph:

> This memorandum focuses on facts, inferences, and theories that demonstrate that beginning no later than March 21, 1973, the President joined an ongoing criminal conspiracy to obstruct justice, obstruct a criminal investigation, and commit perjury....

This contention is directly contrary to President Nixon's essential Watergate defense (which Dean vigorously supports in his recent book)— that Nixon didn't fully appreciate what had been going on before his March 21st meeting with Dean, after which he began trying to get to the bottom of it. In contrast, WSPF prosecutors asserted that Nixon had joined the cover-up conspiracy upon learning of it.

Frampton recounts the prosecution's version of the events of March 21—on the president's instructions, Haldeman called Mitchell after the meeting with Dean and told him to instruct LaRue to meet Hunt's blackmail demand, which LaRue did that evening—and then sets forth the prosecution's theory of Nixon's criminal liability:

> The actions and statements of the President set out above are sufficient to show that the President joined and became an active participant in a conspiracy to make cash payments to Howard Hunt and others in order to influence their testimony before various tribunals.
>
> The President's counsel has argued that the President did not specifically instruct anyone on March 21 to make the payment to Hunt and that in any event the $75,000 paid on that same night was not paid on a direct chain of instructions emanating from the President. Despite this argument, there is certainly sufficient evidence—consisting of the undisputed facts listed above together with a single inference that a reasonable man could certainly draw therefrom in light of all the surrounding circumstances—to permit a jury to conclude beyond a reasonable doubt that the President did instruct that Hunt be paid and that the President's instructions were communicated by a direct chain of communication from Haldeman to Mitchell to LaRue, thereby becoming the causal force of the payment that evening. [pp. 16–17]

Frampton goes on to say that, even if they couldn't prove a direct casual connection, a jury could still find beyond a reasonable doubt that the president "threw his lot in with the conspirators and had made their purpose his own," and that, even if there had been no seventy-five-thousand-dollar payment at all, "there probably would be sufficient evidence upon which the jury could find Presidential liability." While his intent was to cover all of the bases, the main thrust of Frampton's report was WSPF prosecutors' belief in the Frampton Supposition, which he repeated:

> Given the entire chain of circumstances, given the President's urgent concern about Hunt's threat on the morning of March 21, and given Haldeman's role as the President's chief of staff ordinarily charged with communicating the President's desires directly to those who were required to take highly significant action, a jury could certainly draw the inference that Haldeman did pass along the President's feelings as instructions to Mitchell. Such an inference completes the causal chain. [p. 27]

This revised memorandum indicates in the clearest terms the WSPF prosecutors' nearly exclusive reliance on the Frampton Supposition as the primary evidence of the president's personal guilt and their eagerness to convince the House Judiciary staff of their conclusions.

But if we pause to reexamine the Frampton Supposition in the cold light of day, we can see it for what it was. It was not, in fact, "a single inference that a reasonable man could certainly draw...in light of all the surrounding circumstances" but an argument with absurd implications. By making this one reasonable leap of faith, Frampton maintains, a jury could conclude beyond a reasonable doubt that Nixon did what no actual evidence shows he did. As we shall see, the reasonableness of that single inference did not hold up when challenged in court, and their theory was quietly abandoned, but only after the damage had been done.

Armed with Frampton's revised Prosecutive Report, WSPF staff connived to convey its full import to John Doar, lead counsel to the Judiciary Committee's impeachment inquiry. Ben-Veniste and Frampton describe how they pulled this off:

> Within a few days John Doar became aware of the existence of this memorandum. Doar demanded the document and

told the Special Prosecutor and his deputy that he would recommend to the full Judiciary Committee that it be subpoenaed if necessary. Doar was told, in response, that we believed it would be unwise to have a copy of this document go to the committee physically, as it was an internal prosecution document. Since it was obviously relevant to the impeachment inquiry, however, Doar would be permitted to examine it in our offices if he agreed to withdraw the "threat" of a subpoena. Several late evenings that week Doar pored over the memorandum in Ruth's office, taking copious notes.[18]

What Ben-Veniste and Frampton omit is that Doar's supposed demand for the report and the WSPF's response are documented by three letters, all dated the same day and all helpfully bearing the notation "By Hand," as though this exchange of letters really had occurred over the course of a single day. The unlikelihood of such an exchange raises a suspicion that these documents were created after the fact to give the appearance of propriety to the prosecutors' sharing their report with Doar.

Ben-Veniste and Frampton also neglect to point out that, by supposedly following this procedure (and avoiding the formality of a subpoena), WSPF information was conveyed to the impeachment inquiry staff in secret. The president's lawyers, unaware of these meetings, had no opportunity to challenge them or to refute the memorandum's assertions. Since the WSPF's assistance to the House impeachment inquiry was kept secret, it could not be reviewed by a court of law.

Frampton's revised report certainly did the trick. The WSPF prosecutors' certainty of Nixon's guilt easily carried the day. Don't take my word for it—you can get it straight from the special prosecutor. In Bob Woodward's notes from his December 5, 1974, interview of Leon Jaworksi, he asserts again and again that the contribution of the WSPF was determinative in the House Judiciary Committee's impeachment recommendations (see Appendix B).

On July 27, the Judiciary Committee voted twenty-seven to eleven to adopt the first article of impeachment, for obstruction of justice, which provided in pertinent part:

> The means used to implement this course of conduct or plan included one or more of the following:...
>
> (5) approving, condoning, and acquiescing in, the surreptitious payment of substantial sums of money for the purpose of obtaining the silence or influencing the testimony of witnesses, potential witnesses or individuals who participated in such unlawful entry and other illegal activities.

In essence, the Frampton Supposition provided the substantive underpinning for WSPF prosecutors' assurances—to the grand jury and to the House Judiciary Committee—that Nixon was personally involved in authorizing the final Hunt payoff. When it came time to prove their thesis in an actual court of law, subject to rules of evidence and the opportunity to confront and cross-examine witnesses, WSPF prosecutors failed miserably and the Frampton Supposition was quietly abandoned. But it was not for lack of trying.

THE COVER-UP TRIAL: CONVICTING NIXON IN ABSENTIA

President Nixon may have been pardoned and thus out of reach of WSPF prosecutors, but the cover-up trial gave them the opportunity to prove their prosecutorial theory. Nixon was not an actual defendant at this trial, but he was certainly being tried in absentia as a principle target of WSPF prosecutors.

Proving the Frampton Supposition was one of the prosecution's paramount goals at this trial. Nixon, they argued, would have revisited Hunt's blackmail demands with Haldeman right after Dean left their meeting at 11:55 a.m. on March 21, 1973. The president would have told Haldeman to contact Mitchell in New York to order that Hunt's demands be met. For this scenario to work, Fred LaRue would have to have talked with Mitchell in the *afternoon* of March 21 (that is, subsequent to Haldeman's phone call, which clearly followed Dean's meeting with Nixon).[19]

To perfect their scenario, the WSPF had to corral its witnesses into telling a consistent story about a matter that had not been so critical when they testified before the Ervin Committee and subsequent grand juries. Ideally, Dean and LaRue would testify that their conversation occurred on March 21, and not before, precluding any alternative interpretations.

But Dean's recollection up to this point, reflected in WSPF documents, had been that his conversation with LaRue had occurred on March 20. The July 1974 draft of Dean's anticipated testimony noted with asterisks (*) any significant discrepancies with Dean's prior testimony or that of other government witnesses:

> On March 20 or 21, Dean had a conversation with LaRue in which LaRue asked Dean what should be done about Hunt's demand and Dean said that Dean wanted nothing more to do with money and would not tell LaRue what to do. LaRue replied that LaRue would not pay any money to Hunt without instructions or authorization from someone else; Dean suggested that LaRue contact Mitchell if he wanted authorization.*
>
> *Dean believes this conversation was on March 20. If LaRue got authorization from Mitchell on March 21, however, it appears more likely that Dean and LaRue spoke on March 21.
>
> LaRue recalls this as a telephone conversation. Dean recalls that LaRue came to Dean's office.
>
> Dean recalls that LaRue was already aware of the threat, presumably through O'Brien. O'Brien denies telling LaRue. LaRue should be questioned about this closely.[20]

Note the challenges to the WSPF desired scenario that are reflected in this document: LaRue remembered this as a telephone conversation of indeterminate date. Dean remembered it as a face-to-face meeting on the evening of March 20. It was troubling—and remains so today—that the government's two witnesses did not even agree on the date or on the format of this critical conversation.

The specific date was finessed in the finalized WSPF memo, which carefully did not predict Dean's actual testimony:

> 3/20 or early 3/21/73

> Dean and LaRue discuss Hunt demand. Dean says "I am not going to have anything to do with it—take it up with Mitchell." LaRue said o.k. and left.
> GJ 11/20/73, 87
> GJ 2/14/74, p. 16
> House Jud II 249–250[21]

We have no access to the grand jury testimony that is cited, but we do know that it was John Dean who appeared before the grand jury on November 20, 1973. It is not clear whether the February 14, 1974, appearance was that of Dean or LaRue. Dean's written statement before the Ervin Committee had finessed the matter entirely. He did not allude to any meeting or conversation with LaRue on either March 20 or 21.[22]

In Ben-Veniste's opening statement at trial he also finessed the date of the Dean-LaRue communication—placing it on either March 20 or 21—and whether it was a telephone conversation or in-person meeting:

> Now, either that evening or on the morning of March 21st, before meeting with the President and H. R. Haldeman, Dean informed LaRue of the fact that Hunt was asking for this enormous sum of money.[23]

By the time Dean actually testified at the cover-up trial, however, he must have felt more confident of not being challenged on any inconsistency with his earlier statements to prosecutors, for he was now more open to the possibility that his conversation with LaRue had occurred on March 21. Here is his exchange with James Neal, who was guiding him through his direct testimony:

> Q: Mr. Dean, before we go further on this, I want to ask you to back up to just before you had your conversation with the President about what you just testified and ask you if you had occasion to talk with Mr. Fred LaRue?
> A: Yes sir; I did.
> Q: About Mr. Hunt's demands?
> A: Yes sir; I did.
> Q: Tell us when this was?
> A: Mr. Neal, that was either on the evening of the 20th there was possibly a telephone call on the evening of the 20th but my best recollection is there was a very brief meeting with Mr. LaRue and myself on the morning of the 21st.
> Q: Was that before your meeting with the President?
> A: Yes sir.

While Dean had now done his part and altered his recollection (in conflict with his earlier testimony), LaRue's testimony about the timing of his conversations with Dean and Mitchell remained problematic. Here is LaRue's exchange with Ben-Veniste, who was guiding him through his direct testimony:

> Q: Now, did there come a time on or about the 21st of March, Mr. LaRue, when you learned of additional requests for money from the defendants?
> A: Yes.
> Q: And what were the circumstances of that?
> A: This was a conversation—this was a phone call I had from Mr. Dean.
> Q: Can you fix the time?

A: The best of my recollection, the phone call was that morning.

Q: What did Mr. Dean say to you?

A: Mr. Dean said that he had a request for funds for Mr. Hunt. The amount was approximately $130,000, broken down, as I recall, to $60,000 for his living expenses for a year, approximately $75,000 for legal fees.

Q: Sixty and 75 is different than 130.

A: It would be 135. Mr. Dean told me that—or I asked Mr. Dean if he thought I should pay this money. At that time I had that much cash on hand.

Mr. Dean informed me that he was not any longer in the money business, that he was very apprehensive about this operation, he was withdrawing from it and would no longer be involved with anything having to do with money and Watergate affairs.

I told Mr. Dean that I would not undertake to make any payments unless I had some authorization from someone.

He said: Why don't you call Mr. Mitchell.

Q: Did you call Mr. Mitchell?

A: Yes, I did.

Q: Can you fix the time of day?

A: Again, the best of my recollection, it would be the morning of the 21st.

Q: Do you know whether you actually spoke with Mr. Mitchell on the morning of the 21st?

A: I know I placed the call, whether I talked to him at the time I placed the call or he called me back, I don't know.

Q: Can you say with any certainty whether it was the morning or afternoon that you spoke with Mr. Mitchell?

A: I cannot say with any degree of certainty, no.[24]

This was not the answer that Ben-Veniste wanted. The LaRue-Mitchell conversation had to have occurred *after* the conclusion of Dean's

March 21st meeting with the president—which had ended at 11:55 a.m.—for the prosecutors' scenario involving Nixon to be feasible. That is why LaRue's recollection of a morning call was so devastating—and why Ben-Veniste introduced the idea that maybe the call had not gone through.

Ben-Veniste had pushed LaRue as hard as he dared, even to the point of asking leading questions on direct examination in a desperate attempt to align LaRue's testimony with the revised testimony of John Dean, but LaRue's responses had hardly been helpful.

While the defendants themselves did not appear to appreciate the critical importance of these exchanges with respect to President Nixon, they did get LaRue to reconfirm his testimony on cross-examination by John Wilson, Haldeman's defense counsel:

> Q: Going to the March 21st meeting, you said your best recollection was that you called Mr. Mitchell in the morning?
>
> A: That is correct.
>
> Q: And you testified that you told Mr. Mitchell that they needed $75,000 is that correct?
>
> A: Yes.
>
> Q: And you fixed the figure of $75,000?
>
> A: That is correct.
>
> Q: And I take it, according to your testimony, that he then asked you what it was for; is that right?
>
> A: That is correct.
>
> Q: And what did you tell him?
>
> A: I told him it was for legal fees.[25]

But it really was much worse. When LaRue was asked why he had asked Mitchell only for authority to pay the seventy-five thousand dollars of legal expenses (instead of Hunt's total demand of $135,000), LaRue responded that they had never paid the full amount requested by any defendant and had always cut it back by some amount. He volunteered that it had been his decision alone to pay only the legal fees portion of

Hunt's demands. This unexpected response totally undermined the Frampton Supposition. It is obvious that if the president had ordered the payment based on Dean's representations that morning, the full $135,000 would have been paid.

Dean had changed his testimony to support the WSPF hypothesis and testified that his communication with LaRue—he still maintained that it had been a brief meeting—had occurred on the morning of March 21. LaRue had been brow-beaten into placing the conversation on March 21, but he still maintained that it had taken place over the telephone, and he was clear in his recollection that the conversation had occurred in the morning.

Without LaRue's testimony that his conversation with Mitchell had not occurred in the afternoon of March 21 (preferably with Mitchell calling him, rather than the reverse, to relay the instructions that Mitchell had allegedly received from Haldeman following the Nixon-Dean meeting of late that morning), and that it was his own idea to cut the payment to seventy-five thousand dollars, the WSPF prosecutors' theory of Nixon's direct involvement in that final payment collapsed. The Frampton Supposition was never advanced again—not in the closing arguments in the cover-up trial and not in the statement of facts or argument in WSPF briefs on subsequent appeals to the D.C. Circuit.

There was no public acknowledgment of the Frampton Supposition's demise, however. It was as though WSPF prosecutors hoped that no one would remember their long-maintained theory of presidential involvement, which they had so forcefully conveyed to the grand jury, had made the basis for the Road Map and for naming Nixon as an unindicted co-conspirator, and had conveyed to the House Judiciary staff as the determining factor in Nixon's impeachment. The Frampton Supposition, which had driven the prosecutors' concerted effort to convince the government's witnesses to change their recollections at the cover-up trial, vanished without a trace—until now.

CONCLUSIONS AND IMPLICATIONS

Much new information has come to light since Nixon's resignation.

We now know that the smoking gun tape has been totally misunderstood, that it did not reveal any criminal interference with the FBI's Watergate investigation, and that it should not have forced the president's resignation.

We also now know that the moving force behind the House Judiciary Committee's first article of impeachment, the WSPF prosecutor's secret and adamant assurance that they had proof of Nixon's own personal involvement in directing the final payoff to Howard Hunt, turned out to be unsupportable.

America lost a great president when Nixon was forced from office. The damage to our nation, wreaked by prosecutorial excess and judicial malfeasance, is now clear for all to see. Let us now turn our attention to how the same sort of judicial and prosecutorial improprieties denied Nixon's senior aides their constitutional right to a fair trial through systematic violations of the due process of law.

PART IV

DENYING DUE PROCESS TO THE WATERGATE DEFENDANTS

We have already identified the essential elements of due process denied to Mitchell, Haldeman, and Ehrlichman during the cover-up trial. The next four chapters consider these elements in greater detail. Any one of these abuses, had it been known at the time, might well have been sufficient grounds for overturning the verdicts.

CHAPTER 6

A FAIR AND IMPARTIAL TRIAL JUDGE

The independence of the judiciary from the influence of the executive was codified in England by the Act of Settlement of 1701. The Founding Fathers made an independent judiciary part of the basic architecture of the government of the United States, establishing the judiciary in Article III of the Constitution as one of the three co-equal branches of government. One of the purposes of this independence is to assure that judges can preside over trials without being unduly influenced by prosecutors.

In the Watergate trials, however, Judge John Sirica effectively joined the prosecution, combining the roles of vengeance and justice in one man. This is the very definition of tyranny and a subversion of the Anglo-American adversarial tradition. The system—reassurances from Carl Bernstein and Leon Jaworski notwithstanding—did not work.

A JUDICIAL INQUISITION: SIRICA'S CONDUCT OF THE BREAK-IN TRIAL

Sirica's conduct of the original Watergate break-in trial was controversial, largely indefensible, and roundly criticized at the time. Among his severest critics was the journalist and lawyer Renata Adler, a former staff member of the House Judiciary Committee's impeachment inquiry:

> A judge, after all, is not meant to be a hero. And judges, under the Constitution, are not meant to ascertain, least of all to prosecute or to coerce by sentencing, the "truth," "for the American people," or even for the jury. They are to preside fairly, under the adversary system, over cases presented to them by lawyers for the plaintiffs and the defendants before them. Anything else, whether it is posturing for the media, or coercing defendants with outrageous "provisional sentences", or working on behalf of some party not before the court, undermines the system. Far from demonstrating that "no man is above the law," it suggests that the judge himself is above it. We do not, under the Constitution, have a system wherein judges are inquisitors.[1]

Anglo-American criminal justice is based on the adversarial system, in which the judge does not investigate the facts himself but acts as an impartial referee between the prosecution and the defense. Each side makes its case to the jury, which determines questions of fact. In the inquisitorial system of the Continental legal tradition, the judge himself conducts the investigation of the facts. Sirica not only acted as an inquisitor by intruding himself into the investigation, as Adler charged; he went further and took the part of the prosecution.

Sirica refused to accept plea bargains that Hunt and the Cubans had reached with federal prosecutors, demanding that they plead guilty to each and every charge brought against them. His justification for that decision was that he was certain of their guilt—somehow having achieved that certainty on the first day of trial before any evidence had been presented.

He cross-examined witnesses in front of the jury, urging them to provide a fuller story and to implicate others. He publicly criticized the prosecution for not aggressively pursuing other possible defendants. At the trial's conclusion, he announced his frustration in not having uncovered the real story, the "truth" as he characterized it, and called for a Senate investigation. He even went so far as to demand that the prosecution bring before the grand jury a list of persons who he believed must know more about the scandal than had come out in his courtroom. His provisional sentences of up to thirty-five years for first-time burglary convictions remain a classic example of judicial excess.[2]

SIRICA'S OPEN-DOOR POLICY: PRIVATE MEETINGS WITH INTERESTED PARTIES

Sirica's prejudicial conduct as trial judge was even worse than anyone knew at the time. He held a series of private meetings with outside parties with interests adverse to the defendants before him in the burglary trial and those who would come before him in the cover-up trial. It was as though anyone with an anti-Nixon interest in Watergate owed it to himself to drop by and discuss the matter with the judge. His door was always open to secret meetings with people on that side of the political battle. Four sets of such meetings have come to light since the break-in trial.

Ex Parte Meetings with Edward Bennett Williams

Edward Bennett Williams (1920–1988)[3] was born and raised in Hartford, Connecticut, in modest circumstances. He attended Holy Cross College on an academic scholarship but really came into his own at Georgetown University Law School, where he was an outstanding student. Upon graduating in 1944, he was hired into the eighteen-man law firm of Hogan & Hartson, he stayed four years before leaving to form his own trial firm, which survives today as Williams & Connolly.

Williams became known as the best and most aggressive criminal defense lawyer on the East Coast, if not in the country. Over the course of his forty-four-year career, he represented an amazing cross section of the prominent and the powerful of both parties. His clients included Teamsters presidents Dave Beck and Jimmy Hoffa, on corruption charges; Treasury Secretary John Connally, on Watergate-related bribery charges; Mafia kingpin Frank Costello, on racketeering charges; Bernard Goldfine, whose gift of a vicuna coat had cost Eisenhower's chief of staff, Sherman Adams, his job; CIA Director Richard Helms, on charges of lying in congressional testimony; Senator Joe McCarthy, who was censured by the Senate; Congressman Adam Clayton Powell, the controversial and flamboyant New Yorker who was expelled from Congress; New York Yankees owner George Steinbrenner, on Watergate-related campaign finance charges; and Robert Vesco, who was indicted with John Mitchell and Maurice Stans on Watergate-related campaign finance charges.

This hugely successful attorney cast a long shadow in Democratic political circles, especially as a frequent advisor to President Johnson. At the same time, Williams was an owner of the Washington Redskins football team and entertained lavishly in his box at RFK Stadium. He was counsel to the *Washington Post*, whose cub reporters Woodward and Bernstein were writing Watergate-related stories on almost a daily basis. Perhaps as importantly, he was treasurer of Democratic National Committee, whose offices had been the target of the Watergate burglars.

Within three days of their arrest on June 17, 1972, Williams had filed a three-hundred-page civil suit on behalf of the DNC against CRP. His aggressive deposition schedule, which had all the characteristics of front-running the Watergate grand jury's investigations, was halted by judicial order on September 21, 1972, just days after the Watergate burglars had been indicted, but not before severe damage had been inflicted on the Nixon White House. It's no wonder that he was considered to be "White House Enemy Number One," the title of the opening chapter in Robert Pack's biography of Williams.[4]

In short, it would have been difficult to identify a lawyer more closely identified with the opposition to the Nixon administration or more involved in efforts to bring about its demise.

Williams was also exceptionally close to Sirica. While he is mentioned only once in Sirica's book (in connection with the incident we will explore below), Williams was Sirica's career mentor and saved him from his unsuccessful solo practice. It seems that when Williams left Hogan & Hartson in 1949 to form his own criminal defense firm, he arranged for his former partners to hire Sirica as his replacement, a man some sixteen years his senior but a fellow graduate of Georgetown Law School. As Pack put it, Sirica never forgot who saved him and his legal career, which he had been tempted to give up entirely:

> Instead, Sirica spent eight years at Hogan & Hartson, then was named a U.S. district judge in 1957. As a result of his close friendship with Williams (Williams and his wife were godparents of Sirica's daughter), Sirica has disqualified himself from hearing any of Williams's cases, except for routine motions.[5]

Their friendship is of interest because of something that happened in the fall of 1972. There was a lull in Watergate reporting following the burglary indictments on September 15. While the government's criminal investigations continued and the Watergate grand jury was still active, the *Post*'s stories were losing their immediacy and sense of urgency. Woodward and Bernstein then hit upon the idea of interviewing several of the Watergate grand jurors, but when they tried, one of them complained to the prosecutors. When Sirica was informed of their actions, he brought it to a halt by admonishing the two reporters. A number of books have covered this incident, but there is more here than is immediately apparent. Woodward and Bernstein undertook these interviews with the full concurrence of the *Post*'s management and, it appears, with the advance knowledge of the newspaper's outside counsel—Edward Bennett Williams and his equally well-connected partner Joseph Califano.

In late November, Woodward talked someone in the clerk's office at the U.S. courthouse into letting him review the list of grand jurors. He was allowed to look but not to take notes. Over the course of the morning, however, he managed to memorize and record all twenty-three names, as well as their contact information.

This list was discussed, dissected, and debated by the *Post*'s management team, who identified the most promising members. Over the first weekend in December, working independently, Woodward or Bernstein approached at least six of the jurors, supposedly without success. But on Monday morning, one of those who had been approached complained to Earl Silbert, an assistant U.S. attorney, who then informed Sirica.

None of the published accounts contains the specifics of how the meeting came about, but Williams was promptly dispatched to see his old friend Judge Sirica on the *Post*'s behalf. Another biographer, Evan Thomas, offers this description of Williams's appeal to Sirica:

> Fortunately, Williams and Sirica were old friends, fellow Catholics and criminal lawyers from the fifties. Williams was godfather to one of the judge's children. Williams took the tack of agreeing with Sirica that reporters were irresponsible nuisances, but he argued that the grand jurors had not actually leaked anything, so there had been no breach of grand jury secrecy. He promised that the two young reporters would behave in the future. Sirica agreed to let them off with a verbal reprimand.[6]

Perhaps that is how things really are handled in Washington. Prominent counsel, perhaps the Nixon administration's most ardent opponent, meets privately with his old friend, the very judge who is about to rip that administration limb from limb, to smooth over this unfortunate incident. It is incidental that this same lawyer is lead counsel in a pending civil suit against the president's re-election committee and seeking damages for its responsibility for the very break-in that is the subject of the criminal trial then before this judge. Regardless, everything is finessed and there's no harm done—at least to the one side.

Here is how Sirica described this incident and its resolution in his own book:

> The newspaper had performed an invaluable public service in keeping the spotlight on the Watergate case, but now they had gone too far, interfering, I thought, with the administration of justice.
>
> The newspaper's attorney, Edward Bennett Williams, assured me that the *Post* management had admonished the eager young reporters and that no further incidents like this would occur. I settled on a stiff lecture in open court, reminding everyone present that to approach a grand juror and solicit information about a case being investigated was to ask for a citation for contempt. I praised the grand jurors for their refusal to co-operate and recessed the proceeding to let the message sink in. In their later book, about their reporting efforts, Woodward and Bernstein said that after the lecture, "they felt lousy... they had sailed around [the law] and exposed others to danger. They had chosen expediency over principle...." I agree. Had they actually obtained information from that grand juror, they would have gone to jail.[7]

How reassuring. Here is yet another instructive example of how a considerate and resolute judge has assessed an unfortunate incident and dealt with it in a prompt and proper manner—from the lips of the very judge who acted so responsibly. And he knows the reporters were contrite about what they had done because they said so in their bestselling book.

The only trouble is that much of this story turns out to be completely untrue.

Sirica's remarks to the overreaching journalists were hardly a "stiff lecture in open court." Having collected members of the press in his courtroom on December 19, 1972, he informed them that "a news media representative" had improperly approached grand jurors, a trespass he characterized as "extremely serious." He took no action against the two reporters, warning only in the most general way that seeking out grand jurors could, potentially, place people in contempt of court.

Gordon Liddy, who had been indicted by this same grand jury and was soon to stand trial before this very judge, complained in his memoir that Sirica "had knuckled under to the *Post*'s powerful lawyer, Edward Bennett Williams," pointing out that far from singling out Woodward and Bernstein for their unacceptable conduct, Sirica had never even mentioned their names.[8]

This was not the only ex parte meeting that Williams had with Sirica at that time:

> Shortly after Sirica's lecture to the press against seeking out grand jurors, a potential witness in the case mistakenly understood Woodward to have identified himself as an FBI agent when he tried to interview her. Williams again had to argue on behalf of Woodward and Bernstein to Sirica, who placed additional restrictions on the two eager reporters.[9]

So we have not one but two instances of private meetings between Sirica and Ed Williams, about whose friendship the judge was so punctilious that he would not allow Williams even to practice before him in court. Of course, we do not know the full content of the meetings—since they were secret and no record of their conversation was kept—so we don't know what else might have been said during the course of their discussion. It seems fair to assume, however, that these were not quick, five-minute conversations.

We only know that if the defendants' counsel had been made aware of these meetings, as they should have been, they would have insisted that they be conducted in open court and on the record so that everyone would know what had been said and they could have been assured that their clients' interests had been protected.

This was how matters stood until April 29, 2012, when an article by Jeff Himmelman was posted in the online edition of *New York* magazine.[10]

Himmelman, who had been Woodward's research assistant and lived on the third floor of Woodward's house, had agreed to help Ben Bradlee, the ninety-year-old former editor of the *Washington Post*, who was considering writing another book. Bradlee, who died in October 2014, subsequently decided to have Himmelman write the book on his own and opened all of his files to the young researcher.

The article, soon followed by the book itself, *Yours in Truth: A Personal Portrait of Ben Bradlee*, contained a number of remarkable revelations. To begin with, in a talk on March 15, 2011, Woodward said that the *Post*'s lawyers had approved their efforts to interview the Watergate grand jurors:

> In the Watergate investigation, Carl Bernstein and I went to talk to grand jurors. *We had legal advice saying we could do it.* It was very risky. It is not something I'm sure I'd do all the time, but when you're convinced the system of justice has collapsed, I think you have to be very aggressive. But we didn't say we were from the U.S. attorney's office. We identified ourselves as *Washington Post* reporters—and we got nothing from the grand jurors [emphasis added].[11]

This is rather startling news, since Williams had vehemently denied ever giving advance permission for this initiative. It also does not sound like the contrition that Sirica bragged about having inspired with his skillful handling of this breach of grand jury sanctity.

Himmelman also disclosed that Williams himself had strongly objected to the description of his meeting with Sirica that appeared in Woodward's and Bernstein's blockbuster book, *All the President's Men*:[12]

> Williams didn't like the idea of a back room deal with Sirica and objected to its publication in *All the President's Men*; just

before the book came out he appealed to Simon and Schuster to have it eliminated from the manuscript. When it made it into the final draft, Williams refused to talk to Woodward for two years.[13]

Williams was right to be seriously concerned. Much more attuned to the Rules of Professional Responsibility than the two reporters, the eminent lawyer had realized all along that his meeting with Sirica could have been characterized—and criticized—as a back-room deal. But Woodward's and Bernstein's description was an entirely different matter. Williams knew the responsibilities and obligations regarding ex parte meetings between lawyers and judges and feared that the disclosure of such a meeting in the reporters' book would be seen as a clear violation of both legal and judicial ethics and lead to real trouble. It is no wonder that he was so aggressive in his efforts to have that section removed and that he reacted so strongly when it was not. The disclosure could have gotten him hauled before the bar association's ethics committee and perhaps even disciplined as a result.

Himmelman's most interesting disclosure, however, was that Bernstein had, in fact, succeeded in interviewing at least one of the Watergate grand jurors. She turns out to be the source that the two reporters misleadingly described in their book as "Z," with the implication that she was a CRP secretary.[14]

Bradlee's files contained seven pages of typed notes from Bernstein's interview with that grand juror on December 4, 1972. This appears to confirm that Bradlee himself knew of Bernstein's success, and it suggests that the evidence of this breach of grand jury sanctity had been deposited with Bradlee for safekeeping when Silbert was tipped off about the reporters' attempted interviews. If they were questioned, Woodward and Bernstein could deny having anything incriminating in their possession. While one hesitates to question the ethics of these heroic journalists, the cynically minded might ask in what other particulars the veracity of their reporting might be doubted.[15]

Finally, Himmelman found the following notes from the files of Alan Pakula, the director of the movie version of *All the President's Men*:

> Barry Sussman [the editor in charge of the *Washington Post*'s Watergate coverage], to Pakula: "Some of their writing is not true...that they never got something from a Grand Jury member. Barry thinks that's wrong. They did get information from one person and Carl planned to meet with that person again."[16]

There is considerable basis, therefore, for believing that the *Post*'s entire newsroom had been lying about the grand juror incident for forty years. It also contains the tantalizing possibility that Edward Bennett Williams not only knew and approved of the initiative in advance but may also have known about the successful interview with one of the grand jurors when he assured Sirica that Woodward and Bernstein had obtained no information from any of them.

The reporters' interview with at least one Watergate grand juror was highly improper, and their lying about it for the subsequent forty years only adds to these concerns. A zealous prosecutor could have framed the interview as an obstruction of justice and the participation of the *Post*'s management and its counsel as part of a conspiracy to obstruct justice. But that sort of prosecutorial zeal was reserved only for Nixon and his associates.

Williams's ex parte meetings with Sirica were equally improper and clearly influenced the judge to react much less aggressively than he might otherwise have done. But for Williams's personal and private intervention with Sirica, we might have learned far more about this troublesome breach of the sanctity of the Watergate grand jury. Some cover-ups, it seems, are successful.[17]

Moreover, if it could have been shown that the grand jury's secrecy had been breached and that the breach had led to further adverse publicity about potential defendants, the necessity of moving their subsequent trial to another jurisdiction might have been undeniably apparent.

If plaintiffs can informally dispose of problems through friendly chats with a judge who is remorselessly exacting with the defendants in a parallel case, then we must seriously question whether the trials over which that judge presides meet the standards of fairness demanded by the Fifth Amendment.

Ex Parte Meetings with Clark Mollenhoff

Clark Mollenhoff[18] is not a name many people know today, but it once was—at least among members of the Washington press corps. Before the legend of Woodward and Bernstein made investigative reporting a hallowed profession, Mollenhoff (1921–1991) was the dean of Washington's investigative reporters. The Institute on Political Journalism still bestows its annual Clark Mollenhoff Award for Excellence in Investigative Reporting on the author of the best investigative journalism in a newspaper or magazine.

Born and raised in Iowa and a 1944 graduate of Drake University law school, Mollenhoff was admitted to practice in Iowa, in Washington, D.C., and in the federal courts up to and including the U.S. Supreme Court. He was a reporter, yes, but also an active member of the legal profession and subject to its rules of professional responsibility.

Mollenhoff had worked for the *Des Moines Register* since his college days and was assigned to its Washington bureau following his year at Harvard as a Neiman Fellow. A nationally syndicated columnist and the author of several books, Mollenhoff had won the Pulitzer Prize for his reporting on the influence of organized crime in American society before joining the Nixon White House staff as special counsel in 1969. After leaving the White House, he authored six more books, including *Game Plan for Disaster* (1976), about Watergate, and a college textbook, *Investigative Reporting* (1981), whose highly disturbing disclosures will be the focus of our attention. Like Edward Bennett Williams, Mollenhoff was a close friend of Sirica, who mentions him twice in his own book.

Like many of the more prominent reporters in the capital, Mollenhoff was not content merely to report on the news; he felt compelled to help shape newsworthy events themselves. For example, in July 1974, as

Watergate spiraled toward its unhappy conclusion, Mollenhoff became so troubled about Vice President Ford's continued support of Nixon that he took it upon himself to counsel the vice president:

> I called Ford on the telephone. In a brief, friendly conversation, I expressed my views and listed the reasons for my opinion that the evidence established a serious criminal case of obstruction of justice against Richard Nixon. Ford offered no rebuttal to the facts I cited or to my legal considerations.
>
> It was not my desire to urge him to criticize President Nixon, but I did suggest that it was in neither his best interest nor that of the country for him to engage in a public defense which was without merit.[19]

The man on the phone with the vice president was not a reporter—much less a reporter's reporter. This was a man of action, one who knew what public officials ought to be doing and was not shy about telling them so directly.

Similarly, Mollenhoff modestly credits himself with talking Jeb Magruder into coming clean about his own role in Watergate and its cover-up. Mollenhoff sought him out in April 1973, after Judge Sirica had read James McCord's letter, to share his views about Magruder's deteriorating situation. Having first talked to Magruder's attorney, Mollenhoff took it upon himself to help Magruder to switch sides; that is, to become a prosecution witness. When they met, Mollenhoff writes,

> I told him...that I planned "to write a column indicting you in connection with the Watergate affair."
>
> When I entered his office, at 2:00 P.M., Magruder had been reasonably confident that he could "ride it out," but when I left, at 2:30, he was nervous and uncertain, making frequent reference to assurances his lawyers had been giving him for some months. As a parting shot, I tossed another ingredient into his stew: "I don't know who your lawyers are

and I don't want to know, but if they are paid for by the Nixon re-election committee, you had better ask yourself whether they are really looking out for your interests or whether they are using you to protect some higher-ups."[20]

The day after his meeting with Mollenhoff, Magruder came clean with his lawyers, which quickly led to his agreement the evening of April 13 to plead guilty to a single felony count and to become a prosecution witness.

Mollenhoff injected himself into the heart of the scandal at the precise moment that the cover-up was collapsing, creating the appearance, at least, that he was more interested in breaking the cover-up and bringing down the Nixon administration than in Magruder's personal welfare. Mollenhoff was, as they say, an interested party, and he acted not as a reporter but as an active participant in the Watergate drama.

Among Nixon's most dangerous enemies, Mollenhoff was unusual. He wasn't a product of the Eastern Establishment with a lifelong antipathy to everything that Nixon represented. In fact, he had joined the administration in its early days, but the disappointment he suffered there may explain the zeal with which he turned on Nixon in the end.

Mollenhoff had managed to convince Nixon that if he was serious about running the cleanest administration in recent memory, he would be well advised to have an ombudsman on his White House staff, someone who could sniff out problems before they became scandals, who could speak truth to power—someone, that is, very much like Mollenhoff himself.

Nixon went for it, and Mollenhoff joined the White House staff in August 1969. He didn't get all he wanted, however. He didn't get an office in the West Wing, and he was not one of Nixon's few direct reports. Instead, he was put in the Executive Office Building, given the title of deputy counsel, and told that he would be reporting to the president through Ehrlichman, then counsel to the president.

Mollenhoff devoted over a hundred pages at the beginning of his Watergate book to documenting his frustration at not seeing the president whenever he thought it appropriate and at having to communicate through Haldeman and Ehrlichman, the infamous "Berlin Wall." Mollenhoff complained that he saw the president on only five occasions during his ten-month stay. He was particularly chagrined by Haldeman's and Ehrlichman's use of the phrase "the President would like" when communicating orders to him. Unless Mollenhoff got his instructions from the president's own lips, he frequently responded, he would not accept them at face value.

Finally, on May 29, 1970, Mollenhoff left in frustration, carrying with him a deep and abiding resentment of Haldeman and Ehrlichman— and of the president. He became chief of the Washington bureau of the *Des Moines Register* and resumed his nationally syndicated column, wielding new authority because of his experience as the president's special counsel. With his insider's knowledge of the White House, he was a respected player among Washington insiders.

It was Nixon's great misfortune that one of his fiercest critics also enjoyed a close friendship with Judge Sirica going back to 1957.[21] Mollenhoff maintained the friendship during his time in the administration, even inviting the good judge to dine with him in the inner sanctum of the Staff Mess, Sirica's first meal at the White House.

Their relationship became critically important as the tides of Watergate began to engulf the president and his administration. Mollenhoff believed that Sirica was the only man who could frustrate the "complete cover-up of the Watergate affair and...the continuation and expansion of the corruptive doctrine of executive privilege,"[22] and he was determined to exercise his influence to ensure that Sirica did not fail:

> I hesitated to write or speak of my conviction that Judge Sirica would be a trustworthy and aggressive judge. This reluctance endured despite long conversations with him in the fall of 1972 in which we talked of the importance of honest government and I expressed a belief in the eventual triumph of right over wrong. We did not speak of the merits of the cases before him, but I was sure that he was lonely and

in need of assurance that if he did precisely what he believed to be right, at least one individual would remember it and record it in historic perspective.[23]

It is important to appreciate what Mollenhoff is saying here. He initiated a series of meetings with the very judge who had appointed himself to preside over the Watergate burglary trial (and later the cover-up trial). Mollenhoff's goal, which he certainly accomplished, was to convince Sirica that he alone was in a position to thwart the cover-up and to uncover the truth, but only if he took aggressive action as the presiding judge.

But Mollenhoff also had a special message to deliver to his friend: Mollenhoff knew the Nixon White House from the inside and had strong opinions as to what must have happened. In addition, he had a unique inside story that he was eager to share. He had secured an interview with Maury Stans, Nixon's former secretary of commerce who was chairman of CRP's finance committee, and Dick Moore, special counsel to the president, who was working on Watergate matters. Unfortunately, that interview had been off the record, so Mollenhoff could not quote them directly.

The thrust of what Mollenhoff most likely shared with Sirica, however, can be derived from the chapter on Watergate from his 1981 textbook *Investigative Reporting*, where he wrote about confiding his views with Stan Greigg, the deputy chairman of the Democratic National Committee:

> The understanding I had of the internal workings of the White House and the relationships of the various members of that staff was important in my early analysis of the Watergate matter. For example, I knew that Jeb Magruder, a former White House staffer who was deputy director of CREP, was likely to be Haldeman's puppet. If CREP had financed the burglary, it was likely that it had the approval of Haldeman. I knew that Magruder, ambitious and eager to

please Haldeman, was clearing all but routine matters with Haldeman personally.

I told Greigg that it was my view that Haldeman controlled the reelection committee through Magruder, and that Magruder would not have initiated such a burglary on his own....

The [White House] "game plan" was apparent to me. There would be the addition of some minor figures with White House connections indicted to give the impression of a forthright investigation, but even those indictments would be a part of an obstruction of justice unless they included Magruder, Haldeman, and Stans.

As a result of the Stans interview [on September 14, 1973, the day before the burglary indictments were handed down], I now knew that Richard Nixon was involved in planning and directing a cover-up that was being executed by John Dean in the White House.[24]

Since Mollenhoff was already peddling his insights to others, there is every reason to suppose that he shared the same views with Judge Sirica. This is the most harmful and indefensible sort of ex parte meeting with a sitting judge. Mollenhoff was clearly not there in a journalistic capacity; he was in no sense interviewing Sirica. No, he was seeking to influence his conduct and to even the score with Haldeman and Ehrlichman, the men who had cut off his access to Nixon three years before.

Sirica ate it up. Mollenhoff was telling him how important he was in the whole scheme of things—describing the role he was destined to play and promising to write columns lauding his heroism. He was also sharing his inside information and opinions, in secret, with the judge who would preside over the Watergate trials:

In reviewing the facts of those cases with Judge Sirica prior to writing my column, I sensed the same pride in honest, non-partisan action that I had felt throughout our association.

It made me more confident as I wrote: "If the seven men indicted in connection with the burglary of and bugging at Democratic headquarters in the Watergate complex expect to have an easy time because Judge Sirica is a lifelong Republican appointed in a Republican administration, they should give more study to Sirica's background."[25]

Mollenhoff's meetings with Sirica were egregiously improper for a multitude of reasons:

- A man who had worked as a lawyer on the Nixon White House staff and who bore a personal grudge against people he believed ought to have been named as the principal Watergate defendants conducted a series of meetings with the judge who would preside over the Watergate break-in case.

- Even Mollenhoff admitted that his meetings with Sirica were not press interviews. His purpose was to speculate on who else might be involved and to encourage Sirica's sense of his importance in history.

- The meetings were secret and no records were kept. That is why ex parte meetings are so suspect. No one can ever know for sure what was actually said, but we certainly know what was on the men's minds at the time.

- Neither the defendants nor their counsel were aware of these meetings. They were thus denied the right to confront and cross-examine this witness about what had been said. They could not introduce contrary evidence or even seek to have Sirica removed as hopelessly compromised.

- The very action that Mollenhoff admits that he urged on Sirica—the search for truth—was hugely improper. Our system of justice requires that judges stay above the fray; that they preside and not investigate.

- It was likewise highly improper for Sirica to listen to Mollenhoff. It is axiomatic that judges cannot discuss cases before them with any outsider—except in open court, in the presence of opposing counsel, or in chambers, in the presence of a court reporter. Anything else prevents the maintenance of a complete and accurate record for challenge on appeal.

Sirica compounded the impropriety of his meetings with Mollenhoff by following his advice. The judge played the intrepid searcher for truth rather than the role that the law assigns to him: of impartial presider over an adversarial process. Mollenhoff gloated over the perversion of justice that he had encouraged:

> With control of the Justice Department, the Nixon White House was confident that not even independent Judge Sirica could penetrate the stone wall of silence created by the prosecution's theory that Gordon Liddy was the mastermind and that there was no criminal responsibility at a higher level. But Judge Sirica was to demonstrate that he was hardly an average judge in his aggressive search for the truth.[26]

Though Mollenhoff claimed credit for influencing Judge Sirica's conduct of the Watergate cases, he nevertheless stated that he did not discuss the merits of the case then before the judge. But he didn't have to. Those poor souls were caught red-handed in the Watergate burglary. Mollenhoff's whole point was that these defendants could not have acted alone, that they had to have been directed by higher-ups—higher-ups whom Mollenhoff believed he could identify because they had run everything else in the Nixon White House. He had been there and he had seen how their system worked.

It would be difficult to imagine a more blatant violation of due process than this series of ex parte meetings. But secret meetings with Sirica were not Mollenhoff's only inexcusable conduct. While Nixon's ombudsman, Mollenhoff had obtained and reviewed the tax returns of some twelve persons, including seven federal judges, acts that became public in 1977. When Mollenhoff's boss at the *Des Moines Register* obtained the names of the aggrieved parties, he discovered that "they were people that Mollenhoff either had written about before or after his White House stint or else had had others in the [*Register*'s] bureau write about."[27] Mollenhoff was quietly fired for unethical conduct, but the reason was kept confidential until I uncovered it.

Ex Parte Meeting with Earl Silbert

As principal assistant U.S. attorney for the District of Columbia, Earl Silbert[28] was an ideal and idealistic prosecutor. In pursuing the Watergate burglary, he directed a complex investigation, sought indictments in those cases he knew he could prove, laid out his strategy for his superiors in a timely and convincing fashion, explaining clearly how he might go after any higher-ups once the initial convictions had been obtained, and put on a most convincing case on the government's behalf at trial.

Silbert and his associates are responsible for breaking the cover-up—and they did so in a thoroughly proper and professional manner. Later, however, they were treated shoddily by the special prosecutor—relieved of their responsibilities and gagged so they could not even respond to press inquiries—and by many in the media, but their hands are clean and their reputations are intact.

Silbert's professional and ethical prosecution was not good enough for Sirica, however. He felt constrained being on the bench when he very much wanted to participate as a member of the prosecution team. One of the ways he tried to fulfill this desire was to seek a private, ex parte meeting with Silbert. We know about this meeting only because Sirica describes it in his own book. Here's what he wrote:

> I like Earl Silbert. I think he's a good lawyer. I wanted to be helpful, to share with him some of my experiences which I felt might give him some guidance through what was obviously a tough situation.

A few days before the trial started, he was in my chambers discussing an administrative problem unconnected with
the Watergate case. I said to him, "Earl, look, you've got a
great opportunity in this case if you go right down the middle, let the chips fall where they may. Don't let anybody put
pressure on you."

Before he left my office, I gave him a bound copy of the
hearings conducted back in 1944 by a select committee of
the House of Representatives into the activities of the Federal
Communications Commission. I wanted the young prosecutor to know just how white-washers were engineered. And I
wanted him to know that I had had direct experience with
cover-ups while serving as chief counsel to that committee.[29]

It takes a fairly arrogant judge—as Sirica clearly was—not only to
take a seasoned prosecutor aside condescendingly to let him know just
how the case should be tried, but to brag about having done so in his
memoir.

Despite Sirica's assurance that his conversation with Silbert came
about casually, it is clear from the context that he had prepared for the
encounter. Sirica had been chief counsel in 1944 to the House Select
Committee to Investigate the Federal Communications Commission but
had resigned in protest when the committee decided to close the remainder of the hearings to the public—an action Sirica saw as a whitewash.
Sirica thrust the records of those hearings into Silbert's hands and urged
him to study them. Indeed, earlier drafts of Sirica's memoir in the Library
of Congress make it clear that he viewed his experience of thirty years
earlier as instructive for his pursuit of the truth in the break-in trial.

As with other ex parte meetings, we have only Sirica's benign version
of his meeting with Silbert, but it was seriously improper for the meeting
to take place at all. Judges may not privately instruct prosecutors on how
to put on cases before them. At the very least, it clearly demonstrates
Sirica's prosecutorial bias. If the defense had learned of this meeting,
Sirica would have had to recuse himself from further involvement in the

break-in case. But the meeting was secret, there was no record of it, and no one knew about it.

I intend no criticism of Earl Silbert. By this time, he was no doubt used to Sirica's prosecutorial bent. He would have shrugged this off and continued his prosecution precisely as he saw fit. The initiative for this illicit conversation was Sirica's alone. It was the judge who denied the defendants their right to a fair trial by trying privately to instruct the prosecutor on how to try his case.

It does not excuse Sirica to point out that he merely instructed Silbert to "go right down the middle"—that is not the point. We have no idea of what was actually intended or said. Sirica arranged the meeting, and his giving *any* advice or instruction was per se improper.

Ex Parte Meeting with Samuel Dash

Sam Dash[30] was a man with a mission. The Ervin Committee's newly appointed chief counsel, he needed witnesses to fill the public hearings that were scheduled to begin on May 17, 1973.

The Georgetown law professor had built a distinguished legal career, graduating from Harvard Law School in 1950 and becoming district attorney of Philadelphia at the age of thirty, but now he faced a major challenge:

> I turned my attention to the problem of how to begin developing some cracks in the wall of silence which the Watergate burglars had constructed and maintained. I had no doubt that our investigation was confronting a major cover-up conspiracy. It seemed obvious we would need the help of an insider—an informer to successfully expose this conspiracy. Some extraordinary tactic had to be employed to induce one or more of the burglars to start talking.[31]

On March 23, Sirica would announce his sentences in the burglary trial, and Dash saw an opportunity for the judge to help him. "Other judges had used the sentencing power as a carrot-and-stick strategy to provide an incentive for a convicted defendant to turn informer,"[32] and

Dash figured Sirica could do the same. In a political corruption case against Martin Sweig, Dash had actually opposed "provisional sentencing"—temporarily imposing a severe sentence with the offer to reduce it in exchange for the prisoner's cooperation—before the Court of Appeals for the Second Circuit. "But I had lost," he writes. "Although I still believed the practice was wrong, the Sweig case was a legal precedent that a trial judge could use the sentence as a pressure tactic on the defendant."[33]

In the Sweig case, however, the trial judge was seeking to encourage the defendant's cooperation with prosecutors. Dash now had in mind a whole new objective: to use the possibility of future sentence reduction to encourage the defendants' cooperation with a political investigation by the Senate that had no legal connection with the prosecution of them in the U.S. district court. It is a crucial distinction—in law and in fact—that seems to have been missed by all commentators to date.

Dash was almost gleeful in explaining how he maneuvered himself into an ex parte meeting with Judge Sirica:

> As chief counsel of the Senate committee, I had no standing in the criminal case before Judge Sirica. But I had a committee reason to meet with him prior to the sentencing date. Senator Ervin had earlier requested Sirica to let the committee inspect the grand jury minutes of the Watergate case. On further review of the law I had concluded that Sirica could not legally grant this request. Ervin concurred with my opinion and had asked me to withdraw his request. This could have been accomplished by letter, but it gave me the opportunity to talk to Judge Sirica in his chambers. Sirica and I had been friends for years as faculty colleagues at Georgetown University Law Center.[34]

In the privacy of the judge's chambers–cum–Georgetown faculty club, Dash communicated the scheme to his friend with a wink and a nod:

When I met with Sirica I was careful to emphasize I was not recommending anything regarding his sentencing of the Watergate defendants, but I expressed the hope that one of them might give us information about the cover-up and I referred him to the Sweig case. Judge Sirica responded that he understood the committee was not making any request of him, as it had no right to do, and that he would study all the law and would sentence as he determined the interests of justice required.[35]

This meeting was a flagrant violation of legal and judicial ethics. The commentary to Canon 3 of the Code of Conduct for United States Judges addresses this situation directly:

Canon 3A(4). The restriction on ex parte communications concerning a proceeding includes communications from lawyers, law teachers, and others who are not participants in the proceeding.

If word of the meeting with Dash had gotten out, Sirica would have had to recuse himself from the sentencing. But no one found out for many years (Sirica omitted any mention of the meeting in his own book), and Sirica proceeded to adopt Dash's idea as his own, imposing sentences of up to thirty-five years on the hapless first-time offenders.

The convicted defendants had every right to know what was being said about them to the judge who was about to sentence them. As with Sirica's other ex parte meetings, no record was kept, so there was nothing to review on appeal. Apart from the justice or injustice of provisional sentencing, Dash's scheme called for improper coordination between the judicial and legislative branches. No other court before or since has conditioned a criminal sentence on a defendant's testimony before a congressional committee.

Sirica's ex parte meetings with interested parties—Williams, Mollenhoff, Silbert, and Dash—remained a secret until Watergate was safely consigned to the history books (and John Sirica enshrined in America's judiciary pantheon). But the misconduct that was publicly known at the time (most recently detailed in Gaughan's law review article cited in Chapter 6), standing alone, ought to have resulted in his removal from the case.

SIRICA'S EX PARTE MEETINGS WITH THE SPECIAL PROSECUTORS

Secret meetings with interested parties are bad enough, but Sirica repeatedly violated the defendants' rights to due process through a series of meetings with the Watergate special prosecutors themselves. We have already detailed his meeting with Silbert, but we now know of at least eight other such secret meetings, including two with Archibald Cox, the original special prosecutor, and six with Leon Jaworski.

In their attempt to have Sirica removed as presiding judge in the cover-up trial, the defendants cited two newspaper accounts—dated June 19 and July 18, 1973—indicating that Sirica had met privately with prosecutors while Cox was still the special prosecutor. In the earlier article, the Associated Press had reported, "After Cox met with newsmen, he conferred privately for 15 minutes with U.S. District Court Judge John J. Sirica and Sirica, without further explanation, scheduled a hearing for today." This was about the time that Dean's scheduled testimony before the Ervin Committee was postponed because of the visit of the Soviet leader Leonid Brezhnev. It is possible, then, that Cox's private visit dealt with his continuing concern that Dean's public testimony would taint the jury pool in the District of Columbia. Since the defendants' request for an evidentiary hearing to explore Sirica's ex parte contacts was denied and no one ever divulged their subject matter, we will never know what was actually discussed.

Sirica's subsequent series of secret meetings with Jaworski and senior members of his staff have already been discussed. During the tenures of both Cox and Jaworski, then, Sirica indulged a bad habit of meeting privately with government prosecutors. His fidelity to the norms of fair and balanced judicial conduct was hopelessly tainted.

SIRICA'S FALSE SENTENCING PLOY

Perhaps the clearest indication of Sirica's prosecutorial bent was his attempt to influence the verdict in the cover-up trial by enhancing the credibility of the government's principal witnesses, John Dean and Jeb Magruder, through manipulative sentencing. Sirica kept his ploy a secret for several years until he confessed it without shame in his book in 1979.

On August 16, 1973, Magruder pleaded guilty to a single felony count before Sirica. As is customary with government witnesses, his sentencing was postponed until the conclusion of the trial in which his testimony was needed by the government. This is done so that defendants testifying against their former colleagues don't have a sudden change of heart after receiving a reduced sentence in anticipation of their coopera-tion.

Dean pleaded guilty to a single felony count before Sirica on Octo-ber 19, 1973, and his sentencing was similarly postponed until after the cover-up trial. Indeed, Dean's formal plea bargain specified:

> The Government will join with you in urging that Mr. Dean's sentencing be deferred until after the trial of others implicated by Mr. Dean's testimony and that Mr. Dean be permitted to remain on bond or in recognizance pending sentence in order to facilitate his cooperation with the Government.[36]

John Mitchell and Maurice Stans were acquitted on April 28, 1974, in the Vesco case, in which Dean had been one of the principal govern-ment witnesses. Part of the prosecution's problem, as *Congressional Quarterly* reported, was Dean's lack of credibility:

> The defense lawyers claimed…that prosecution witnesses were not telling the truth.
>
> In interviews after the verdicts were announced, the jurors said that they had voted to acquit Mitchell and Stans because they could not believe the testimony of key government

witnesses. They used the words "incredible" or "unbelievable" when they talked about John W. Dean III [and other] major government witnesses.

"I don't want to say Mr. Dean was lying, but he was often unbelievable," said Sybil Kucharski, the 21-year-old forewoman of the jury.[37]

Shortly thereafter, on May 21, 1974, Sirica reversed course. Apparently on his own initiative, he went ahead and sentenced Magruder to a prison term of ten months to four years, ordering his surrender to custody on or before June 4. He likewise decided to move up Dean's sentencing. Court records reflect a good deal of scurrying to finalize the pre-sentence report, particularly to obtain Dean's financial statement, since the judge had become quite eager to impose sentence. All was completed by the end of July, and at the hearing on August 2 Sirica sentenced Dean to a prison term of one to four years—a harsh sentence from any perspective—with confinement to begin on September 3, 1974, just a week before the scheduled opening of the cover-up trial. Sirica made no public comment as he imposed the sentence. There was no lecturing of the defendant; there was no advice on how to reform himself. Sirica simply and succinctly announced Dean's sentence and left the bench.

There was speculation at the time that the accelerated schedule and the harshness of the sentences were a reaction to the acquittals in the Vesco trial, which had been blamed on Dean's lack of credibility. Dean confirmed these suspicions in his book when he recounted an exchange with James Neal, the lead prosecutor on the Watergate Task Force:

[Dean:] "I can't figure it [his harsh sentence] out, Jim. I guess either Sirica just doesn't like me or maybe he believes all that crap the White House put out about how I invented the cover-up and ran it single-handed."

[Neal:] "No, I don't think that's it. He gave you a hefty sentence because he wants to make you a credible witness. I tell you, I think Charlie's [Shaffer, Dean's lawyer] going to be in good shape when he files a motion to reduce. He's just got to wait awhile."[38]

The idea was that if Dean had already been given a harsh sentence, he would appear to have nothing to gain by pleasing the prosecution with his testimony in the upcoming cover-up trial, thus coming across to the jury as more credible than he seemed in the Vesco trial. Neal's comment suggests he might even have known more about Sirica's approach than he was willing to let on. No one ever dreamed that Sirica would be obtuse and arrogant enough to acknowledge his sentencing ploy, yet that is what he later did in his book:

> When Dean was on the stand in the New York [Vesco] case, the defense attorneys had suggested from time to time that he was testifying against Mitchell and Stans in order to get a lighter sentence from the court in Washington. It was a legitimate way for those attorneys to try to discredit Dean, given the fact that he hadn't yet been sentenced by me. *But I didn't want the defense to use the same tactic in the cover-up case.* Dean had already made his plea bargain with the prosecutors. As long as he appeared to testify fully and truthfully, I knew that what he said on the witness stand was not going to make any difference in the sentence I handed down. *So to prevent the suggestion that he was testifying in the hope that I would reduce his sentence, I decided to give Dean that sentence well before the trial* [emphasis added].[39]

It is entirely possible that the idea of hurrying Dean's sentence originated with people within the special prosecutor's office, but we may never know for sure.

For his own part, Dean later wrote that he was devastated by the harshness of Sirica's sudden sentence:

I was absorbing Sirica's words. "He threw the book at me? The most he could have given me was five years, and he gave me four. Why'd he do that?"

"I don't understand it," Charlie [Shaffer] said, over and over. "This is my fault, John. I should never have allowed you to plead to Sirica. I'm sorry. I didn't know. I don't understand." Charlie was as shaken by the sentence as if it were his own.

"How can he do that?" I asked plaintively. "I figured I'd get something like Krogh—six to eighteen months, maybe a year at the most. He hit me harder than Magruder. Even Colson didn't get the sentence I got. It can't be, Charlie."

"How could he do that?" Mo shrieked hysterically. She was sobbing, out of control."[40]

Dean was subsequently incarcerated, as ordered, but not sent to prison as Sirica had seemingly indicated in his order—or even kept in a jail cell. He spent his nights at a witness holding facility at nearby Fort Holabird, Maryland, at the request of the special prosecutor and with the concurrence of the Bureau of Prisons. And where did Dean spend his days? He recounted his conversation with Henry Ruth, Jaworski's deputy who succeeded him as special prosecutor in October 1974, about the office he was using in the special prosecutor's suite:

"John, I really don't think this is appropriate." Hank Ruth, Jaworski's replacement as Special Prosecutor, was frowning. "If the press got hold of this, they'll go crazy." He threw a "JOHN DEAN" office name plate down on my desk and waited for an answer.

"Well, Hank," I sputtered. I didn't know whether to take his remark seriously. "I didn't put that on the door. One of the secretaries did it as a joke. They think I'm almost one of the guys."

"I know," he said flatly. "But we can't afford this kind of stuff. I'm already catching a lot of flak about the office you've got."

"Okay, I understand."

I knew there was some resentment that I had fared so well in the office shuffle at the Special Prosecutor's K Street headquarters. When the Watergate trial team had moved to the courthouse, I had been assigned Neal's old office on the ninth floor—a corner location with lots of windows.[41]

Dean has confirmed on a number of occasions that he never went to jail. In a 1995 deposition he stated, "For example, when I was first incarcerated, I went to a witness protection facility in Maryland. I was brought in on almost a daily basis from that facility to the prosecutors' office [on K Street in downtown Washington]. That continued through the trial. Through a lot of the trial I was also in the courthouse for the benefit of the prosecutors [who had moved to the courthouse for the trial's duration]."[42]

In a discussion with Brian Lamb on C-SPAN in 2004, he elaborated:

> BRIAN LAMB: And during that time you went to prison for a couple of months?
>
> JOHN DEAN: I actually technically never went to prison. I had—I was in the witness protection program. They were worried about keeping me alive at the time. And so I was in a safe house and then spent most of that time actually in the prosecutor's office. And it was 120 days that I was sort of in confinement, but I actually had—I was in the witness protection program for over a year.[43]

In another interview in 2004, Dean expanded upon how he served his supposedly harsh one-to-four-year sentence that had been so publicly imposed by Judge Sirica:

> JOHN DEAN: Technically, let me correct you. I really never did go to prison. I was 127 days in the custody of the U.S.

Marshalls because I was in the Witness Protection Program. The government was very concerned about keeping me alive. I really have not let that get corrected over the years. It's out there on the web. It's on different sites.

AMY GOODMAN: Weren't you in prison?

DEAN: I was not in prison.

GOODMAN: Weren't you in jail?

DEAN: I was not in jail.

GOODMAN: In detention?

DEAN: I was in custody and would stay in a safe house at night. I spent most of that time in the U.S.—excuse me, in the Watergate Special Prosecutor's office. I was driven to the office every day from the safe house. I was actually during the time that the trials were going on, I was in the courthouse in the prosecutor's office.

GOODMAN: Wasn't it a sentence?

DEAN: It was part of a sentence—well, yes. It became the sentence, the judge after—had sentenced me just before the trial started, and after 127 days later, said time served.

GOODMAN: And that time you had served in the prosecutor's office?

DEAN: More or less.

GOODMAN: You never served a night in any kind of detention facility?

DEAN: Well in a safe house, yes.

GOODMAN: With other people?

DEAN: There were other government witnesses in that facility, yes. My next door neighbor happened to be a former mafia hit man who once told me, you know, John, I always liked Richard Nixon until I realized he wasn't a very good criminal.

GOODMAN: Is that place still a house of detention?

DEAN: I don't know. They don't—they don't advertise it. It's part of the witness protection program. Well? Anyway, a technical point that I just thought I would clear up.[44]

Finally, in a more recent interview with Chapman University's campus newspaper, *The Panther*, on January 29, 2012, Dean made it clear that he went into the prosecutor's offices in the District of Columbia each and every day:

> THE PANTHER: Once the trial was coming to a conclusion and you were sentenced to jail time, what was that time like?
>
> JOHN DEAN: I was in the witness protection program the whole time. I never really served time. I stayed within the witness protection program in a safe house. Every day of the four months I was in confinement I was driven into Washington to the prosecutor's office—not exactly hard time.[45]

Here Dean was stretching the truth. He was not in "the" Witness Protection Program at all. That program is used to provide key witnesses with brand new, permanent identities, such that they can relocate and live without fear of retaliation after their testimony—usually against the Mafia. Dean was provided protection by the U.S. Marshal Service, at the request of the special prosecutor, prior to his testimony but not anything close to a new identity. Dean had been sentenced to a prison term of one to four years—and was under that sentence at all times that he was testifying in the cover-up trial. Supposedly for the convenience of the special prosecutors, he was confined to a witness holding facility in Baltimore named Fort Holabird, which had been founded as a U.S. Army post in 1917.

We also might ask, however, what Dean meant by "not exactly hard time"? We already know that he was not just sitting around the courthouse, waiting to be prepped by the trial team that had moved there weeks earlier. Dean himself tells us that he was housed back at their K Street location, using the spacious office that had formerly been occupied by the lead prosecutor. What was he doing during those three months—only one week of which was actually spent on the witness stand—which he spent in the special prosecutor's offices while seemingly beginning his prison sentence of one to four years? We can get some inkling from the financial disclosure statement that he submitted to his sentencing officer in July 1974:

> I signed a contract with the Bantam Book Publishing Co., to write two "non-Watergate" books about government. It is my hope to write whenever I am not being called upon by the government to testify, and hopefully complete the first manuscript by March of next year.[46]

So while the jurors and the rest of the American public thought that Dean was sitting in prison for his central role in the Watergate scandal, he was writing his book (supposedly a "non-Watergate" book) and palling around the prosecutors' offices with his new best friends.

Dean was the prosecution's principal witness in the cover-up trial that began on October 1, 1974. He was on the stand for over a week and was the only witness who could connect Haldeman and Ehrlichman (and President Nixon) to the cover-up, which he had helped to run. His testimony was all the more credible since he had pleaded guilty to the felony of conspiring to obstruct justice, had been sentenced to a harsh prison term, and appeared to be testifying while serving that sentence. The theme was as simple as it was direct: We were all in this together; I've 'fessed up and have been severely punished. These were my colleagues. You should see to it that they are punished too.

It was particularly critical for Dean to appear to have been harshly sentenced—along with Magruder—following President Ford's unconditional pardon of former President Nixon. Jurors in the cover-up trial might have concluded that it would be unfair to send Nixon's aides to prison when he himself had gotten off scot-free. They might have felt the same way if Nixon's lesser aides also were treated lightly. So as far as the public knew, Dean and Magruder were serving one-to-four-year terms.

Here is how the two of the members of the Watergate Task Force describe the effect of Dean's testifying from prison:

Moral balancing aside, the realpolitik of the situation was that Dean would not be an effective witness at trial if he got a free ride. His credibility would be substantially diminished…if the prosecutors completely forgave his own deep involvement. The evident effect of Dean's prison sentence, later, on the jurors at the Watergate cover-up trial confirmed our tactical judgment. As a man who was already serving a long jail term for doing what he testified he had been instructed to do by Haldeman and Ehrlichman, Dean made a measurably greater impression than if he had never been charged or punished for his acts.[47]

Dean, that earnest and handsome young man, the hero of the Ervin Committee hearings, the one with the beautiful young wife—he was the one the jurors should believe. Not the vilified and disgraced Nixon henchmen, depicted nightly on the news as having tried to steal democracy, along with their equally disgraced president. No, the jury's choice of whom to believe was simplified by Dean's and Magruder's apparent incarceration.

And Judge Sirica was determined that that carefully crafted appearance should not be compromised. When defense counsel's opening statement raised the possibility that government witnesses could look forward to favorable treatment in return for testimony that was agreeable to the prosecution, Sirica promptly shut him down:

> MR. BRESS [counsel for defendant Robert Mardian]: The first [class of witnesses] will be witnesses who have already pleaded guilty to one or more felonies and have been sentenced but look forward to some consideration in the future for their present governmental cooperation.
>
> JUDGE SIRICA: There isn't any evidence that is a fact. You will have to come up to the bench on that.
>
> [At the bench]
>
> JUDGE SIRICA: Now what is the basis for a statement like that? There isn't anything in this case that they can look

forward, they have been sentenced. You talking about Mr. Dean? He has been sentenced. I sentenced Mr. Magruder.

Now what kind of argument—You can't make that argument, Mr. Bress. You may do it on cross-examination, if I think it is proper.

MR. BRESS: I intend to back this up with—You want me to respond?

JUDGE SIRICA: Yes, I want to know what you have to justify that kind of statement in an opening statement.

MR. BRESS: Talking about weight of evidence, credibility.

JUDGE SIRICA: I am talking about—hoping for consideration, expecting consideration.

MR. BRESS: They hope.

MR. NEAL: You said expecting.

MR. BRESS: They hope, expect, what is the difference? I don't say there is a deal, but I am saying that from my own experience as a prosecutor I know that when the matter comes up before the Parole Board, inquiries are made of the Government, the prosecution offers as to whether or not there has been or any factors that would warrant favorable consideration in granting parole. And I want to show, and this statement, they can criticize me on the closing argument if I fail to do it, but I have good reason to believe, Your honor, that these people are cooperating fully with the view that that will redound to their benefit by reason of favorable comments to come from the prosecutor's office to the Parole Board.

Now, if I don't establish that, they can criticize me.

JUDGE SIRICA: You can't establish it by an opening statement. I won't permit you to do it. At the proper time you will not ask that question in presence of the jury, you will first come to the bench out of the presence of the jury. I will not permit it now.

You will not do what—This was a matter in the Mitchell case in New York. Mr. Flemming walked into the courtroom and said, Mr. Dean have you been sentenced yet; and so forth and so forth. That is not the situation. Mr. Dean has been sentenced.[48]

Dean was the government's lead witness, and the lead prosecutor wasted no time in emphasizing Dean's supposed incarceration. Here is the opening sequence, as recounted by Ben-Veniste and Frampton:[49]

> MR. NEAL: You are Mr. John W. Dean?
> MR. DEAN: Yes, I am.
> MR. NEAL: Mr. Dean, what is your present employment status and residence?
> MR. DEAN: Mr. Neal, I am presently serving a prison term at Fort Holabird, Maryland.
> MR. NEAL: A prison term for what offense?
> MR. DEAN: Conspiracy to obstruct justice.
> MR. NEAL: In connection with what?
> MR. DEAN: With my involvement in the Watergate cover-up.
> MR. NEAL: What was your last position prior to being in a federal prison?
> MR. DEAN: The last position I held was that of counsel to the President of the United States.
> MR. NEAL: What was the President's name?
> MR. DEAN: Richard Nixon.

There was no mention of the witness protection program or a witness holding facility. There was no disclosure of his spending each day in WSPF offices working on his book. Just as Sirica and WSPF prosecutors had intended, Dean was on the witness stand testifying for the government, already harshly sentenced and apparently imprisoned for his part in this conspiracy, eager to talk about the involvement of his former colleagues. At the end of the three-month trial, on January 1, 1975, the jury convicted Ehrlichman, Haldeman, and Mitchell on all counts.

One week later, on January 8, 1975, apparently upon his own motion, Sirica reduced Dean's and Magruder's sentences to "time served." After four months of technical confinement, Dean was a free man—no parole, no probation, no further restraint whatsoever. Magruder, who had been confined about six months, was likewise set completely free.

Let's return to Sirica's explanation of why he sentenced Dean to prison before his testimony had been given, breaking from normal government procedure and from what had been agreed upon when Dean pleaded guilty in the first place:

> Dean had already made his plea bargain with the prosecutors. *As long as he appeared to testify fully and truthfully, I knew that what he said on the witness stand was not going to make any difference in the sentence I handed down.* So to prevent the suggestion that he was testifying in the hope that I would reduce his sentence, I decided to give Dean that sentence well before the trial [emphasis added].[50]

If we take Sirica at his word, Dean testified just as he was expected to do, so there was no reason for Sirica to reduce his sentence after he had so testified. The only reason to have imposed the harsh sentence on Dean before his cover-up trial testimony, as the judge himself seems to have admitted and as the special prosecutors confirmed in their own book—was to increase Dean's credibility with the jurors.

Let us be clear about this: Dean and Magruder's false sentencing was a deliberate act of fraud on the jury and on the American public. This deception, stemming from the need to secure convictions at any cost, was perpetrated by Sirica and concurred in by WSPF prosecutors.

A hanging judge, his head turned by the new attention of an adoring media, decided that he alone could fashion justice. In single-mindedly pursuing what he thought was justice, however, John Sirica acted as though he was above the law. In so doing, he undermined the foundation of the American justice system—the due process of law.

CHAPTER 7

EVENHANDED, NONPARTISAN PROSECUTORS

E qual protection of the law implies even-handed prosecutions for criminal conduct. But highly partisan WSPF prosecutors targeted Nixon's top aides, charged them with highly questionable "thought crimes," and improperly hid exculpatory evidence from their defense counsel.

CONSTITUTIONAL WEAKNESSES OF SPECIAL PROSECUTORS

The phrase carved into the west pediment of the Supreme Court building, "EQUAL JUSTICE UNDER LAW," nicely captures the constitutional expectation of equal protection: the even-handed application of the laws. This is particularly true with regard to criminal laws, where the Fifth and Sixth Amendments come into play and prosecutions are expected to be nonpartisan.

JACKSON'S ADMONITION

The prosecutor's challenge—and dilemma—was best articulated by Attorney General Robert Jackson back in 1940 in his address to the second annual conference of United States attorneys in the Great Hall of the Department of Justice. Soon to be appointed by President Roosevelt to the Supreme Court, where he served with distinction until 1954, Jackson would also the lead the U.S. prosecution in the war crimes trials at Nuremberg following World War II.

Jackson began his speech by asserting that U.S. attorneys, as federal prosecutors, have more power over individual Americans' lives, liberties, and reputations than any other officials in the country. It is a question of discretion, he added, since there are so many federal offenses that could be prosecuted. And it is that discretion that poses a U.S. attorney's greatest challenge.

If prosecutors can pick their cases, Jackson pointed out, they can also pick their defendants. That discretion is the greatest danger for American citizens, because a determined prosecutor can always find some charge to bring against an individual or group that he has decided he doesn't like. It matters not whether the prosecutorial dislike stems from being unpopular with those in power, from holding the wrong political views, or even from somehow being in the way of the prosecutor himself.

Jackson emphasized that the greatest threats come in times of fear, when various groups might hunger for the scalps of people with whose views they disagree. He singled out "subversive activities" as being especially dangerous to civil liberties, since there was no agreed-upon definition for such actions. Jackson even observed, "We must not forget that it was not so long ago that both the term 'Republican' and the term 'Democrat' were epithets with sinister meaning to denote persons of radical tendencies that were 'subversive' of the order of things then dominant."

Jackson's words still rang true three decades later. In all periods relevant to the Watergate prosecutions, Jackson's speech was featured prominently in the introduction to the United States Attorneys' Manual, and it set the standard under which the laws of the United States were to be enforced by the Department of Justice.

But something changed in the years since Jackson's admonition. A contemporary account by the lawyer, prosecutor, and novelist George Higgins describes the targeting of specific persons that characterized the Watergate prosecutions—which embodied everything that Jackson had warned against some three decades earlier.

> The course of human events being what it is, the people who knew how to prosecute, in 1973, were people conditioned (directly or at second hand) by the Kennedy Justice methodology. Imperfectly articulated as it was, that methodology was developed on the premise that law enforcement should not be passive, but aggressive. The governing hypothesis was that there is an ineradicable difference between good guys and bad guys, apparent to, and actionable by, the good guys. Out of that came targeted law enforcement: upon identification as a bad guy, the suspect may resign himself to merciless investigation, reinvestigation, indictment and reindictment, trial and retrial, until at last the Government secures a verdict which ratifies the prosecutor's assessment of the defendant as a bad guy.
>
> Nevertheless, the targets—people—of the alternative process are selected on an ad hoc basis. It is terribly personal. It is not monitored by a disinterested custodian of the due process of law.
>
> Cox...arranged the Special Prosecution Force on the aggressive model of law enforcement, which evolved from the development of the Organized Crime and Racketeering Section.
>
> Mating the investigative and prosecutive functions, it adds to the territorial designation two further letters of marque and reprisal: designation of prospective suspects (no longer does the prosecutor decide whether to prosecute by

asking: "Can we prove he did it?"; he begins with the decision
to prosecute at least half made, and reasons: "We know he
did something, and as soon as we can prove it, we indict the
bastard").[1]

THE WSPF: DESIGNED FOR ABUSE

In my earlier book, I documented the case that the members of the
Watergate Special Prosecution Force did not observe the minimum standards of due process,[2] but a summary of the problems inherent in the
force is useful here.

The WSPF was an extra-legal expedient, imposed by the Democratic
majority of the Senate Judiciary Committee as a condition for the confirmation of Elliot Richardson as attorney general. It was led by Democrats who had worked together in Robert Kennedy's Department of
Justice and staffed by Democrats selected for their predisposition to
oppose President Nixon. It enjoyed all of the investigative and prosecutorial authority of the Department of Justice but operated with total and
unreviewed independence. The only person to whom the WSPF could be
said to answer was Edward Kennedy of the Senate Judiciary Committee.

Because of its total independence, the WSPF was unconstrained by
the rules of conduct and independent levels of review to which prosecutors were ordinarily subject in the Department of Justice. The United
States Attorneys' Manual, for example, did not bind WSPF prosecutors.
There were no internal departmental reviews by the appropriate assistant
attorney general, the deputy attorney general, or the attorney general
himself, and the independent review and concurrence of the office of the
solicitor general was not required before filing or responding to circuit
court appeals.

In essence, WSPF prosecutors operated in the manner that Attorney
General Jackson had deplored in his 1940 speech. They identified their
chosen defendants and tailored the charges they would bring against
them. Jack Farrell, an investigative reporter for the *Boston Globe*,
summarized the investigative approach that animated the Watergate
prosecution:

Cox and his zealous staff had gone to work with an obvious aim—to get Richard Nixon—and with an array of prosecutorial tactics that would become so familiar to Americans as a series of "independent" counsels, in collusion with Congress and the media, hounded presidents of both parties over the next twenty-five years. Like his successors, Cox did not limit his investigations to the crime at hand—the burglary and wiretapping of the Democratic headquarters. Instead, he chose a suspect first and then used a nigh-unlimited budget, his team of 150 investigators, lawyers and support personnel, and his broad subpoena power to find a crime. To generate public support for the process, Cox's office deftly leaked to the press: over the summer [of 1973], the media reported that Cox's team was examining Nixon campaign fund-raising; corporate favors; the President's tax returns; and government financed improvements to Nixon's homes in Florida and California.[3]

MORRISON V. OLSON

Judge Laurence Silberman[4] of the D.C. Circuit detailed the risks inherent in an independent prosecution in his opinion in *Morrison v. Olson* (1988), holding that the independent prosecutor established by the 1978 Ethics in Government Act was an unconstitutional delegation of prosecutorial discretion:[5]

That very independence from presidential and Justice Department supervision and guidance that Congress deliberately fashioned for independent counsel has troubling consequences for those who find themselves the target of the independent counsel's attention. A person occupying this statutory office has, it seems to us, unique incentives to seek an indictment. Our concern is based on the self-evident proposition that the whole raison d'être of the independent counsel is not to administer the criminal law across a wide population, but rather to focus on one individual or group of individuals targeted at the inception of the office. In effect, an entire self-sufficient government agency is created from scratch to investigate and perhaps prosecute a single individual. The need to justify even the expense of an office dedicated solely to one goal must generate a reluctance to decide against indictment or to conclude the investigation absent near certainty that no indictment is possible or that no further leads remain. And inevitably, the success of the office itself, in the public's eyes, at least, must turn to some extent upon whether indictment and conviction are obtained. The independent counsel is thus "subject to formidable public—and perhaps self-imposed—pressure to indict in the one case he was appointed to pursue."

At least the Ethics in Government Act, which formalized the position of independent prosecutor, was a statutory scheme enacted into law by both Houses of Congress. The Watergate Special Prosecution Force, by contrast, was merely an ad hoc political arrangement.

PARTISAN STAFFING OF THE SPECIAL PROSECUTOR'S OFFICE

Cox's biggest challenges when appointed special prosecutor at the end of May 1973 were staffing the Watergate Special Prosecution Force and dealing with the threats to a fair trial posed by the Ervin Committee's public hearings in the Senate. His unsuccessful efforts to deal with the latter are detailed in the next chapter. What we will cover here is the decidedly partisan nature of his office staffing. As I detailed in my earlier book:

Archibald Cox (Harvard, '34; Harvard Law, '37; clerk for Judge Learned Hand) was a Triple Crown Kennedy clan confidant: He had headed JFK's issues analysis and speech-writing teams during the 1960 campaign; he was second in command in RFK's Department of Justice as solicitor general; and he had worked closely with Teddy Kennedy on numerous matters, particularly the campaigns to defeat Nixon's Supreme Court nominees (including Haynsworth and Carswell, who were defeated, and Berger, Powell, and Rehnquist, who were confirmed). The most recent exchange of Cox-Kennedy correspondence—concerning the landmark Supreme Court abortion ruling *Roe v. Wade*— had occurred less than a month before Cox was named special prosecutor.

Cox's first two appointments were his closest colleagues from the Harvard Law School: Philip Heymann (Yale, '54; Harvard Law, '60; clerk for Justice John Marshall Harlan), his former student, who had served with him in RFK's solicitor general office; and James Vorenberg (Harvard '49; Harvard Law, '51; clerk to Justice Felix Frankfurter), who had headed RFK's Office of Criminal Justice and written position papers for George McGovern's 1972 presidential campaign. These two were instrumental in completing the staffing and establishing the direction of the fledgling special prosecutor's office before they returned to Harvard in the fall of 1973. Vorenberg came back to Washington in August 1974 to help with the possible indictment of Richard Nixon following his resignation, and again in the fall of 1975 as primary author of the *Watergate Special Prosecution Force Report.*[6]

It was Vorenberg who took the lead in staffing the office, and to do so quickly, without getting bogged down in Department of Justice hiring procedures, he sought out only friends or friends of friends. While this simplified matters considerably, it also assured that everyone who was hired held President Nixon and his administration in extremely low regard.

Vorenberg's staffing, which is illustrated on the chart at Appendix K, fell into three categories:

Leadership: Seven of the eight top WSPF attorneys had worked together in Robert Kennedy's Department of Justice. They were competent lawyers, to be sure, but all ardent Democrats and adherents to its aggressive targeting-of-individuals approach to law enforcement.

Line prosecutors: Many of the line prosecutors had worked for the U.S. attorney for the Southern District of New York, Robert Morganthau (a hold-over from the Kennedy-Johnson administrations, whose father had been Franklin Roosevelt's treasury secretary), where they developed considerable experience in prosecuting organized crime. Indeed, they used many of the scorched-earth tactics designed for going after the mob in prosecuting Nixon administration officials.

Younger lawyers: Most of the younger lawyers on the staff were recent graduates of elite Ivy League law schools and had opposed Nixon's conduct of the Vietnam War.

This brand new, totally dedicated prosecutorial team really was Prud'hon's Nemesis—dedicated political opponents of Nixon and his aides and determined to pursue them to the ends of the earth.

As the adjoining charts show, it wasn't just WSPF prosecutors who came from the Kennedy-Johnson Department of Justice. Key figures on the staffs of both the Senate Ervin Committee and the House Judiciary impeachment inquiry did too. Perhaps not surprisingly, defense counsel for two of the major Watergate criminal figures (Charles Shaffer, who represented John Dean, and William Bittman, who represented Howard Hunt) also came out of this group.

Among Cox's first official acts was the replacement of the career prosecutors from the U.S. attorney's office, whose extensive investigative work had broken the Watergate cover-up, with his new team of partisan Democrats. A threshold question was what to do with Dean, who had been intimately involved in the Watergate scandal from its outset but was also the only man through whom they could reach their top targets—Mitchell, Haldeman, and Ehrlichman (along with President Nixon himself).

For his part, and to his credit, Cox had severe reservations about Dean:

Archie Cox was particularly firm in his personal determination that Dean be prosecuted no matter what. Dean became an *idée fixe* for Cox. True, as a witness Dean would cement otherwise weak cases against Haldeman and Ehrlichman. But Cox preferred, if forced to choose, to take the relatively sure shot at Dean rather than the long shot against Dean's superiors. When the Saturday Night Massacre loomed close, it might have been propitious for Cox to make a deal with Dean and secure Dean's testimony against President Nixon as another weapon to hold the President off. Even then, Cox's determination did not waiver. With all the uncertainties of Watergate that swirled around him—the weakness of evidence against Nixon's top aides without Dean's testimony, the possibility of Presidential culpability, the problems of obtaining White House evidence and of dealing with "national security"—Cox saw Dean's guilt as the one enduring constant. During a particularly difficult period Archie remarked to us, "If everything else goes down the drain the one thing I can cling to is Dean's venality."[7]

But once Cox had been fired in the Saturday Night Massacre, the spirit of revenge crowded out any lingering concerns about Dean. He was allowed to plead guilty to a single felony count and supposedly sentenced to one to four years in prison, though he never spent a day there. When he finally got around to disclosing that he had destroyed evidence that Hunt said would exonerate him, there was no follow-up investigation and he was never prosecuted. When an internal comparison of Dean's sworn testimony before the Ervin Committee about his meetings with President Nixon with the tapes of those meetings disclosed some nineteen material discrepancies (see Appendix L), there was never any thought of charging him with perjury or of sharing such analysis with Watergate defense counsel. Their actions were precisely the opposite: WSPF prosecutors (along with the media) consistently and constantly praised Dean for the precision of his memory and the extent of his cooperation.

GRAND JURY ABUSE

Grand juries began in England under Henry II and were recognized in the Magna Carta, but they exist today only in the United States, enshrined in the Fifth Amendment. Their original purpose was to determine if a crime had been committed and to act as a brake on overzealous prosecutions. But by the 1970s grand juries had become nothing more than a prosecutorial tool.

Grand jurors are not screened for bias, they hear only the side of the story the prosecutor wants them to hear, there is no judicial supervision of their operation, and witnesses must appear before them without their counsel's even being allowed into the room. Such procedures lend themselves to abuse by partisan prosecutors, but since all proceedings (except indictments) are kept sealed forever, there is almost no opportunity for abuses to surface.

Nonetheless, the weaknesses in the grand jury system are well known. A chief judge of New York State's highest court famously observed that grand juries are so malleable that any prosecutor worth his salt could get a grand jury to "indict a ham sandwich." A former federal district judge in Chicago once complained that "the grand jury is the total captive of the prosecutor who, if he is candid, will concede that he can indict anybody, at any time, for almost anything, before any grand jury."[8]

Watergate prosecutors made extensive use of grand juries, subpoenaing dozens of Nixon administration employees to appear before three grand juries devoted to their exclusive use. They of course did all the work, picked all the witnesses, prepared all the questions, and drafted all the indictments, as well as the special report known as the Road Map. It was a reign of terror unprecedented in the American justice system. Forty years later, in spite of my best efforts, those grand jury proceedings remain sealed.[9]

SHAPING THE COVER-UP INDICTMENT

We have already seen how collusion between the WSPF prosecutors and Judge Sirica enabled him to appoint himself to preside over the subsequent trial and to implicate President Nixon. Let us now see how they shaped the indictments to assure convictions of their principal targets: Mitchell, Haldeman, and Ehrlichman.

"THOUGHT CRIMES"

Civil libertarians have long decried the use of "thought crimes" by aggressive prosecutors to pursue defendants they don't like. Typically, federal crimes have specific elements, each of which must be proved before a case can be made. Usually this involves the introduction of hard evidence, such as a murder weapon, medical reports, injury photographs, etc. But thought crimes have no such precise definitions, and if there are any specific elements, they require the trial jury to determine what was in the mind of the defendant at the time the alleged crime was committed. The most familiar thought crime, and the one prosecutors turn to most, is conspiracy.

Under federal criminal law (18 U.S.C. § 371), a conspiracy is an agreement between two or more persons to commit a crime in the future. There are two theoretical grounds for the statute: first, the belief that concerted action by a group of persons poses a greater danger than the criminal designs of someone acting alone, and second, the parallel belief that society ought to be able to stop a crime before it is committed and still punish the persons who were intent on its accomplishment.

The elements of the crime of conspiracy are different from those of substantive criminal offenses mainly because the law is designed to punish intent alone. The three elements of conspiracy are an agreement, an overt act in furtherance of the conspiracy, and a specific state of mind.[10]

While the agreement itself is the gravamen of the crime, there is almost never an explicit agreement, such as a formalized document or a bargained-for commitment. Most conspiracy convictions, therefore, are based on inferences from circumstantial evidence, including the conduct of the defendants. There need not be an actual meeting or a uniform start date. The conspirators need not know each other or even know of each other's existence. A conspiracy can be found to exist even where there is no express communication of agreement. All that is necessary is that the jury conclude that there was an agreement to commit a crime. Once that agreement has been found to exist, case law requires only slight additional evidence to link a particular defendant to that conspiracy. The law of conspiracy, then, can turn what a man can lawfully think about into a crime if that same thought becomes a part of an agreement with another person.

At least one of the parties to the agreement must then make an overt act in furtherance of that agreement—or, in the words of the federal statute, "[A]nd one or more of such persons do any act to effect the object of the conspiracy...." This element of the crime is largely inconsequential, since the act can be committed by any member of the alleged conspiracy and need not be substantial or even criminal. Almost anything done by any member can be seen as having put the agreement into motion.

There must, however, be a "buy in" by each of the defendants; there must be a meeting of the minds (which is an analogy to contract law). The mental component of the conspiracy, however, involves two distinct states of mind. First, the defendant must understand and appreciate that an agreement has been reached and, second, the defendant must understand and appreciate that achieving the object of the agreement will involve some sort of criminal activity. Put a little differently, it must be shown that there was an intent to agree, as well as an understanding that a criminal offense was the desired outcome of that agreement. This particularized desire has been characterized as a requirement of *specific* intent.

If you have followed this description thus far, you should begin to see how ephemeral conspiracy concepts are—and how confusing such prosecutions can be to jurors.

Criticisms of prosecutors' use of conspiracy statutes are common. Professor Paul Marcus wrote what for our purposes is the definitive article in 1976—"Conspiracy: The Criminal Agreement, in Theory and in Practice."[11] The basis for the article was a detailed questionnaire of over thirty issues, which Marcus sent to over 1,600 judges and practitioners—including both prosecutors and members of the criminal defense bar. Half of those questioned responded in a substantive manner. The questionnaire was then followed up with face-to-face interviews with a variety of lawyers and judges in fourteen major U.S. cities.

Marcus opened his article with contrasting statements about conspiracy statutes, the first by Justice Felix Frankfurter in a 1961 opinion:

> [C]ollective criminal agreement—partnership in crime—presents a greater potential threat to the public than individual delicts. Concerted action both increases the likelihood that the criminal object will be successfully attained and decreases the probability that the individuals involved will depart from their path of criminality. Group association for criminal purposes often, if not normally, makes possible the attainment of ends more complex than those which one criminal could accomplish.

Frankfurter's approving view of conspiracy prosecutions is contrasted with that of Clarence Darrow, who stated in his 1932 biography, "If there are still any citizens interested in protecting human liberty, let them study the conspiracy law of the United States."

Richard Harris, writing in the *New Yorker*, went further:

> In the view of most civil libertarians, conspiracy laws are basically pernicious, and should be either rewritten or taken off the books altogether. During conspiracy trials, moreover, prosecutors are permitted wide procedural latitude in presenting evidence, such as the right to introduce information that is based on the assumption that a conspiracy exists, though its existence has not yet been proven, while defendants are deprived of ordinary courtroom protections, such as the inadmissibility of hearsay evidence.[12]

Marcus poses two troubling questions:

> First, if the purpose of a primary rationale for the conspiracy
> law is to enable the government to intervene before the crime
> itself has occurred, why are prosecutors allowed to bring
> conspiracy charges *after* the crime itself has occurred?
>
> Second, doesn't conviction on both the conspiracy charge
> and the underlying crime constitute dual punishment (a sort
> of double jeopardy) for the same crime?

Marcus suggests the reasons for prosecutor's widespread use of
conspiracy statutes after posing the following question:

> If the theoretical basis for convicting persons of both the
> substantive offense and the conspiracy is not supportable,
> and if in practice the conspirator rarely receives consecutive
> sentences, why do prosecutors charge and attempt to prove
> two offenses at trial? Surely there must be an advantage to
> counteract the disadvantages of time consumption and con-
> fusion engendered by more complex jury instructions.
> According to defense counsel, the advantage is higher con-
> viction rates.

By far the most important advantage of including a conspiracy
charge alongside the substantive count is the exception to the hearsay
rule for any statement of any conspirator made during the course of the
conspiracy. Such statements are admissible at trial against all conspirators. As Marcus documents in a footnote,

> The out-of-court declaration of a coconspirator may be used
> as substantive evidence against the defendant as long as the
> declaration was made during the course of the conspiracy and
> in furtherance of it. The rationale for this exception to the
> hearsay rule is that the coconspirators are agents of one

another, and any such statement by one is the statement of all.

Marcus dramatically illustrates the perceived advantages of this exception in his table of responses to the following question:

Question 10: What would be the result of eliminating the hearsay exception where conspiracy is charged or where it is the uncharged basis for the charged crime?

The view of virtually all practitioners was that there would be a dramatic—almost catastrophic—decline in convictions were this exception to the hearsay rule to be eliminated.

The enormous influence of this hearsay exception on obtaining convictions, Marcus concludes, was almost universally accepted. And this is not only the exception to evidentiary rules that a conspiracy charge opens up. Marcus points out that the admissibility of acts of co-conspirators at trial also is hugely influential and is seen as a distinct advantage by almost 80 percent of his survey respondents.

Marcus identifies other advantages of bringing conspiracy counts:

The survey shows that these advantages are important, but it also establishes that other reasons encourage prosecutors to charge conspiracy: the reaction of the jury or judge to the alleged danger of group activity, jurors' confusion that may lead them to convict all defendants, longer sentences, and improved plea bargaining positions.

A final point is pertinent to Watergate. The case law on conspiracies has been developed primarily in prosecutions for illegal gambling, narcotics distribution, or organized crime. In such cases, mere membership in the corrupt organization is evidence of an evil state of mind. Thus, once a conspiracy has been shown to exist, virtually no additional proof is necessary to add additional defendants to that conspiracy, since there is no innocent reason for them to be a part of that group. When the organization in question is a legitimate one—such as the White House staff or a political committee—in which people could well have gone about their daily lives without being confronted with first having to join a criminal enterprise, a criminal prosecution framed in terms of conspiracy can easily produce unjust results.

	Significant Reduction in Convictions	Small Reduction in Convictions	No Effect
Prosecutors	61.7	24.4	14.0
Defense Attorneys	72.1	22.7	5.2
Appellate Judges	56.5	32.6	10.9
Trial Judges	42.4	49.2	8.5
Law Professors	51.8	42.9	5.4
Average for all Respondents	62.6	27.8	9.6

It is easy to see why conspiracy was the first count named in the cover-up indictment brought by WSPF prosecutors. But a conspiracy charge becomes particularly troublesome when the underlying substantive charge is obstruction of justice, which is also a thought crime.

The definition of the crime of obstruction is exceedingly broad, encompassing interference in some way with an official investigation or court procedure. The Watergate cover-up defendants were charged under 18 U.S.C. § 1503, Influencing or injuring officer, juror or witness generally ("Whoever corruptly...endeavors to impede any witness..." as the statute read at the time) and § 1001, Statements or entries generally ("Whoever...knowingly and willfully falsifies, conceals or covers up...a material fact..."). Obstruction is typically committed by lying to investigators (perjury or false statements), by getting others to lie to investigators (subornation of perjury), or by destroying evidence (even if not then under subpoena).

With such a broad and open-ended definition, almost any act could be alleged to constitute an obstruction of justice. The only safeguard, such as it is, is the requirement of specific intent to obstruct or otherwise interfere with a judicial proceeding. The defendant, then, must not only know of the legal proceeding but must appreciate the connection between his act and that proceeding.

For our purposes, it is the reason behind the act in question, the defendant's intent, which would pose the greatest challenge for the jury. To find guilt, the jury would be required to look into the mind of each defendant to determine his motive and the rationale for his actions.

Coupling a charge of conspiracy to obstruct justice with a charge of the obstruction itself doubles down on the key issue—to find one would be to find the other. This is particularly true when evidence—the acts and statements of co-conspirators, which become admissible only because of the conspiracy charge—will influence the jury's deliberations on the obstruction charge.

Mitchell, Haldeman, and Ehrlichman were also charged with perjury under 18 U.S.C. § 1621, which provides, "Whoever, having taken an oath before a competent tribunal...willfully and contrary to such oath states or subscribes any material matter which he does not believe to be true, is guilty of perjury...." Federal prosecutions for perjury are quite rare, however, because of the difficult burden of proof. The government must show that the untruth involved something material to the investigation, and the untruth must be proved from two independent sources.

Similarly, 18 U.S.C. § 1623 punishes false declarations before a grand jury or court with penalties of up to five years. Materiality is still required, but prosecutions do not require any particular number of witnesses or documentary evidence.

Under either section, the trial jury must decide what was going through the defendant's mind at the time of his allegedly false testimony, a task that is particularly difficult if the defendant's response to a question was that he could not remember.

SELECTING THE COVER-UP DEFENDANTS:
THE ABUSE OF PROSECUTORIAL DISCRETION

There were lots of possible defendants for the cover-up's comprehensive indictment. Students of Watergate have long wondered how these seven,[13] and no others, were selected for the political trial of the century. Documents which I have only recently uncovered tell a most interesting tale.

In early 1974 the prosecuting attorneys on the Watergate Task Force, then headed by Richard Ben-Veniste, held a series of meetings with the senior staff lawyers in the Office of the Special Prosecutor—Special Prosecutor Leon Jaworski, his deputy, Henry Ruth, and Special Counsel Philip Lacovara. What we know about these meetings comes from the handwritten notes taken by Peter Kreindler, the special prosecutor's executive assistant. The notes are so detailed and revealing that they read like an account of a jury's deliberations.

In the initial meeting on January 11, they discussed Richard Kleindienst, the former attorney general; Patrick Gray, the former acting director of the FBI; Jack Caulfield, Dean's assistant, who had helped with the alleged "hush money" payments; and Herbert Porter, the young CRP staff member who had testified falsely before the grand jury about Gordon Liddy's budget. No decisions were made, except that Gray would not be indicted. He had shown, they felt, bad judgment but was not involved in the conspiracy.[14]

Kreindler summarized the deliberations: "Watergate [Task Force] views core as Mitchell, Haldeman, Ehrlichman and Mardian. Questions, in addition to Bittman & Parkinson, are Colson, Kalmbach & Strachan."[15]

In the next meeting, on January 31, they discussed Caulfield, who a year earlier had tried to induce James McCord not to testify against members of the administration. The special prosecutor had offered to recommend a suspended sentence for Caulfield if he pleaded guilty to a conspiracy charge, but now there was some concern about setting such a precedent. Jaworski agreed to stand by the agreement, but wanted to avoid any announcement and to let the matter drift for the time being.

The discussion then turned to Kenneth Parkinson, a lawyer who had passed messages about the defendants' payment needs to CRP and the White House. He also had been told the story of the break-in by Magruder and had made extensive notes. When Mitchell denied Magruder's story, Parkinson had destroyed those notes and helped to prepare Magruder for his grand jury testimony. Ben-Veniste said Parkinson's background "couldn't be cleaner. Pillar of bar & community, etc.," but he had to be indicted because the "core of whole case is about money. Parkinson caught up in money." Jill Volner, another task force prosecutor, added that Parkinson "has nothing to offer as a witness & would be counter-productive." She added that the U.S. attorney prosecuting the Vesco case in New York, where Parkinson had initially represented Stans, "believes that Parkinson has lied to them." The conclusion: "Watergate recommends including Parkinson as a defendant. Have decided tentatively, though, not to charge him with perjury. Only charge principals w/ perjury (Haldeman, Ehrlichman, Mitchell, Strachan)."

Next on the agenda was William Bittman, Hunt's defense lawyer. Jaworski stated that he knew the case well and had read all the memos. He stated that he was "troubled because of Bittman's record."[16] When Volner said Bittman knew well what was going on, Jaworski responded "from his experience that it may not have dawned on Bittman that he was doing something criminal," (a state of mind that could have applied to most of the Watergate defendants). The matter was left unresolved, since Jaworski had agreed to meet with Bittman's attorney to hear his side of the argument.

The next potential defendant was Gordon Strachan. After recalling that Strachan had "lied extensively to GJ in 4/73 about transactions with [Fred] LaRue," the task force recommended that he be included in the conspiracy count and charged with perjury before the Senate. It was noted that there would be legal problems, since that testimony had occurred under a grant of use immunity.

The group then turned to Charles Colson. Jaworski opened the discussion: "LJ [Jaworski] said he is familiar w/ facts—talked to Colson and Shapiro at length. [David Shapiro was Colson's law partner and represented him in the criminal case.] LJ does not see strong case, but sees possibility of plea because of concern about indictment." Kreindler goes on to observe:

> RB-V [Ben-Veniste] thinks conspiracy could be won. PAL [Lacovara] raised problem of Colson getting caught up in larger conspiracy.
>
> PMK [Kreindler] stated 8/72 perjury seems more solid & better case than major conspiracy. Perjury alone and/or conspiracy recognized as possibilities.
>
> HR [Ruth] points out that no one testifies as to promise to Hunt of clemency—Dean pitted against 4 other witnesses.
>
> LJ said if there are significant doubts, Fielding break-in [the Plumbers trial] may be way to proceed.

Colson appears to be a rather close case, and the matter remains unresolved, but the DOJ standard for indictment (which the special prosecutor announced he would meet) is that the prosecutor must believe a conviction is probable, which requires more than a fifty-fifty chance.

Kreindler's notes conclude:

> LJ has seen memos on Haldeman, Ehrlichman, Mitchell and Mardian & expressed no problem. Conspiracy & substantive count against each. Perjury against 1st three.

The next meeting occurred on Saturday, February 16. In response to a question about the order of the defendants, Jaworski directed that the indictment "name defendants 'Mitchell, Haldeman & Ehrlichman' and then alphabetically." The discussion then focused on the timing of the indictment, Kreindler noting that "Sirica does not want indictment delayed." This reference suggests that it was rather well known to prosecutors that Sirica faced a deadline in appointing himself to preside over the cover-up trial. Jaworski then inquired about indicting Colson for perjury before the grand jury. Ben-Veniste opposed such a charge, saying there was enough to indict on the conspiracy charge, with a fifty-fifty chance of conviction. Ruth opposed naming Colson at all because the evidence would show that he was trying to get the story out after February 1973. Kreindler records that Ben-Veniste would start summing up the following Tuesday, when they would resolve questions about Colson and Bittman, and the meeting concluded.

If such a subsequent meeting occurred, we do not have Kreindler's notes from it, but the WSPF file contains a two-page typed memorandum titled "Watergate, Final Decisions" and dated February 20, 1974, a Wednesday (see Appendix M). The first half-page reads in pertinent part (emphasis in original):

1. Ruth has decided to include *Parkinson* in indictment. LJ said he agrees with it but did not want to make that decision but will sign indictment.
2. On basis of Ben-Veniste's assessment of chances of conviction of *Colson* on the evidence, LJ has decided that he should be included. Ben-Veniste said evidence shows he is a member of conspiracy and there is a 50-50 chance of conviction. Ruth dissents.
3. Mardian is to be included, according to LJ, because of his *early* involvement in incriminating activities, even though he withdrew later.
4. There are no doubts about inclusion of *Mitchell, Ehrlichman, Haldeman* and *Strachan*.

The next page and a half is devoted exclusively to Bittman:

LJ has decided not to charge him; he was appearing [before the grand jury] as defense counsel acting for a guilty client [Howard Hunt], but one he had an obligation to do his best for. His conduct was unsavory, but his role is that of defense counsel and his actions are subject to several interpretations, including those consistent with representing his client's interests.

There followed extensive push-back from members of the Watergate Task Force, who had unanimously recommended Bittman's indictment. Their questions for Jaworski include: How can you indict Parkinson, a man of sterling reputation, who was also acting as counsel, and not Bittman? How can you indict Colson, when chances of conviction are "no more than 50-50," and not indict Bittman? But Jaworski held firm, and Bittman walked free.[17] In a two-page memorandum to Jaworski, Lacovara made one last attempt to convince him not to include Colson, noting that both Ruth and Kreindler shared his concerns, but to no avail (see Appendix N).[18]

From this internal debate, it seems reasonable to conclude that Mitchell, Haldeman, and Ehrlichman were named first in the indictment to make clear—even to the most casual observer, but certainly to the jury—that they were the central defendants. They were deliberately named first. Although specific perjury counts could have been brought against each of the defendants, they were filed only against these three, who were characterized as "principals" not because they were principals in the cover-up but because they were Nixon's closest associates. Indeed, after all the verdicts had been rendered and the appeals had concluded, only these three stood convicted of the cover-up. Everyone else named in the original indictment had been acquitted or had seen his charges dropped.

Lawyers retained as counsel were held to a higher standard (the phrase used by Jaworski), but that standard was unevenly applied. Kenneth Parkinson, a Republican who represented CRP in a civil case, was indicted. William Bittman, a Democrat who represented Hunt in a criminal case, was not. Parkinson, it should be noted, was the only defendant acquitted by the trial jury.

Charles Colson was included in the indictment even though the Watergate Task Force rated the chances of his conviction at no better than fifty-fifty and Jaworski's entire staff opposed including him. Colson

Nixon meets in the early months of his administration with his two closest aides, H. R. Haldeman and John Ehrlichman, at the Western White House in San Clemente, California. The two were later convicted on all counts in the Watergate cover-up trial and sentenced to terms of two and a half to eight years. (Richard Nixon Presidential Library)

Nixon meets in the Oval Office with Attorney General John Mitchell, who later headed his re-election campaign. Mitchell was convicted on all counts in the Watergate cover-up trial and sentenced to two and a half to eight years. (Richard Nixon Presidential Library)

Clark Mollenhoff in the Oval Office in 1969, when he was special counsel to the president. Mollenhoff left after only ten months and harbored deep resentments against Haldeman and Ehrlichman, which he shared privately with Judge Sirica. (Richard Nixon Presidential Library)

Charles Colson, with Nixon in the Oval Office, was renowned as a political in-fighter but was only peripherally involved in the Watergate scandal. Prosecutors knew their case against Colson was not strong, but they included him in the cover-up indictment believing that he would seek an early plea bargain, which he did. (Richard Nixon Presidential Library)

John Dean, counsel to the president and "chief desk officer" for the Watergate cover-up. In seeking immunity from prosecution, he changed his story and became the lead witness against his former colleagues. Nominally sentenced to a term of one to four years, Dean spent only four months in a witness holding facility before Sirica set him free one week after the cover-up trial. (Richard Nixon Presidential Library)

The author, then a White House Fellow, in the Oval Office with Nixon and the fellows program's executive director, Hudson Drake, July 1970. (Richard Nixon Presidential Library)

The author (at head of table, on right), now associate director of the Domestic Council, meets in the Cabinet Room with (clockwise around table): Nixon, Attorney General William Saxby, presidential counselor Bryce Harlow, assistant to the president for congressional relations William Timmons, counsel to the president Leonard Garment, Republican National Committee co-chairmen George H. W. Bush and Anne Armstrong, and Vice President Gerald Ford. (Richard Nixon Presidential Library)

Chief District Court Judge John J. Sirica, July 1973. His series of secret meetings with each of the Watergate prosecutors and with other interested parties undermined the validity of the convictions obtained in the cover-up trial. (Bettmann/Corbis/AP Images)

Earl Silbert, principal assistant U.S. attorney, whose prosecution of the Watergate break-in defendants brought about the collapse of the cover-up. He and his team were later treated shabbily by the special prosecutor's office. One of the few real Watergate heroes, Silbert was later confirmed as U.S. attorney for the District of Columbia. (Bettmann/Corbis/AP Images)

Sam Ervin of North Carolina, chairman of the Senate Watergate Committee, with the committee's chief counsel, Samuel Dash, March 18, 1973. Dash met privately with Judge Sirica to urge harsh temporary sentences for the Watergate defendants to encourage them to testify before his committee. (Associated Press)

Archibald Cox, Kennedy confidant and Harvard law professor, was the original Watergate special prosecutor and brought with him two other Harvard professors. They assembled a highly partisan Democratic staff, whose overriding goal, as described by Cox's successor, was to get Nixon "at all cost." (Associated Press)

Leon Jaworski, Cox's replacement as special prosecutor, on his way to court with two of his top assistants: Philip Lacovara, counsel to the special prosecutor, and Richard Ben-Veniste, head of the Watergate task force. All met privately with Sirica. (Associated Press)

Edward Bennett Williams, a renowned trial lawyer, was counsel to the Democratic National Committee and the *Washington Post*. An inveterate foe of the Nixon administration, he was Sirica's patron and godfather to his daughter. Williams met privately with the judge on at least two occasions in successful efforts to protect the *Post* reporters. (Associated Press)

John Mitchell and Maurice Stans after their acquittal in the Vesco trial in New York City on April 28, 1974. John Dean was a principal government witness against them, but jurors told the press that they didn't find him credible. (Bettmann/Corbis/AP Images)

Nixon's top Watergate defense attorneys—James D. St. Clair, trial counsel, and J. Fred Buzhardt, inside strategic counsel—in a rare light-hearted moment as the Nixon presidency wound toward its unhappy conclusion. (Associated Press)

was indicted not because he was central to the cover-up conspiracy but because, as Kreindler recorded, Jaworski saw the "possibility of plea [bargain] because of concern about indictment." Jaworski was right. Colson was indicted (in both the cover-up and the Plumbers cases) and was the first to agree to a plea bargain and to become a witness for the government.

The WSPF's decision about whom to indict for the cover-up reeked of political manipulation and brings no credit to Jaworski as special prosecutor. In a textbook case of prosecutorial abuse, he punished his political enemies and rewarded his political friends.

HIDING THE BALL: NON-DISCLOSURE OF EXCULPATORY EVIDENCE

The record of the WSPF prosecutors was tarnished by highly questionable acts and omissions with regard to their two principal witnesses, John Dean and Jeb Magruder. The duty of the prosecution to disclose possibly exculpatory evidence to the defense is a well-settled element of due process. The Supreme Court developed this doctrine in three cases that bear on the Watergate prosecutions.

In one of its landmark decisions in the criminal law, the Warren court overturned a murder conviction in *Brady v. Maryland* (1963) because the prosecution had not shared possibly exculpatory evidence in its possession with defense counsel. The Brady doctrine, as it came to be known, was considerably expanded in two subsequent decisions.

In 1972, the Court held that the prosecution must inform the jury if its witness has been promised immunity in exchange for his testimony.[19] And in 1976, the Supreme Court held in *United States v. Agurs* that undisclosed evidence is material if it would create a reasonable doubt of guilt that did not otherwise exist.[20] Since the appeal from the Watergate cover-up trial was argued before the D.C. Circuit Court on January 6, 1976, and decided on October 12, 1976, the *Agurs* rule applied.

The case for disclosure was even stronger for reasons that only a lawyer could love. *Agurs* itself was appealed to the Supreme Court from the D.C. Circuit, which had ruled that withholding *any* material evidence violated due process.[21] Thus, during appeal of the Watergate cover-up convictions, the disclosure standard within the D.C. Circuit was even more expansive than that ultimately adopted by the Supreme Court on June 24, 1976.

As discussed below, it appears quite likely that the Watergate prosecutors violated the Brady doctrine by keeping from the defense material that could have undermined the testimony of the prosecution's chief witnesses, Dean and Magruder.

THE BRADY DOCTRINE AND JOHN DEAN

The newly recruited Watergate Special Prosecution Force built its case against the cover-up defendants almost entirely around Dean's testimony. Richard Ben-Veniste and George Frampton described Dean's importance to their case:

> The Watergate Task Force regarded the securing of Dean as a government witness to be the key to our entire case. Haldeman and Ehrlichman had acted almost exclusively through him. Without Dean, there were few direct witnesses against either Haldeman or Ehrlichman. There was no one else who could testify of his own personal knowledge to the full spectrum of their activities in the cover-up.[22]

Dean's cooperation was so important to the Watergate Task Force that they did not charge him with destruction of evidence when he admitted to them on November 3, 1973, that it was he who had destroyed the notebooks and other materials taken from Howard Hunt's safe. Dean's admission to the prosecutors came within three weeks of Sirica's approval in open court of his formal plea bargain. While the prosecutors did make Dean's admission public right away, they took no action against him in response.

Nor did the special prosecutor take action against Dean when a good deal of his sworn testimony before the Ervin Committee turned out to be in substantial error. One of the White House's goals in releasing transcripts of the tapes on April 30, 1974, was to highlight the errors and omissions in Dean's Senate testimony. Indeed, several days later, on May 4, the White House Office of Communications released a thirty-two-page report detailing some nineteen instances where Dean's assertions before the Ervin Committee were contradicted by the tapes themselves—particularly with regard to what he had told the president before their "cancer on the presidency" meeting of March 21, 1973.

But WSPF prosecutors already knew of such problems with Dean's testimony. Following Jaworski's assertion on February 3, 1974, on ABC's *Issues and Answers* that prosecutors had full confidence in Dean's veracity, Watergate Task Force attorney Peter Rient submitted a three-page analysis to Ben-Veniste, dated February 6, 1974 (see Appendix L), identifying some sixteen "material discrepancies" with the White House tapes then in their possession (the ones they had received from Sirica on December 12). We know that Jaworski was aware of this analysis because a copy of the memo was found in his confidential Watergate files. Nonetheless, Jaworski asserted on February 14 that WSPF prosecutors had concluded that Dean had made no "material misstatement in his testimony." At a hearing the next day, Judge Gesell cautioned counsel for both sides to cease the public debate concerning Dean's veracity, but WSPF prosecutors never stepped back from their firm public assertions of Dean's credibility.[23]

The indictments of Haldeman and Mitchell—handed down within three weeks of these events—included perjury counts for similar erroneous testimony before Congress, but comparable charges against Dean were never contemplated.

This selective prosecution is powerful evidence that highly partisan WSPF prosecutors were out to get President Nixon and his senior aides "at all cost." They labored over the preparation of prosecutorial reports on Mitchell, Haldeman, and Ehrlichman that ran into hundreds of pages, uncovering every possibility for charging them with perjury in connection with their Ervin Committee and grand jury testimony. But no one lifted a finger against Dean. Nixon and his senior aides were their enemies; Dean was their friend.

As we saw earlier, Cox had expressed strong concerns about Dean and his actions during the cover-up, but Cox was gone, and the single overriding goal was to get Nixon and his top aides. To do so, they had to rely on Dean—and that required fully buying into Dean's story that he was only doing what he had been told to do by his White House superiors. The problem was that there was evidence to the contrary, and it was sitting in their own files—evidence that was not disclosed to defense counsel, as required under the Brady doctrine.

Dean or his criminal defense counsel Charles Shaffer met or talked with one or more of the career prosecutors from the U.S. attorney's office—Earl Silbert, Seymour Glanzer, and Donald Campbell—more than fifteen times in the days and weeks following the cover-up's collapse (between April 2 and May 5, 1973), and before the appointment of the Watergate special prosecutor. In these negotiations, everyone knew that Dean would not testify against his former colleagues without the promise of immunity from prosecution. While immunity was never formally granted, they agreed informally that the prosecutors would not bring charges against Dean for what was revealed during the course of these meetings.

Dean's initial offer, through his counsel, was to testify against Mitchell and Magruder, but the prosecutors were not impressed with the value of such testimony. They countered that they already had enough testimony against Mitchell from Magruder. Dean then removed exceptionally sensitive information from the files in his counsel's office and presented these files to prosecutors as bargaining chips.[24] When this failed to secure his desired immunity, Dean's own lawyer, Charles Shaffer, told him that since the prosecutors were targeting him on the break-in, he had to enhance the importance of the cover-up and make himself indispensable to their case. Dean describes the conversation in *Blind Ambition*:

DEAN: Goddammit, Charlie. I don't want to meet with those bastards.

SHAFFER: Listen, John, we don't have any choice. The cat's out of the bag. We've got to pump them full of the cover up now. I've got to up the ante with them to have a shot at immunity. That's your only chance not to be the fall guy.

[Two paragraphs later:]

DEAN: I think your strategy of getting immunity is more important than ever now.[25]

Thus, toward the end of their series of meetings, Dean began to make accusations against Haldeman and Ehrlichman. In May, following his termination, Dean first began to make accusations against President Nixon himself. Silbert later characterized Dean's somewhat fluid story as having "escalated" over the course of this critical month.

The career prosecutors were never willing to grant Dean the immunity he sought, since they remained concerned with the seriousness of his own criminal culpability. Dean nevertheless agreed to appear before the Watergate grand jury on May 5, but it turned out that he and Shaffer had also been negotiating for immunity from the Ervin Committee. That grant of immunity seemed to be within his grasp, and on May 4, the evening before Dean's scheduled grand jury appearance, Shaffer called Glanzer at home to say that Dean had changed his mind and would not appear before the grand jury as previously agreed.

The prosecutors from the U.S. attorney's office took careful notes during their lengthy interviews with Dean and Shaffer (available today for review at the National Archives). But those prosecutors, who had secured the burglary convictions and broken the cover-up, were removed from the Watergate case upon the appointment of the special prosecutor and creation of his independent office. The original prosecutors' first-hand knowledge of what had happened up to that point was then lost to the prosecution.

Those meetings from April and May 1973 between the career prosecutors and Dean took on new importance in the fall, when

Watergate Task Force attorneys were trying to formalize their plea deal with Dean. As the negotiations progressed, WSPF prosecutors became concerned that Silbert, Glanzer, and Campbell might have extended an informal offer of immunity to Dean that could preclude his actual prosecution under any circumstances. They decided, therefore, to meet with the career prosecutors to find out more about their spring interviews with Dean and Shaffer. The meetings with which we are concerned are those with Seymour Glanzer and Donald Campbell, conducted by Peter Rient and Judith Denny of the Watergate Task Force in Glanzer's office on September 18 and October 10, 1973. They asked Glanzer and Campbell about each of their April and May meetings, pressing them for details about the scope of the discussions—what was said, when, and by whom. Rient and Denny took extensive notes, which they memorialized in a joint memo to the files dated November 15, 1973 (see Appendix O).[26] The following excerpts from that memo present troubling issues regarding the WSPF's compliance with the Brady doctrine in the prosecution of Haldeman and Ehrlichman:

> April 6: Shaffer talked only about Dean's knowledge of Mitchell and Magruder. There was nothing said about Ehrlichman, Haldeman, Colson or Nixon.
>
> April 8: Dean did not mention his subsequent meeting with Haldeman at this time.[27] He gave no information at all about Haldeman or Ehrlichman.
>
> April 9: Dean never acknowledged a cover-up or conspiracy or paying the defendants for silence until after he was fired (April 30, 1973).
>
> April 9: Dean said that at some time Parkinson and LaRue had come to Dean's office with a sheet of paper with money requests from Hunt on it, but Dean never said that the money was for Hunt's silence.
>
> April 9: Dean mentioned the McCord letter complaining about a CIA defense being contemplated. Ehrlichman told

Dean to "stroke" McCord. Also Bittman visited Colson and discussed clemency. Again the response by Ehrlichman and Haldeman was that Colson should "stroke" Bittman, but make no promises.

April 9: Campbell remembers that Dean told of the March 21 meeting where Dean attempted to tell the President about the situation, but that the President didn't understand.

April 23: Glanzer says that by this time, the discussions had turned into a political game. Dean was bargaining with the Senate for immunity and the prosecutor's attempts at agreeing on a plea were in vain.

April 29: By the end of April, Dean had become much more antagonistic toward Haldeman and Ehrlichman in his discussions with the prosecutors and also in public, issuing the "scapegoat" statement. Before that, the impressions he gave of Haldeman was of a "great devoted public servant," clean and hard working. He had been restrained in his praise of Ehrlichman.

May 2: [Dean] said Colson could corroborate the meeting on June 19th where Ehrlichman gave the order to tell Hunt to leave the country. (Dean became antagonistic toward Colson when Colson did not corroborate).

May 3: On May 3, Dean began focusing on Presidential involvement, thus changing dramatically from his previous stance.[28]

May 3: Dean was somewhat concerned about being arrested for turning over the documents since he never had control of them.[29]

May 3: Months before Dean's March 21 conversation with Nixon, Dean had discussed the cover-up with [White House special counsel] Dick Moore. Although Moore suggested going to Nixon then, Dean did not do so.

End of Memo: Glanzer thinks the prosecutors' effort was neutralized by the appointment of a special prosecutor and

the Senate Committee coming into being, and that they began
to lose control over the case.

These portions of Rient's and Denny's memo, reflecting the views of
the original Watergate prosecutors—the career prosecutors from the U.S.
attorney's office who met with Dean when he first approached them in
pursuit of immunity—contained evidence that would have raised substantial doubts about the special prosecutor's case against Haldeman and
Ehrlichman (as well as any case against President Nixon). In short, the
contents of this memo were—and remain—critically damaging to Dean's
credibility as a witness.

Dean mentioned no conspiracy early on. He said nothing about the
payment of money's being for silence. He did not allege the involvement
of Haldeman and Ehrlichman in the course of over a dozen meetings and
phone calls with prosecutors. It was not until a full month after the meetings began—and only after he had been terminated from his job as
counsel to the president—that Dean first began to mention these matters
or to accuse President Nixon of any wrongdoing.

It seems clear from the quoted portions of this memo from the
special prosecutor's own files that Dean's story changed considerably
during his month-long pursuit of immunity. It would be difficult to
imagine a more devastating document, especially in the hands of
defense counsel seeking to raise reasonable doubts about the consis-
tency and credibility of Dean's accusations against their clients. Dean
was the principal accusatory witness, and Rient's and Denny's memorandum undercut his story.

The WSPF ought to have revealed the Rient-Denny memorandum
to the defense under the Brady doctrine. It unquestionably raises reasonable doubts about Dean's story. The memo was not attorney work product, which might arguably have been exempt from disclosure. These
career prosecutors were interviewed as witnesses about what had happened during their early meetings with Dean and Shaffer. Withholding
this memo from defense counsel was a clear violation of the due process
of law guaranteed to the defendants.

But the conduct of the Watergate Task Force appeared even more troubling when I found (in the National Archives) and reviewed Rient's and Denny's original handwritten notes from their two meetings with Glanzer and Campbell. It became clear that WSPF prosecutors had altered Glanzer's and Campbell's recollections when they summarized them in the memorandum of November 15, 1973.

The typed memo reads:

> By the end of April, Dean had become much more antagonistic toward Haldeman and Ehrlichman in his discussions with the prosecutors and also in public, issuing the "scapegoat" statement. Before that, the impressions he gave of Haldeman was of a "great devoted public servant," clean and hard working. He had been restrained in his praise of Ehrlichman.

The handwritten notes from the October 10th meeting read as follows (see Appendix P):

> 5/2—5/3 Silbert, Glanzer & Campbell meeting with Dean & Shaffer—
> Situation in state of flux because of Senate Committee & Cox after 4/15. Dean becomes antagonistic toward E & H, whereas before he had given the impression that H was clean & was restrained as to E's involvement. This was around time of "scapegoat" statement by Dean.

It is clear from a comparison of these two documents that someone in the prosecutors' office re-interpreted the plain meaning of the handwritten notes, changing "H was clean and was restrained as to E's involvement" to read "Haldeman was a 'great devoted public servant,' clean and hardworking. He had been restrained in his praise of Ehrlichman." This constitutes the deliberate alteration of evidence in the possession of the prosecution. Altering the records of witness testimony normally would get an attorney fired and perhaps even disbarred.

It might be objected that the omission of these documents—both the handwritten notes and the finalized typewritten memo—from material turned over to defense counsel was mere oversight by the Watergate Task Force, but even if true it makes no difference. It is clear from the Supreme Court's opinions discussed above that the prosecutor's intent doesn't matter. It is a denial of due process whether the omission is intentional or unintentional.

Besides, it is highly unlikely that the Rient-Denny memo was kept from defense counsel accidentally. On the concluding page of handwritten notes from the Glanzer and Campbell interviews are four "Additional Question[s] for Glanzer & Campbell," including "Escalation by Dean." Silbert first used the term in his eighty-seven-page briefing memo of May 25, 1973, to Cox, describing how Dean's testimony gradually "escalated" to include President Nixon and his two top White House aides.

The deliberate change in wording from the handwritten notes to the typed version suggests that the authors—and possibly others—appreciated how important these observations were. It seems unlikely, moreover, that both Rient and Denny, having conducted the interviews and signed the final memo, would have overlooked this information or the applicability of the Brady doctrine.

WSPF prosecutors were clearly alert to the possibility of a challenge to Dean's testimony on the grounds that it had changed over the course of his early meetings with the prosecutors from the U.S. attorney's office. On the opening day of the cover-up trial, James Neal of the Watergate Task Force wrote an internal memo asking for an immediate and thorough review of Dean's statements to the career prosecutors in case the defense counsel raised questions about how Dean's story "escalated" as the series of interviews progressed.[30]

Even after this concern was raised, the prosecution insisted on the opening day of trial that it had turned over all that was required:

> MR. NEAL: May it please the court; as we have said time and time again both in court and out to Mr. Hall [counsel for

John Ehrlichman], we have turned over volumes of materials relating to each witness. We have turned over to defense counsel months ago each and every document, and at the same time those matters that we believe we are obligated to turn over under 18 U.S.C. 3500 [the Jencks Act], and under the doctrine of Brady versus Maryland, we have turned over more than we think we are obligated to do, and as far as we are concerned, that is all we are going to do.[31]

MR. WILSON [Haldeman's defense counsel]: I would like, through you, to ask Mr. Neal is the government withholding from the defense, documents which might be helpful to us in the cross-examination of Mr. Dean or that might be relevant to that cross-examination?

JUDGE SIRICA: Mr. Neal looks like he is itching to answer that question.

MR. NEAL: May it please the court; I am too cautious to answer something like that. I don't know what would be helpful to Mr. Wilson in cross-examining Mr. Dean. All I am saying, Your Honor, we have turned over everything that we are obligated to turn over.[32]

The prosecution compounded its violation of the Brady doctrine on the subsequent appeal when Rient and Denny, the members of the Watergate Task Force responsible for the memorandum about Dean's evolving story, both signed the appellate brief, which asserted that "the prosecution thoroughly reviewed and voluntarily produced all documents and other materials even remotely relevant to the issues to be tried."[33]

Not alerting defense counsel to the existence of this memo or of the handwritten notes, which could have raised reasonable doubt as to the credibility of key aspects of Dean's testimony on behalf of the prosecution, was a violation of the Brady doctrine. This omission alone, if known at the time, could have been the basis for reversing the convictions and remanding for a new trial.

THE BRADY DOCTRINE AND JEB MAGRUDER

The WSPF prosecutors' handling of Jeb Magruder, its other principal witness, raises a separate set of questions about the ethics and conduct of the prosecution.

Handsome and engaging, Magruder joined the Nixon White House staff in mid-1969 as deputy director of communications. He left that position in May 1971, one of the first people assigned to help organize the Committee to Re-Elect the President. He functioned as acting chief of staff until John Mitchell's arrival the following March.

When Gordon Liddy showed up at CRP talking about spending a million dollars or more on a campaign intelligence plan, Magruder responded that only Mitchell had the authority to approve expenditures at that level—and he was still attorney general. Thus Mitchell's involvement in the two fateful meetings, on January 27 and February 4, 1972, in which Liddy presented his campaign intelligence plans to Dean, Magruder, and the attorney general, was, ironically enough, the result of Magruder's *budgetary* concerns.

Magruder knew a great deal about the events that led to the Watergate break-ins:

- Magruder had not only been at the planning meetings of January 27 and February 4, he had also presented Liddy's wiretapping plan at the third meeting—with Mitchell on March 30 in Key Biscayne—the meeting at which, Magruder later asserted, Mitchell had approved the Liddy plan.[34]
- Magruder had authorized the funds that had been disbursed to Liddy to effectuate his plan.
- Magruder had received the fruits of the one Watergate wiretap that worked.
- Magruder was the one who allegedly ordered Liddy to take his team back in to repair the wiretap that was not operating correctly.[35]

The trouble was that he didn't know much about any possible involvement of Haldeman or Ehrlichman in the cover-up itself. His main involvement was in covering up his own criminal conduct, including his having given perjured testimony (with coaching from Dean) on two occasions. When the cover-up collapsed, Magruder was desperately eager to be helpful to the prosecutors, but he had little of substance to offer. His primary role, as the WSPF prosecutors saw it, was to support Dean's lead testimony. Magruder, however, could not corroborate anything Dean said about Dean's meetings with Haldeman and Ehrlichman, since Magruder had not been present, at least not after the June 17th break-in, and Dean's own recollections kept evolving.

In the thirty-month period between Magruder's first grand jury testimony and his testimony at the Watergate cover-up trial, he had offered sworn testimony before Watergate grand juries on at least five occasions and had been subjected to in-depth interviews by prosecuting attorneys on at least sixteen separate occasions. He had told and retold his story so many times, each time with slight variations, that he may not have been able to remember with any precision what had actually happened. He only knew that he wanted to please the prosecutors, the ones who held his fate in their hands. He appears to have adopted the protective posture of telling them whatever he thought they then wanted to hear.

It would not be odd for Magruder's various re-tellings to contain minor variances, but the situation was far worse than that. James Neal, the lead prosecutor in the cover-up case, once shared his concern with President Nixon's own Watergate defense lawyer, J. Fred Buzhardt, saying that he was not at all sure that the prosecutors could put Magruder on the witness stand in good faith, since they had substantial doubts about his veracity. Magruder, Neal explained, was so scared of going to prison that he was liable to say anything that he felt the prosecutors wanted.[36] It was an ethical issue, as well as a question of possible prosecutorial misconduct, since lawyers are not allowed to put witnesses on the stand when they know they are going to lie.

There is a hint of this same concern in Dean's book:

> Neal looked disgusted. "I'll be honest with you. [Magruder's]
> a crybaby. All he does is bitch, bitch, bitch. I don't like him

very well. Any man who slants his testimony to satisfy a prosecutor is weak, and I don't have much respect for your friend Jeb."

I had already known that Jeb's testimony had vexed the prosecutors; Jill Volner [another attorney on the Watergate Task Force] had complained often about his eagerness to tailor his story to the prosecutors' needs.[37]

The material discrepancies in Magruder's various recollections were laid out in an internal memorandum prepared for WSPF counsel to use in guiding him through his testimony in the cover-up trial. The undated and unsigned forty-four-page document is titled "Jeb Stuart Magruder— Direct Testimony" and is contained in the special prosecutor's Magruder file at the National Archives.

The memo identifies fifty-seven topics to be covered during Magruder's direct testimony and provides summaries of what Magruder is expected to say with regard to each topic.[38] The memo helpfully identifies the source for each expected response—particularly when it comes from earlier sworn testimony, either before the Senate Watergate Committee or the grand jury. It also notes where Magruder's expected testimony might conflict with the sworn testimony of another government witness. The trouble for the prosecutors is that the memo identifies some *four dozen* potential discrepancies.

For example, Magruder met with Mitchell and his assistant Fred LaRue in Key Biscayne on March 30, 1972. Magruder had prepared thirty action memos for discussion, the last of which concerned Liddy's scaled-down intelligence plan. Magruder contended that Mitchell approved the plan at this meeting, but his previous testimony differed as to how or in what form the plan was presented. The memo describes Magruder's expected testimony about this meeting:

> Liddy plan memo was last: it was a $250,000 budget on plain paper, probably on several sheets,* with operational figures and it clearly indicated the intended purchase of electronic

surveillance equipment and called for wiretapping and photographing documents and entry.

The asterisk, however, points to problems with Magruder's current story:

> * It was not in the orginary [sic] action memo form because there was no notation typed on it for "approve, disapprove, comment." Magruder has waivered [sic] as to whether there was a new budget typed for $250,000 or the old $500,000 was just verbally altered (he now thinks there was a new $250,000 budget and says he waivered due to [Robert] Reisner's [Magruder's assistant at CRP] testimony that he told R to tell Liddy "First half approved." Since Reisner and Sloan saw a paper with a $250,000 total and Mason says she typed a budget on plain paper around 3/17 for $100,000, there probably was a new budget for $250,000, but query whether it was one or several pages (Reisner says one; Sloan and Mg several).

Magruder was then to be asked about the specifics of Mitchell's approval of Liddy's plan. About a third of Mitchell's testimony at the cover-up trial was devoted to contending that he had not approved the plan at this meeting and therefore had nothing to cover up. LaRue, another government witness, also testified that Mitchell had not approved money for Liddy's plan at this meeting. Magruder's testimony was to the contrary, but again Magruder was uncertain as to the details. The memo notes some of the problems:

> Magruder recalls that LaRue was negative.... Magruder's memory was jogged by LaRue's Senate Select Committee testimony and [now] does remember that Mitchell was initially inclined to delay approving the budget, as was Mitchell's wont in some cases. It was in that context that Mitchell

orally and reluctantly approved the plan and said, "Well, let's give him this much and see what he can do with it," or words to that effect*

* But see [this portion is redacted, probably because it refers to non-public grand jury testimony—but clearly indicates the prosecution is aware of contrary or conflicting testimony by Magruder or some other government witness.]

Magruder has no recollection of LaRue being there or not being there when budget approved. LaRue may have gotten up to take a phone call in the other room, as he had done once or twice during the day. Omit?

Mg goes back to hotel. Tries unsuccessfully to call Liddy. Calls GS* [Gordon Strachan, Haldeman's assistant] and tells him all results of KB [Key Biscayne] mtg, including JM's approval and targets selected. Calls Reisner and tells him (1) to have Liddy contact Mg in Florida or (2) tells him to tell Liddy his project is approved.**

* Hotel Records show 2 calls to WH on 3/30—1 for 16 minutes and 1 for 29 minutes. But SS 1983 [Magruder's Senate Watergate Committee testimony] and [reference redacted, which must be Magruder's grand jury testimony] says Mg spoke to GS after return to D.C. SS 2036 says call may have been from Key Biscayne.

** [redacted reference, again probably to Magruder's grand jury testimony] Mg said was (2). Reisner's testimony is that Mg told him to tell Liddy it was approved in person and he's not sure it was after KB, but, says it is only logical that it was. R's diary is consistent with possibility Mg tried calling Liddy or having R tell Liddy to call him and having failed to reach him from Florida, then telling R to give message to L after he had returned from Florida.

Despite the obscurities here, it is clear that Magruder had sworn that he called Strachan to inform him of the results of all thirty action items, either before he left Key Biscayne or after he returned to Washington. This would have been a rather long call, and Magruder's failure to remember when he had made it did not help his credibility. Similarly, Magruder's testimony differs from Reisner's as to whether he instructed Reisner to have Liddy call Magruder or instructed Reisner to tell Liddy that the plan had been approved. Magruder now seems insistent that he instructed Reisner not to use the phone but to talk to Liddy in person once they had returned from Key Biscayne.

One more example should suffice to illustrate the thicket of contradictions from which the prosecutors had to extract Magruder. What really undermined Mitchell's denial of having approved Liddy's plan was a call that he had subsequently received from Maurice Stans, chairman of CRP's finance committee, questioning the large sums of money that Liddy was requisitioning, which Mitchell then approved. Here, too, Magruder's testimony changed as to the specific circumstances. The memo reads:

> Shortly thereafter Mitchell asked Magruder to explain Liddy's request, which Magruder did. Magruder said that the disbursement was "front money" for equipment and personnel for the intelligence plan which Mitchell had approved. JM said he'd tell Stans. [JM in Mg's presence told Stans it was ok to give L $] (NEW! Omit if possible)

Here Magruder has suddenly and for the first time recalled that he was present in Mitchell's office when Mitchell called Stans to approve the disbursement to Liddy. He had never made such an assertion before, and if it came out at this late date, it would further undermine Magruder's credibility with the jury. Hence, the advice to omit any reference to this if possible.

The WSPF memo goes on, working its way through dozens of such discrepancies, which—if defense counsel had but known of them—could have been devastating to Magruder's credibility. Prior inconsistent statements are a godsend to defense counsel, who don't really care which statement is correct. They simply point out the inconsistency and ask, "Were you lying then or are you lying now?" One or two inconsistencies can be enough to severely undermine a witness's credibility before the jury; four dozen would be like shooting fish in a barrel.

The prosecution, however, chose not to share this information with defense counsel—at least not as it was detailed in the memorandum it had prepared for use in its own direct examination of one of its two star witnesses.

Did this lack of full disclosure constitute another breach of the Brady doctrine, or was the Magruder testimony memorandum protected attorney work product? It would have been interesting to watch members of the Watergate Special Prosecution Force defend this lack of disclosure before a fair and impartial judge.

A PARTING QUESTION

Prosecutorial abuse is hardly unheard of, but since Watergate there have been a number of instances committed by Democratic prosecutors out to even political scores with Republican office holders. Recent examples include the 2008 prosecution of Senator Ted Stevens of Alaska by the Department of Justice's Public Integrity Unit; the indictments of Senator Kay Bailey Hutchison of Texas (1993), House Majority Leader Tom DeLay (2005), and Governor Rick Perry of Texas (2014) by the Travis County (Texas) district attorney; the scorched-earth prosecutions of New Orleans police officers following Hurricane Katrina by DOJ's Civil Rights Division (2011); and the massive and secret "John Doe" investigation of Wisconsin Governor Scott Walker's campaign by the Milwaukee County district attorney (2012).

In most of these instances, however, judges or appellate courts—perhaps helped along by vigorous media coverage—responded to the abuse by investigating and invalidating the improperly obtained verdicts.[39]

But the Watergate prosecution turned out differently. It featured a hanging judge reveling in his new-found celebrity and willing to bend every rule to assist the prosecution, and highly partisan prosecutors, working in secret collusion with that judge, charging selected persons with thought crimes and withholding exculpatory evidence to secure their convictions. These were the conditions faced by the cover-up defendants. Could other elements of due process, including trial before a jury of their peers or their automatic right of appeal, provide any of the constitutional safeguards guaranteed by our Bill of Rights?

CHAPTER 8

AN UNTAINTED AND UNBIASED JURY

Jury trials have provided an essential element of fairness in criminal prosecutions at least as far back as ancient Greece and Rome and have long been viewed as a check on over-zealous prosecutors. The right to a trial before a jury of one's peers was confirmed by the Magna Carta (1215) and reconfirmed over five hundred years later by the Sixth Amendment to our Constitution, which requires "an impartial jury" in all criminal trials.

From the very outset of the Watergate scandal there were serious questions as to whether, after the massive adverse pretrial publicity, such a jury could be found within the District of Columbia—and with good reason.

THE D.C. JURY POOL

The boundaries of the original District of Columbia formed a perfect square, ten miles on each side and canted like a baseball diamond, with its corners pointed north, south, east, and west. It consisted primarily of low-lying tidal lands contributed by the contiguous states of Maryland and Virginia. Most of the portion donated by Virginia, that to the west of the Potomac River, was returned to the state just prior to the Civil War, forming what is now Arlington County and leaving the District with an area of just over sixty square miles. No point in the District is more than five miles from the state line of Maryland or Virginia and a different political jurisdiction and federal circuit.

In 1970, Washington's population of 750,000 was just over 70 percent black and predominantly lower middle class. The city had been exceptionally hard hit by white flight and the riots that followed Martin Luther King's assassination. One reason for the District's low socio-economic profile was that virtually all of the area's desirable suburbs were located across state lines in Maryland (Potomac and Bethesda) or in Virginia (Arlington and Alexandria).

At the time of the Watergate trials, Washington was not yet the cosmopolitan city of today. Wags joked that it combined Northern charm and Southern efficiency. It was a one-industry town, the vast majority of its residents working for or in connection with the federal government. The dominant topic of conversation was politics, and the newspapers reflected this. Almost without exception, local news was relegated to a separate, inside section.

Because of the growth of the federal government that began under President Franklin Roosevelt and the long dominance of the Democratic Party in Congress, it was a totally Democratic town. The Congress, its professional staff, the civil service, the city's law firms, think tanks, and news organizations—all had been dominated by Democrats since 1932.

The District typically delivered better than 80 percent Democratic majorities in presidential elections. Even in Nixon's sweeping re-election victory of 1972—when he won the second-highest percentage of the vote in American history (61.2 percent)—the District had voted 78 percent

Democratic and, with Massachusetts, supplied Senator George McGovern's only electoral votes. Simply put, no jurisdiction in the nation was more completely dominated by one political point of view than Washington, D.C.

Was it possible in such an environment to impanel a jury that could impartially try men who were as prominent and notorious Republicans as the defendants in the Watergate cover-up trial, particularly after two and a half years of massive adverse pretrial publicity and the resignation in disgrace of the president they had served?

This question involves two issues: jury taint and jury bias. Had the jury pool—the list of registered voters from which the jurors would be selected—been so thoroughly exposed to news about Watergate that they could not be expected to approach the question of the defendants' guilt with an open mind? And was that jury pool so politically biased against the defendants that a jury taken from it could not be expected to render a fair verdict in a case with such political overtones?

THE TAINT OF PRETRIAL PUBLICITY

The likelihood of a tainted jury pool was among Special Prosecutor Cox's primary concerns when he arrived in late May 1973. The Ervin Committee's public hearings had begun on May 17 and soon dominated American television. They were initially carried live by all three national networks—ABC, CBS, and NBC—though they soon moved to rotating coverage. The hearings also were rebroadcast at night on local Public Broadcasting System affiliates and carried live by National Public Radio. In all, over three hundred hours of hearings were broadcast, and 85 percent of American households watched at least some portion of them. Even today, most Americans' first-hand knowledge of Watergate stems from what they saw coming from the Senate caucus room on their television in 1973.

When the Ervin Committee declined Cox's request to suspend its public hearings until their potential adverse effect on the defendants' criminal rights could be sorted out, he submitted a thirteen-page

"Memorandum on Behalf of the Special Prosecutor on Application for Orders Conferring Immunity" to Sirica, asking that grants of immunity to potential prosecution witnesses be conditioned on their not testifying in public hearings. Cox summarized his concerns in the opening paragraph:

> [T]he continued conduct of public and televised Senate hearings creates a very serious danger: (1) of impeding investigation of the Watergate affair and associated misconduct; (2) of widespread, pretrial publicity which might prevent bringing to justice those guilty of serious offenses in high government office.

The memorandum detailed why Cox believed that Sirica had not only the authority to condition the court's grants of immunity to Dean and Magruder on their refraining from public testimony but the obligation to do so. Cox had his eye on the trials to come:

> From the standpoint of the integrity of grand jury proceedings and the fairness of any subsequent trials, the most appropriate order would be one requiring the testimony be taken in executive session without subsequent publication. Bearing in mind the decision of the Select Committee to push forward with public hearings, the most appropriate condition would seem to be the exclusion, during the giving of compelled self-incriminatory testimony, of live or recorded radio, television, and other coverage not permitted at a criminal trial.

Cox specified the potential damage which he was seeking to avert (all case citations omitted):

> In the absence of conditions restricting the publicity accorded statements compelled by this Court, it now appears likely that the testimony will be carried on nation-wide television, reaching into millions of homes. While it is impossible to judge at

this time the precise impact of this publicity on the conduct of the forthcoming cases, there is, at the least, a significant possibility that the Committee's proceedings will imperil the government's ability to empanel an unbiased jury for the trial of any offenses charged. *Cf. Delaney v. U.S.*

The proposed testimony would raise difficulties, exceeding even the traditional problems associated with pretrial publicity, since what is expected is the dramatic, broadcast confession of these witnesses, implicating themselves and others in a variety of criminal acts. This compelled, incriminating testimony would, of course, be inadmissible at trial against the witnesses. *Cf. Miranda v. Arizona.* Its availability to prospective jurors prior to trial might make it impossible to provide a fair trial at all. See *Rideau v. Louisiana.* If the anticipated publicity is given to the testimony of these witnesses, "the risk that the jury [that may be called upon to try them and others] will not, or cannot, follow instructions [to disregard the extra-judicial confessions] is so great, and the consequences of failure so vital, that the practical and human limitations of the jury system cannot be ignored." *Bruton v. U.S.*

Granting of the protective relief we request is consonant with long established and well recognized principals of judicial power and responsibility to preserve the integrity of criminal trials. "Judicial supervision of the administration of criminal justice in the federal courts implies the duty of establishing and maintaining civilized standards of procedure and evidence." *McNabb v. U.S., Jenks v. U.S.,* Hill, *The Bill of Rights and the Supervisory Power.*

Speaking in the context of inflammatory pretrial publicity, the Supreme Court and the courts of appeals have emphasized the absolute necessity for the exercise of these supervisory powers. The Supreme Court has described the right to a fair trial as "the most fundamental of all freedoms" which "must be maintained at all costs" (*Estes v. Texas*), and has directed the trial courts to take all necessary action to "protect their process from prejudicial outside interferences" which pretrial publicity may inject into criminal proceedings. *Sheppard v. Maxwell.* See also *ABA Standards Relating to Fair Trial and Free Press.*

The proposed public testimony of the witnesses Dean and Magruder on nationwide television would in all likelihood present a clear and present danger (1) to the ability of other persons whom they may implicate to obtain a fair trial, [and] (2) to the validity of any indictments which are handed up during the period.

While, ordinarily, techniques which "include continuance, change of venue, sequestration of jurors, sequestration of witnesses, voir dire of prospective jurors and cautionary instructions" may suffice to avoid the effects of pretrial publicity, "in many cases, particularly those of a highly sensational nature, the use of these traditional procedures has not proven sufficient to assure the defendant a fair trial." *Report of the Judicial Conference Committee on the Operation of the Jury System on the "Free Press Fair Trial" Issue.*

Cox then issued what he assumed was the ultimate threat—failure to shut down the Ervin Committee's public hearings, at least for the government's principal accusatory witnesses, could result in the defendants' getting away entirely: "The result of an unconditional grant of 'use immunity' in this matter, therefore, may well be the award of complete amnesty to these witnesses and all those who acted in concert with them."

Cox made a forceful, cogent, and scholarly argument against open Senate hearings, but he was talking to the wrong people. To Judge Sirica and the senators on the Ervin Committee, the expected publicity wasn't everything (as Vince Lombardi might have put it), it was the only thing.

Besides, Sirica was the one who had so dramatically called for creation of the Senate committee in the first place.

Brushing aside the serious concerns Cox had raised, Sirica ruled against him with no more concern about the effect on future prosecutions than the Senate committee had shown. Indeed, Senator Ervin later asserted that informing the American public was the more important goal, even if later prosecutions were precluded as a result.

The Ervin Committee hearings, of course, were only part of the media's saturation coverage of Watergate from the original break-in arrests in June 1972 until the opening of the cover-up trial in October 1974. It would be difficult to point to another story that received such extensive coverage for so long. In addition to the Ervin hearings, the press covered the Watergate burglars' arrests and trials, the collapse of the cover-up, the resignations of the president's top advisors, the confirmation hearings for Elliot Richardson that led to the appointment of the Watergate special prosecutor, the fights over the White House tapes, the collapse of the Stennis compromise and the Saturday Night Massacre, the House Judiciary Committee's impeachment inquiry, the indictments in the cover-up case, the release of selected tape transcripts, the Supreme Court's decision ordering the release of sixty-four additional tapes, the "smoking gun" transcript and Nixon's resignation, President Ford's pardon, and the release of the final report of the Ervin Committee—all culminating in the opening of the Watergate cover-up trial on October 4, 1974.

It was estimated that some fifty-two thousand column inches of Watergate stories had been printed in D.C. newspapers—at a time when most people were still getting their news from those sources—85 percent of which had cast President Nixon and members of his administration in an unfavorable light.

POLITICAL BIAS OF DISTRICT VOTERS

When Richard Nixon won re-election two years before the cover-up trial, he was victorious in every state and territory except the

Commonwealth of Massachusetts and the District of Columbia. It was exceedingly convenient for the Democratic prosecutors, therefore, that the trial take place in the District, with jurors drawn from its registered voters, and Sirica made sure that the trial stayed there. President Nixon and his administration may have desegregated the Southern schools, integrated the nation's trade unions under the Philadelphia Plan, broken the District's heroin epidemic, rebuilt its riot corridors, pumped in millions of federal dollars in economic aid, and instituted Home Rule, but it was of little consequence. The jury pool, composed of registered voters, was dominated by people with a lifelong hostility to Richard Nixon and everything that he stood for. Such jurors could no more have put those feelings aside than they could have forgotten their own heritage.

The only two prosecutions of Watergate defendants tried outside the District of Columbia ended in acquittals. John Mitchell and Maurice Stans were acquitted in the Vesco case in New York City in 1973, and Dwayne Andreas, the CEO of Archer Daniels Midland, was acquitted of making an illegal campaign donation to Hubert Humphrey's 1968 presidential campaign—a charge brought by WSPF prosecutors—in a trial in Minneapolis in 1975.

At the same time, convictions were obtained in almost every Watergate prosecution against Republicans brought within the District. Only Kenneth Parkinson and John Connally were acquitted. Parkinson seems to have been the "mercy bait" in the cover-up indictment—a practice, described in John Dean's book,[1] by which an incidental defendant is included in a larger case in the expectation that his acquittal will enhance the credibility of the verdict by showing that the jury made distinctions among the defendants. John Connally, who had been wounded in the shooting of John F. Kennedy, was a lifelong Democrat before switching to the GOP as Nixon's secretary of the treasury. His defense, led by none other than Edward Bennett Williams, featured Lady Bird Johnson as a principal character witness. It would be difficult to maintain that Connally was a typical Republican defendant, and the D.C. jury acquitted him after only token deliberation.

More recent examples of successful prosecutions of Republicans in highly politicized cases include those of President Reagan's national security advisor John Poindexter in 1990; of Vice President Cheney's chief of staff, Lewis "Scooter" Libby, in 2005; and of Alaskan Senator Ted Stevens in 2008—all of whom faced impossible odds in prosecutions brought within the District of Columbia.

The serious disadvantage of prominent Republicans on trial in the District was well known to Supreme Court justices. Bob Woodward's *The Brethren* recounts an exchange between Justices Potter Stewart and William Brennan, in the presence of several of their law clerks, when returning to the Court after lunch and discussing Ehrlichman's conviction in the Plumbers break-in trial:

> In the car on the way back, someone mentioned the Ehrlichman trial. He had been found guilty the day before. Stewart said that, as a white man, he would not want to be tried in the District of Columbia, where the juries were predominantly black.
>
> "You bet your ass," Brennan agreed.[2]

More recently, in 2010, one federal judge observed to me, "I despair of any prominent Republican ever getting a fair trial within the District."

In their book, Ben-Veniste and Frampton mock the inability of the three major defendants to come up with character witnesses who could relate to their D.C. jurors—neglecting to mention that their jury was predominantly Democratic, lower middle class, female, and black— hardly what the common law would have recognized as a jury of their peers.

Consider how the jury composition might have changed had the trial been moved outside of the District of Columbia, say to the nearby city of Baltimore or Richmond. In either city, the jury would in all likelihood have reflected a more varied ethnic, economic, and political mix. The character witnesses that these three defendants might have produced would have been dramatically different and perhaps more effective than they were at the trial in the District.

SIRICA'S RESPONSE TO JURY TAINT AND BIAS

When confronting the problems of jury taint and bias, courts have traditionally taken any of four precautions to secure a defendant's right to a fair trial. First, the court can change the venue of the trial, moving it to a place where the jury pool is less biased or tainted by pretrial publicity. Second, the court can grant a continuance, postponing the trial long enough for passions in the community to subside. Third, the court can exercise special caution in the selection of the jury (a process known as *voir dire*). If close and careful questioning of a prospective juror arouses concern about his fair-mindedness, he can be dismissed for cause, and there is no limit on the number who can be dismissed for cause. If a great number of jurors were so dismissed, the court would need to consider whether the entire jury pool was too poisoned for the trial to proceed. Finally, where bias or taint is a concern, a defendant may be given additional peremptory challenges—that is, the ability to dismiss a potential juror without offering a reason.

Despite the seriously tainted and biased jury pool that the Watergate defendants faced in the District of Columbia, Judge Sirica offered no relief. That jury pool instead became another of Sirica's remorselessly wielded prosecutorial weapons.

On October 1, 1974, 155 veniremen—registered voters summoned for jury duty—were assembled in Washington's largest federal courtroom, with the press and public in attendance, to begin the jury selection process. On the first day, ninety of these citizens convinced Sirica that sitting at a trial of three to six months' duration would present an undue hardship and were excused. After three of the first forty-eight of those potential jurors had volunteered their belief that one or more of the defendants were guilty, WSPF prosecutors asked Sirica to instruct them to confine their responses to whether jury service would constitute a hardship and not to express any belief as to the defendants' guilt. Nonetheless, three additional potential jurors expressed such beliefs.

The next day the seats of the previously excused veniremen were filled with replacements. By the end of the second day, 171 people had been excused for hardship out of a pool of 315, leaving 144 potential jurors who were willing to serve.[3] In practice, this should be seen as a group that was not only willing but eager to be chosen for the panel.

The selection process moved to Sirica's own courtroom on October 3, and the public and press were excluded. There, over the course of a week, the judge posed to each potential juror questions that were designed to ascertain whether he could be impartial in a trial of great notoriety that had been preceded by substantial publicity.

Both WSPF prosecutors and Sirica were eager to form a jury. Since there was no question that the veniremen had heard about the Watergate scandal, the judge and prosecutors considered ways to appear to minimize the effect of that pretrial publicity. The prosecutors urged the judge to ask prospective jurors if they had heard anything about *this particular case*, a strange and unexpected question that would have given pause to even the most closely attuned citizen. The prosecutors hoped that a person's betrayal of some uncertainty about whether he had heard anything about this case in particular could be taken as an indication that he had not been affected by the massive pretrial publicity.

Sirica took an alternative approach, but one aimed at achieving the same result. He would first ask the potential juror whether he had read or heard anything about Watergate. The response was always affirmative, of course, so he followed up by asking whether *anything in particular* about that coverage stood out in his mind. When the person inevitably paused, Sirica would quickly ask if he thought he could set his feelings aside and render a verdict on the evidence that was about to be presented in the upcoming trial. Several admitted that they could not and were dismissed for cause, but the others quickly caught on. All they had to do was assert their expected objectivity and the judge would not inquire further.

Defendants' counsel objected vigorously that such a simple assertion by any given juror was hardly what the case law required, but the objection was overruled. Sirica's generic question was as deceptively simple and deviously clever as the Watergate prosecutors' naming Nixon an unindicted co-conspirator. Even the most dedicated and informed student of the scandal might not have a telling response to the question as Sirica phrased it.[4]

By the evening of October 10, some 315 veniremen had been interviewed, forty-five of whom Sirica had determined to be sufficiently impartial to constitute the pool from which a jury of twelve regulars and six alternates could be selected.

The press and the public were re-admitted to Sirica's courtroom the next day, and the prosecutors and defendants exercised their peremptory challenges to specific jurors. The judge had denied the defendants' motions for a continuance of the trial with the assurance that he would grant them additional preemptory challenges. (The defense would ordinarily have ten and the prosecution six.) The defendants had requested three additional peremptory challenges each and maintained that Sirica's incomplete *voir dire* had denied them sufficient knowledge to exercise their peremptory challenges effectively. In response, the prosecution requested additional peremptory challenges for itself.

In the absence of any agreement among defendants, the judge granted one additional peremptory challenge to each but required that each of the original ten be exercised by the defendants as a group. Sirica knew that the defendants were pursuing different defense strategies, and his ruling made it all but impossible for an individual defendant to exercise much influence over juror selection. Sirica also imposed a complex set of rules for the exercise of these challenges, to which the defendants objected. Mitchell's appellate brief described the Byzantine procedure:

> a. Jurors would be placed in the jury box according to a pre-determined order.

b. The ten joint defense peremptories had to be exercised two at a time.

c. Challenges would alternate between the government and the defense.

d. Two failures to exercise a challenge would bring about forfeiture of that challenge.

e. The government's final challenge would be exempt from forfeiture.[5]

The result of this procedure was that the defendants exercised only three of the five additional peremptory challenges they had been granted.[6] At the end of the tortured proceedings, twelve jurors were impanelled, ranging in age from twenty-seven to sixty-eight. Three-quarters of them were women, and two-thirds of them were black:

Roy V. Carter (27), chief supply officer for George Washington University

Gladys E. Cartier (40), office machine operator at a Washington hospital

Ruth C. Gould (57), loan specialist with the Department of Agriculture

John A. Hoffar (57), retired U.S. Park Service police sergeant, later chosen to be jury foreman

Anita E. King (57), matron with the Washington city schools

Marjorie M. Melbourn (55), retired international relations officer for the Agency for International Development (who lived in a Watergate apartment)

Vanetta N. Metoyer (49), waitress at a dime-store lunch counter

Helen D. Pratt (63), retired embassy maid

Dock Reid (60), doorman at the Burlington Hotel

Jane N. Ryon (63), retired Justice Department secretary

Thelma L. Wells (68), widow

Sandra V. Young (28), pharmacists' assistant

Ben-Veniste and Frampton devoted a full chapter of their book to the jury selection process and their concern to get a jury of their liking. It would take only one holdout to cause a hung jury, and some jurors, it was thought, might feel that since Nixon had been pardoned, his associates ought in fairness to be let off too. The prosecutors also thought it unfair that the defendants had twice as many challenges as the prosecutors did. Above all, the prosecutors were careful that "no rock-ribbed Republican types who still believed Watergate to be a political witch-hunt got on the jury if we could help it."[7] President Nixon's landslide re-election suggested that there were plenty of "rock-ribbed Republican types" out and about in the nation—it was just that none of them had any chance of being included in the District's jury.

The prosecution's imagined difficulties aside, the jury was drawn from a pool that was predominately Democratic and hugely anti-Nixon, people who had been subjected to a non-stop barrage of accusations and disclosures about the prominent defendants whose fate they would hold in their hands.

The chief concern in seating a fair jury is not whether a prospective juror is generally aware of the case at issue but whether that juror is confident that he can put his personal feelings aside and reach a verdict based on what is introduced into evidence at court. In practice, if a person wants to serve on the jury, the appropriate responses to any questioning are quite clear.

Under these circumstances, it is not difficult to see how Sirica could seat the jury he very much wanted, and he ignored the Watergate cover-up defendants' concerns about a tainted and biased jury:

- *Change of venue*: Sirica rejected out of hand the idea of moving the trial. Doing so would have put another judge in charge of the trial, and any subsequent appeals would have gone to the Fourth Circuit, which was notably more conservative than the D.C. Circuit.

- *Continuance*: Sirica declined to postpone the start of the trial, asserting (to the delight of an admiring press) that the Constitution guaranteed a speedy trial and he was going to see to it that the defendants received one. He promised the defendants additional peremptory challenges instead. With great reluctance he eventually postponed the trial for one month at the express urging of the circuit court. President Ford announced his pardon of Nixon on September 9, in the midst of this brief continuance, so the flood of adverse publicity had not abated in the slightest when the trial began on October 4.

- *Careful voir dire*: Adopting procedures urged by WSPF prosecutors, Sirica deliberately omitted any close questioning of prospective jurors and allowed their mere assertion of lack of taint or bias to go unchallenged.

- *Additional peremptory challenges*: After promising additional peremptory challenges to the defendants in lieu of a continuance, Sirica awarded only one to each defendant and imposed procedural rules that effectively vitiated two of those five additional challenges.

The Watergate cover-up trial therefore proceeded before a jury that harbored all the political bias and prejudicial publicity taint that the defendants had feared from the outset. The problems with that jury were compounded by the nature of the charges against the defendants—"thought crimes" that turned predominately on questions of motive and intent—and the multiplicity of defendants, each presenting a different defense theory. The verdict in this complicated three-month trial would come down to whether the jury liked, trusted, and respected the defendants.

Juries are notoriously fickle, and trial lawyers will tell you that any jury trial is a roll of the dice. But these dice were loaded, and the verdict was a forgone conclusion.

You cannot really blame the jurors themselves for the disregard for due process in the cover-up trial. The partisanship of the prosecution, the vagueness of the charges, the complexity and length of the trial, the bias of the presiding judge, and the inherent hostility of the jury pool ensured that these defendants never had a chance.

Thanks to the teamwork of judge and prosecution, the jury was given only one view of the defendants, and the picture was as clear as Prud'hon's painting. The credibility of the government's witness was improperly enhanced, and exculpatory information was improperly withheld. From what the jurors had heard before the trial and were allowed to see during the trial, there was no question who the real criminals were. As the prosecutors intended, the jury considered each of the defendants in the order he was named in the indictment—and the three principal defendants were promptly convicted on all counts.

THE ISSUES ON APPEAL

Judge George MacKinnon of the D.C. Circuit began his dissent in *United States v. Haldeman*, the appeal from the cover-up convictions, "If ever in the history of our country there was a criminal case which by law had to be transferred to another place for trial because of prejudicial pretrial publicity alone, this is that case."[8]

It is not that the issues of bias and taint were not known and argued at the time—both before Sirica and the court of appeals. It is that the defendants' concerns were dismissed out of hand, with virtually nothing being done to ameliorate their predicament. District and appellate judges deliberately turned a deaf ear to the hapless Republican defendants, in clear violation of the requirements of the Sixth Amendment.

CHAPTER 9

THE AUTOMATIC RIGHT TO AN APPEAL

C riminal defendants in the federal court system have the right to appeal a guilty verdict from the district court to the appropriate court of appeals. Generally, questions of fact are presumed to have been resolved by the trial jury, so the only issues on appeal are questions of law and procedure. The defendants in the Watergate cover-up trial had plenty to complain about, but the court of appeals for the District of Columbia was deeply biased against them and their president. In addition, the appeals from the trial before Judge Sirica were frustrated by corruption at the next level.

NIXON'S 1968 CAMPAIGN AGAINST LIBERAL JUDGES

A major theme of Nixon's 1968 presidential campaign was his criticism of liberal judges who were allowing criminals to go free, usually on legal technicalities, a theme that resonated with many Americans in that time of unrest. Frustration with the growing lawlessness was often focused on Chief Justice Earl Warren, under whose leadership the Supreme Court had expanded procedural protections for criminal defendants. The Warren court became the symbol of judicial coddling of criminals.

But Nixon's criticism of the federal courts implicitly included the court of appeals for the District of Columbia, led by Chief Judge David Bazelon, the Supreme Court's primary feeder of federal criminal cases. The District of Columbia had no separate system of local courts, so serious criminal cases were tried in the federal district court, and appeal went to the D.C. Circuit. Bazelon and his liberal colleagues specialized in excusing criminal activity for reasons ranging from misconduct by police and prosecutors (improper search, improper interrogation techniques, coerced confessions, etc.), the unhappy background of the accused, and a vastly expanded definition of insanity that encompassed an increasing number of defendants.

The D.C. Circuit heard more criminal appeals than all other federal circuit courts combined. With its decidedly liberal bias (indeed, Dean had described it as "the most radical court in the land" in his February 28, 1973, meeting with President Nixon), the Bazelon court shaped aggressive new criminal case law, which Warren's Supreme Court accepted and affirmed, imposing it on the entire country. A biographer of Justice William Brennan describes Bazelon's enormous influence:

> To conservative thinkers, Bazelon was one of the most dangerous men in America....
>
> Bazelon was never nominated to the U.S. Supreme Court, but his opinions often became the law of the land. Cynics claimed that it was his personal friendships with the justices that led to so many of his radical rulings being upheld by the Court....
>
> Bazelon was well connected to Washington's power structures.... He often shared a box at the Washington Redskins

games with President Johnson and then–Redskins owner Edward Bennett Williams. Bazelon was not above ensuring the success of his opinions on appeal by befriending new justices on the Court, and that is exactly what happened with Bill Brennan.... He accepted Bazelon's invitation to become a partner in several business deals. Eventually he found himself joining Bazelon for lunch at least twice a week....[1]

In the twilight of his judicial career, Bazelon authored a book, with a forward by Justice Brennan, describing his prominent decisions and defending his court's reversal of so many convictions.

Notions such as "guilty anyway" serve as rationalizations for refusing to admit the deprivations of constitutional rights that occur at trials. This failure to admit what we are doing does not, however, alter the fact. Appellate courts cannot correct errors in past trials to prevent their recurrence in future trials unless we reverse convictions. Incidential observations and nonbinding dicta are just not sufficient. When we allow a conviction to stand despite violations of the Constitution, we conceal a serious problem and nourish the mistaken euphoria that our justice system is alive and performing well. The cost of this concealment is paid in the loss of fairness to individual defendants and in the absence of guidance for police, lawyers, and judges in future cases.[2]

Perhaps tellingly, nowhere in his book does Bazelon mention the series of appeals heard by his court on all of the Watergate cases.

Nixon came to office with a clever plan to reduce the influence of the D.C. Circuit in criminal law. His Home Rule initiative, passed by Congress in 1970, established courts for the District of Columbia that were independent of the federal system. Appeals from the newly established D.C. superior courts would go directly to the Supreme Court (as with appeals from state supreme courts), bypassing Bazelon's court.

Nixon had not only cut the D.C. Circuit out of its precedent-setting position for the nation's criminal justice system, he had been able to appoint his own set of judges for the District's new criminal courts and had enacted anti-crime reforms that had undercut many of Bazelon's earlier decisions. To top it all off, he got popular credit for having done so in the pursuit of home rule for the District's residents. But Bazelon and his liberal brethren on the D.C. Circuit would not forget this slight.

When Archibald Cox was sworn in as special prosecutor in late May 1973, he had to quickly assemble a team of prosecutors to investigate and prosecute the Watergate scandal while dealing with two matters already pending. The first was the Ervin Committee hearings, which opened on May 17 and threatened to poison the jury pool for Cox's later criminal prosecutions. The second was how to handle the appeals from the Watergate break-in trial, which challenged Judge Sirica's conduct.

We have already seen in chapter four how Special Prosecutor Cox arranged a secret meeting with Chief Judge Bazelon to explain how the selection of judges could be manipulated for appeals from the cover-up trial. Let's now see what Bazelon did in response.

BAZELON'S STACKING OF THE APPELLATE DECK

After Bazelon concluded his meeting with Cox in the fall of 1973, he never said anything further about the discussion to his clerk Ronald Carr, but Cox's plan was put into force. The Saturday Night Massacre in October panicked the nation and instilled a sense of urgency in the courts. Cox's plan for the D.C. Circuit to hear all Watergate appeals en banc did not seem so extraordinary after all. In fact, the Cox plan was a nice counterpart to Nixon's court reform that had cut Bazelon's D.C. Circuit out of ruling on criminal appeals. Charles Alan Wright's request for an en banc hearing of the White House tapes case had already established the precedent. All Bazelon had to do was convince his liberal colleagues that they should follow the same procedure for any criminal appeals.[3] If handled adroitly, this approach might not seem so out of the ordinary, but its effect would be dispositive.

Once his liberal bloc was firmly in control of any given appeal, opposition from the remaining judges would be inconsequential. They might vigorously dissent, but they could not overturn. Bazelon was confident that he could convince his liberal colleagues to swallow any concerns about Sirica's denial of defendants' rights. After all, these weren't the sort of downtrodden criminal defendants who deserved the court's special protection; these were Nixon's henchmen, evil men who should never have been allowed into government in the first place. If Bazelon could get his colleagues to see Sirica in a new light—as an activist judge, as one of *them*—then he could assure that these criminal convictions could withstand his court's nominal review.

It is not clear from the D.C. Circuit's own records precisely how Bazelon was able to implement Cox's idea of stacking the appellate deck—the available court records are spotty at best—but it is clear that he was successful (see Appendix Q).

The records show that in October 1973, the court of appeals finally heard the appeals of the break-in defendants, who had been convicted over eight months before. Sirica had kept them in jail pending their appeals. There is a vote sheet dated October 23, 1973, from the clerk of court, Hugh Kline, to the judicial council—composed of all nine circuit judges—asking whether the motions filed in these appeals should be decided by the full court or by the motions division, as would have been the usual practice. The court records do not contain the final votes of the judges on whether the court should precede en banc, but the dockets show that these appeals were disposed of by the full nine-member court sitting en banc.

A non-agenda item for the March 12, 1974, meeting of the judicial council simply notes that the appeals from the convictions of these same break-in defendants would be heard before the full court on June 14, 1974. A memorandum from the clerk to the judicial council, dated April 4, 1974, confirms this without any further details. The dockets show that all matters during this period were considered by the court sitting en banc.

The minutes of the December 10, 1974, judicial council reflect that, in discussing when to schedule the en banc argument in the case of *United States v. Chapin* (the prosecution of one of Nixon's aides for perjury, which had been tried before Gesell and not Sirica), Judge Leventhal questioned whether it was still necessary for the en banc court to consider all Watergate matters. The council decided that the Chapin appeal would be decided by a regular three-judge panel. Even after this notation, however, the court continued to hear those Watergate-related criminal appeals from Sirica sitting en banc through 1976—a total of twelve such appeals.

There were three cases involving the White House Watergate tapes. In the first Watergate-related appeal from Sirica (*Nixon v. Sirica*), the D.C. Circuit upheld the grand jury's subpoena of the first nine tapes. The Ervin Committee's subpoena for the White House tapes was argued before Judge Gesell (*Senate Select Committee v. Nixon*), who dismissed it. The committee's appeal was then heard by the D.C. Circuit, sitting en banc, which upheld Gesell's ruling on May 23, 1974, in an opinion written by Chief Judge Bazelon. The liberal bloc—J. Skelly Wright, Carl McGowan, Harold Leventhal, and Spottswood Robinson—all voted with Bazelon. Judges George MacKinnon and Malcolm Wilkey filed separate concurring opinions. Although Gesell heard at least three Watergate-related criminal matters, this was the only appeal from Gesell that was heard en banc by the D.C. Circuit. The third tapes case, involving the special prosecutor's subpoena of sixty-four more tapes (*United States v. Nixon*), went directly to the Supreme Court, which always sits en banc.

These three cases, balancing the conflict between the judicial system's need for evidence to prosecute criminal conduct and the president's interest in protecting the confidentiality of Oval Office conversations in the name of executive privilege, clearly involved "a question of exceptional importance," as specified in Rule 15 of the General Rules of the D.C. Circuit. It was entirely appropriate, therefore, that the court of appeals sit en banc for the two that came before it.

By contrast, the other Watergate-related appeals involved what WSPF prosecutors described as run-of-the-mill criminal prosecutions. There were no questions of great constitutional moment, yet all twelve subsequent appeals from Judge Sirica's actions, orders, and trials connected with Watergate were heard en banc on the court's own initiative. Sirica was upheld in eleven of them, always with the same five judges voting as a liberal bloc.[4] Seven of the opinions were issued per curiam—that is, no single judge was identified as the author—an infrequent and heavily criticized practice in which no judge is willing to put his name to the opinion.

On the other hand, not one of the three subsequent Watergate-related appeals from actions, orders, and trials by Judge Gesell was heard in such an exceptional manner. Gesell was one of the most liberal of the district court judges in D.C. but also one of the most competent, and his reversal record did not compare to Sirica's. The reason for the differing treatments was not to maximize public confidence in the circuit's decisions—after the massively adverse pretrial publicity and Nixon's resignation, the defendants were among the most loathed figures in America. It was to assure that there was no possibility of reversal on appeal as a result of Sirica's bizarre actions in the trials below.

The en banc procedures were, in short, the direct result of the corruption of the judicial process in the D.C. Circuit that grew out of Cox's secret meeting with Bazelon. That corruption taints every one of its decisions upholding Sirica's questionable actions in the criminal trials below.

THE APPEALS

A closer examination of the appeals from Judge Sirica's court to the D.C. Circuit shows how the Watergate defendants found themselves in a contest with their prosecutors that was rigged against them at every stage.

THE ATTEMPT TO REMOVE SIRICA AS TRIAL JUDGE

The defendants' petition to remove John Sirica as the judge in the cover-up trial was the most important of the criminal matters heard on appeal because it determined the trial's venue, which was the central due-process issue. If the case remained Sirica's, he would certainly keep it in D.C., ensuring that the defendants were tried before a District jury and that all appeals would go to the D.C. Circuit. If Sirica were replaced, the new judge might allow the trial to be moved to Baltimore or Richmond, giving the defendants a less biased judge and a less tainted and biased jury and sending appeals to the more conservative Fourth Circuit. But that's not what happened.

On the very afternoon that the cover-up indictment was handed down by the grand jury—March 1, 1974—Chief Judge Sirica appointed himself to preside over that trial, as the defendants both feared and expected. Watergate was Sirica's ticket to fame, and he was determined to occupy center stage.

Sirica was the defendant's worst nightmare. This was the judge who had presided so aggressively over the break-in trial while repeatedly voicing his suspicions of a cover-up, who had provided prosecutors with a list of people he wanted brought before the grand jury, who had advocated the creation of a Senate investigative committee, and who had refused to avoid the public airing before that committee of accusations against the cover-up defendants prior to their trial. He had presided over a seventy-day evidentiary hearing on the White House tapes, which had so devastated the administration's credibility. And lest anyone doubt Sirica's starring role in the Watergate drama, *Time* magazine named him Man of the Year for 1973.

The defendants now faced a dilemma. They had to get out from under this judge to have any chance of getting a fair trial. But if they tried to have him removed and failed, Sirica's hostility would be aggravated, and he would be all the more difficult to deal with at trial.

They decided to try to remove him, filing on April 10 a request that Sirica recuse himself because of his "unassailable personal bias in favor of the prosecution." The defendants first asked that the question of Sirica's removal be referred to the district court's calendar committee, where the decision regarding a trial judge would be made independently by three other district court judges. Second, they requested an evidentiary hearing to determine the nature and extent of Sirica's ex parte meetings with prosecutors. The American Civil Liberties Union—rarely a supporter of Republican causes—filed an amicus curiae brief in support of the defendants' motion for an evidentiary hearing.

The special prosecutor filed his brief in opposition to Sirica's removal on April 26, calling the allegations against Sirica "scurrilous." As expected, Sirica denied the motion on April 30. He would neither disqualify himself nor refer the question to the independent determination of the court's calendar committee, and he would not tolerate an evidentiary panel to explore his ex parte contacts with prosecutors.

Sirica dismissed the allegation of personal bias for a single reason:

> Every action, decision and comment of the court cited by defendants arose in the course of official judicial activity. Statements concerning the truth or falsity or completeness of testimony at the Liddy trial had their basis in the evidence adduced in court. They reflect, if anything, a judicial state of mind rather than a personal bias. An expressed belief that others might be involved, that a witness had not fully revealed facts known to him, that a defendant had not answered a question truthfully, that all pertinent facts had not been produced before the jury, that the Court had been right in asking questions and an expressed hope that other authorities might uncover all of the relevant facts, are matters that have their roots in the record then before the Court. Such is the case as well regarding encouragement that defendants, following conviction, cooperate with the grand jury and Senate Committee, acquainting the jury with testimony initially taken out of its presence, and the Court's suggestion that certain persons be called before the grand jury as possible sources of additional information. If there be any indication of prejudice in such actions, and the Court perceives none, it is by no means personal as that term is used.

Sirica's stunning assertion is that because every "action, decision and comment" that aroused suspicions of bias occurred in the regular course of court business, they do not affect the constitutional guarantee of a fair trial, which of necessity includes being tried before a fair and impartial judge. Sirica sets up a judicial Catch 22: As long as a judge is acting in his capacity as judge, then his judicial conduct cannot be questioned.

In his insouciance about his ex parte meetings with prosecutors, Sirica was relying on an exception to the rule against such meetings in the Code of Conduct for United States Judges: "A judge may...when circumstances require it, permit ex parte communication for scheduling, administrative, or emergency purposes, but only if the ex parte communication does not address substantive matters and the judge reasonably believes that no party will gain a procedural, substantive, or tactical advantage as a result of the ex parte communication." Sirica's view of this narrow exception for minor housekeeping matters was expansive, to say the least, and it begged the question that the requested evidentiary hearing would address: Did his ex parte communication with the prosecutors concern "substantive matters" or give an advantage to the prosecution? The judge simply asserted:

> In regards to the Court's meetings with Special Prosecution Force personnel, there are no relevant facts to be had. These proceedings included no discussion of evidence bearing on the guilt or innocence of any defendant in this case nor any discussion even remotely of the kind.

This breezy disavowal is similar to those of Clark Mollenhoff and Sam Dash with regard to their own ex parte meetings with Sirica. They may have met with the judge, but they were careful not to discuss any specific evidence in the case before him. Of course, this is not the standard set by the Code of Conduct for United States Judges. It does not say a judge may meet with anyone he chooses as long as he does not discuss specific evidence bearing on the guilt or innocence of defendants. It says there shall be no ex parte meetings.

Sirica also went out of his way to assert that he had acquired no information about the case from outside the courtroom itself: "The Court's acquaintance with information perhaps pertinent to this case has in every instance flowed from court proceedings. *There has not been, nor is there alleged to have been, any extrajudicial source*" [emphasis added]. Regardless of the merits of Sirica's legal arguments, this statement amounts to an admission that such events would be grounds for his removal if they had occurred. Sirica did not admit it at the time, but we now know of at least four such meetings in which he got information and advice from outside parties—namely, his secret ex parte meetings with Edward Bennett Williams, Clark Mollenhoff, Sam Dash, and Leon Jaworski.

CHANGE OF VENUE

It appeared to the defendants that Sirica had pre-judged the question of whether the trial should be removed from the District of Columbia. Sirica's opinion summarized his comments that were the basis of the defendants' concern:

> The fourth category of allegations appearing in the affidavits also treats a single event: statements regarding fair trial made by the Court at the Circuit Judicial Conference in March of this year. Transcripts of the questions and answers, later televised, show that in response to the question, "Is there any doubt in your mind about these men's [defendants at bar] abilities to get fair trials?" the Court stated, "I think they can get just as fair a trial in the District of Columbia as any federal court in the United States. I have no doubt about that. Thank you." When the subject was raised again, the Court responded, "Well, in my opinion, any defendant, any person who happens to be a defendant in this jurisdiction, in my opinion can get just as fair a trial here as any jurisdiction in the country."

In Sirica's view, these statements were informal responses to questions at a lawyer's conference that did not reflect his considered judicial opinion.

In the Alice-in-Wonderland world of the Watergate trials, the statement "I think they can get just as fair a trial in the District of Columbia as any federal court in the United States. I have no doubt about that," did not indicate that the judge who said it had made up his mind on the issue.

APPEAL FROM SIRICA'S RULINGS ON RECUSAL AND VENUE

Five of the defendants filed a petition for a writ of mandamus with the D.C. Circuit on May 9, 1974, asking that court to remove Sirica from the cover-up trial. Their petition made three points:

1. Sirica erred in holding that his alleged bias and prejudice were inconsequential because they "arose in the course of official judicial activity." The defendants argued that the challenged activity "all occurred either in ex parte proceedings or in proceedings to which the present defendants were not parties."

2. Sirica failed to appreciate the disqualifying inconsistency between the judicial role he assigned himself and his role in developing the indictments to be tried in this case.

3. In a situation that demanded every assurance of the most punctilious judicial neutrality, it was not enough for Sirica to consider only the minimal statutory prohibitions as he perceived them.

The joint motion filed in support of their petition detailed the defendants' concerns:

1. Judge Sirica has been personally involved in the investigatory and prosecutorial process leading up to the indictment of defendants, as a result of which there has been a merging of the judicial and prosecutorial functions in this case;

2. Judge Sirica possesses, consciously or unconsciously, a deep-seated and unshakable personal bias in favor of the prosecution;

3. Judge Sirica has a substantial personal interest in the case since establishment of the alleged conspiracy would be viewed as a vindication of his conduct in the 1973 Watergate [burglary] trial;

4. Judge Sirica has met privately with the prosecutors and has pre-viewed the evidence in this case.

In support of the last point, the defendants' affidavit cited newspaper stories of June 19, 1973, and July 18, 1973, indicating that Sirica had met privately with prosecutors. These articles appeared when Cox was still the special prosecutor,[5] so it seems likely that defendants were unaware of any of Sirica's ex parte meetings with Jaworski. But even if they had known what we know today, it would have been difficult for the defendants to state their case with greater specificity.

The special prosecutor filed his reply brief, defending Sirica, with the circuit court on May 20. Three of the four attorneys on the WSPF brief—Jaworski, Lacovara, and Ben-Veniste—had participated in at least one ex parte meeting with Sirica. Would they deny that any such meetings had occurred? Would they admit to one or more such meetings (we now know of at least six)? Would they assert that no one had discussed the evidence? In fact, they simply danced around that delicate issue, ignoring it entirely. They represented to the court of appeals that there were but two issues before it:

1. Whether the affidavits before the respondent Judge which are based almost exclusively on judicial proceedings contain sufficient facts to show that respondent judge has a "personal bias or prejudice" in favor of the prosecution against the defendants as those terms are used in 28 U.S.C. 144.

2. Whether, under the provisions of 28 U.S.C. 455, the district judge...abused his discretion in concluding that he was not so "connected with any party or his attorney as

to render it improper, in his opinion, to preside at the trial."

Without responding to, or even mentioning, the defendants' request for an evidentiary hearing that would reveal the extent of Sirica's ex parte contacts with prosecutors, the reply brief simply asserted that the judge had not abused his discretion. It is arguable that this deliberate disregard of a specific request made by the appellant constituted a fraud upon the court, though it would have seemed trivial in comparison with the secret ex parte meetings, had they come to light. The prosecutors might well then have faced disbarment proceedings.

Reading the prosecution's brief in light of what we now know about the nature and extent of the WSPF's contacts with Sirica, one marvels at their gall. They argued, for example, that defendants need not fear Sirica's hold over one prime prosecution witness, Jeb Magruder, since his sentencing was scheduled to occur before the trial would begin. We now know that John Dean was Sirica's hostage as well. They also argued that Sirica's assertion that the real Watergate culprits had not been identified by the conclusion of the burglary trial did not necessarily mean that he believed that *the present defendants* were the culprits to whom he was referring.

WSPF prosecutors did recognize, however, that the decision about who would preside at the trial could have been referred to the district court's three-judge calendar committee, but they emphasized that such a referral was not necessary:

> On April 26, 1974, the Special Prosecutor filed a memorandum in opposition to the motions and affidavits [when the motion was first filed before Judge Sirica]. We took the position that it might have been appropriate for the judge to refer the recusal motions to the Calendar Committee for deposition, but we argued that, whether the judge or the Calendar Committee passed on the motions, recusal was not legally required.

Despite raising serious doubts about whether they could get a fair trial before Judge Sirica or in the District of Columbia, the defendants' appeal was summarily rejected by the liberal bloc of the D.C. Circuit without an opportunity for oral argument and in an unsigned order. George V. Higgins has summed up the situation nicely:

> Judge Sirica's definition of the bounds of his discretion would have comported nicely with Louis XIV's view of himself as the French State. Having extracted what he thought to be the truth from James McCord, E. Howard Hunt, and others (by the imposition of long prison terms, or the threat thereof) in 1973, Judge Sirica was blandly reassuring when John Ehrlichman, H. R. Haldeman, John N. Mitchell and the rest protested, in 1974, that, really, he shouldn't sit on the trial of their cases on charges of conspiring to effect the cover-up, because he had his mind made up. Sirica found himself to be without bias or prejudice, and six of the nine-judge Court of Appeals for the District of Columbia, preferring not to identify themselves, upheld him.[6]

The liberal bloc—Bazelon, Wright, McGowan, Leventhal, and Robinson—issued a one-sentence, unsigned, per curiam order on June 7. With no oral argument, it was difficult for the media to evaluate the arguments raised by the defendants. With no signed opinion, no judge had to take the heat for the court's abrupt action.

Judge MacKinnon, the only judge on the panel who was decidedly not a member of the liberal bloc, was clearly dismayed by the suddenness with which the order was issued and by the lack of a hearing. In a brief dissenting statement he observed that the defendants had raised substantial issues and he deplored the majority's refusal even to answer the allegations.[7] One month later, on July 8, MacKinnon filed a full dissenting opinion raising both procedural and substantive objections to the majority's disposition of the appeal.

MacKinnon expresses bewilderment as to why the court had handled the petition sitting en banc. His comment that the basis for handling the appeal in that way was "presumably" that the court deemed it "a question of exceptional importance" under the Federal Rules of Appellate Procedure suggests that he was somehow not involved in the decision to hear the case en banc. If the matter was of "exceptional importance," he writes, then the court's response was inappropriate:

> Notwithstanding the recognized importance of this case, a majority of this court deprived petitioners of their right to oral argument, never provided the prior notice required by local Rule 116 and disposed of the matter by a mere one-sentence order denying the petitioner. Such disposition is improper where the case admittedly is of "exceptional importance." These circumstances compel me to raise my single and obviously futile objection to the irresponsible and peremptory manner in which this petition was denied. I simply cannot agree that the majority's handling of this petition was an appropriate method to administer justice in this most important of criminal cases.

MacKinnon goes on to detail the substantive issues raised by the defendants' petition:

> [The defendants] maintain that Judge Sirica must disqualify himself in this case in view of (a) his involvement in the prosecutorial investigation and his prior exposure to evidence, (b) his prejudgment of a material issue [venue], (c) his alleged personal interest in the outcome.... Petitioners also requested the district court (1) to grant them an evidentiary hearing to develop information concerning Judge Sirica's private meetings with the prosecutors and his submission to the prosecution of a list of witnesses to be called before the grand jury, and (2) to refer the disqualification question to the Calendar

Committee of the district court as an appropriate disinterested panel.

Concerns over the first two items form the basis of MacKinnon's substantive dissent. First, he addresses Sirica's prosecutorial bias and previous exposure to the evidence, citing the assertions contained in the defendants' briefs (all citations omitted):

1. Judge Sirica repeatedly and consistently interrogated defendants and witnesses in the Watergate break-in trial "with the zeal of a prosecutor." This interrogation was "an effort to investigate matters beyond the guilt or innocence of the defendants before him."

2. [During the Watergate break-in trial and afterwards,] Judge Sirica expressed the belief that criminal responsibility extended beyond the convicted defendants to higher officials in the Committee to Reelect the President and in the White House. * * * He has expressed the belief that higher officials were involved in the Watergate matter.

3. [Judge Sirica commented] to defendant Liddy suggesting that he was low on the totem pole to be sentenced to thirty years while those who planned, organized and directed the operation walked the streets free.

4. In an admitted effort to coerce testimony from the defendants in the Grand Jury and before the Senate investigating committee which would implicate higher officials, Judge Sirica imposed conditional maximum sentences.

5. Judge Sirica took the extraordinary step of drawing up a list of six Administration officials whom he felt the prosecutors ought to put under oath in the Grand Jury room. Affiants lack specific knowledge of the names included in that list since Judge Sirica ordered it held under seal, but it is reasonable to assume that the names of one or more of the defendants in this case appear on

the list. (The transcript of this chambers conference has since been made available to counsel. Nine names were suggested for further grand jury inquiry. One defendant's name appears on the list, as well as the names of three other persons who were charged and convicted in related cases.)

6. According to newspaper reports dated June 19, 1973, and July 18, 1973, Judge Sirica met privately on at least two occasions with members of the Watergate Special Prosecution Force. The details of these and any other unreported private meetings have not been made public; affiants are therefore unable to state with particularity the number of such meetings which have taken place, or the dates, participants, purposes, or substance thereof.

Reviewing other troubling aspects of Sirica's conduct of the break-in trial, MacKinnon continues:

At times Judge Sirica assumed an even more active role in the prosecutors' investigation of this case. At a chambers conference on January 24, 1973, at which the prosecutors and three attorneys representing defendants in the break-in trial were present, Judge Sirica suggested to the prosecutors that they call nine named individuals before the grand jury. Although he disclaimed any accusatory intent, one of those individuals was indicted by the grand jury and is now a defendant in this case, and three others were subsequently charged and convicted in related cases. Judge Sirica's alleged actions in repeatedly interrogating witnesses concerning the involvement of others, in using the sentencing process to coerce testimony implicating higher officials, and in suggesting further grand jury inquiry of named individuals including a defendant here, publicly demonstrated an accusatory frame of mind that connected the present defendants to the crime with which they are now charged—obstructing the prosecution of the Watergate break-in.

Judge MacKinnon is at pains to point out that the standard of review on appeal must assume that the appellants' allegations are true. The only question for the court was whether, assuming that these allegations were true, they would constitute a sufficient basis for the judge to be disqualified from presiding over the second trial.

MacKinnon's second area of substantive concern is the extent of Sirica's ex parte meetings with prosecutors, about which the defendants had sought permission to have an evidentiary hearing.

In view of their allegations, petitioners are entitled to develop the facts surrounding the ex parte meetings with the prosecutors. A judge, having assisted in the bringing of an indictment, may not consistent with due process of law preside at the trial of that indictment, and such judicial involvement in the prosecutorial process is sufficient to require disqualification under Section 144. The facts alleged by petitioners in this regard may already constitute the requisite "fair support" for a reasonable apprehension of disqualifying bias or prejudice. The denial of petitioners' request for an evidentiary hearing deprived petitioners of the opportunity to demonstrate fully the degree to which the judicial and prosecutorial functions may have coalesced in this case into accusation. An evidentiary hearing concerning the number and nature of contacts between the prosecutors and the judge could be conducted without undue delay and would provide some assurance against reversal after trial on the grounds of bias or prejudice. [Citations omitted.]

The need for an evidentiary hearing is further highlighted by a conversation appearing in the Presidential

Tape Transcripts which were released subsequent to filing of the petitioners' affidavits. [Citing an April 16, 1973, conversation, where Henry Petersen tells the President the following]:

> So they, after they concluded all their questions and names and what have you, they went back and as just a flyer, Judge Sirica when he—in connection with the subpoena issue—hears part of the tapes and hears Chotiner's name. He says to Silbert (Assistant United States Attorney conducting the Watergate investigation), I want these people subpoenaed and that's Murray Chotiner and others. And Silbert says, well he's been to the Grand Jury and this name has nothing to do with it. He (Sirica) has been calling about it ever since— subpoena. No sir. And he—we have no evidence against him. It's become a matter of principle with us. We will not subpoena him. We have no reason to subpoena him. And Sirica wants us to subpoena him just I think for the hell of it.

Also troublesome is the existence of further ex parte contacts between Judge Sirica and the prosecutors, the details of which are unavailable to petitioners or to this court. Petitioners rely on newspaper accounts of at least two private meetings between Judge Sirica and the prosecutors. The opinion denying the motions for disqualification admits meetings with Special Prosecution Force personnel but asserts, "These proceedings included no discussion of evidence bearing on the guilt or innocence of any defendant in this case nor any discussion even remotely of the kind."

MacKinnon concludes this section with the observation:

These allegations suggest repeated ex parte contacts and affirmative investigative conduct by Judge Sirica. The facts developed at an evidentiary hearing may or may not support these allegations and their natural inference of bias in favor of the prosecution, but it is only fair, in order to satisfy not only the fact but the appearance of justice, that petitioners have an opportunity to explore these allegations at an evidentiary hearing.

Having explored the above issues, Judge MacKinnon concludes with the following observations.

In conclusion, I dissent from the majority's summary disposition of this important en banc case without oral argument and without opinion. Moreover, I believe that petitioners have made a sufficient showing to require an evidentiary hearing concerning the number and nature of Judge Sirica's ex parte contacts with the prosecutors. At the very least, Judge Sirica should recuse himself from ruling on the defendants' motions for change of venue—an issue on which he has conveyed the appearance of prejudgment. Finally, I would strongly suggest that Judge Sirica refer to a disinterested panel the question whether the allegations of the affidavits charging judicial involvement in the prosecutorial process and prejudgment of material issues, which allegations cannot be contested, compel his disqualification. The Special Prosecutor and the American Civil Liberties Union concur in this latter suggestion.

But the majority's action allowed Sirica to preside at the cover-up trial. One can only imagine how MacKinnon might have responded he had known of the other secret ex parte meetings with Sirica—with Edward Bennett Williams, with Clark Mollenhoff, with Sam Dash, and the whole series of meetings with Leon Jaworski and his WSPF prosecutors.

THE APPEALS FROM THE BURGLARY CONVICTIONS

Each of the break-in defendants convicted in the first Watergate trial had exercised his automatic right of appeal to the D.C. Circuit. The basis for their individual appeals remains of interest even today.

Gordon Liddy's appeal of his conviction on all counts was a frontal attack on Sirica's conduct of that trial.[8] Both Hunt[9] and the Cubans[10] had filed appeals seeking to withdraw the guilty pleas they had entered at the beginning of the trial, contending that they, like everyone else, had been duped by the people running the cover-up, who had improperly pressured them to enter guilty pleas in order to avoid further inquiry. McCord's appeal combined both of these arguments and sought leniency in return for having written the letter that was credited with exposing the cover-up.[11]

Cox and his staff recognized that these appeals were not without merit, but it would not do for these defendants (the only ones convicted so far) to obtain reversals before those involved in the cover-up had even been indicted.

Fortunately for Cox, but not for the defendants, the court of appeals delayed any hearings on these appeals until June 14, 1974, a full eighteen months after the convictions. The court's decisions, upholding each of the convictions, were not handed down until the fall, almost two full years after the burglary trial and in the midst of the cover-up trial.[12]

THE APPEALS FROM THE COVER-UP CONVICTIONS

It could be argued that the cover-up defendants knew from the outset—at least once it was clear that their trial would be held before a District of Columbia jury and presided over by Sirica—that their convictions at trial were a foregone conclusion and that their only hope was an appeal claiming the essential elements of due process had not been observed in that trial.

The prosecution had gone into the cover-up trial believing it had a strong case on the facts, but the defendants had vigorously contested the prosecution's interpretation of the evidence. The defendants' case was well summarized in the WSPF's appellate brief:

John Mitchell

In essence, Mitchell contended that he had not authorized Liddy's intelligence-gathering plan, that he took no affirmative action in aid of the cover-up, and that he was made the "fall guy" by the White House.

He testified that he had rejected Liddy's intelligence-gathering plans on three occasions and, therefore, believed that he had "turned off" the espionage operation. He also denied having received any fruits of Liddy's operation. As to the cover-up, Mitchell denied suggesting to Mardian or anyone else that [Attorney General Richard] Kleindienst get the burglars out of jail; denied that CRP's June 18 press release was intentionally misleading; denied that he ever suggested the destruction of documents; claimed that he disapproved using CRP money to pay bail for the burglars; denied having discussed use of the CIA either to raise funds or to hamper the FBI's investigation; asserted that he rejected efforts to have him raise money for the Watergate burglars and had no knowledge of the details of payments to them; and swore that he had not advised Magruder to give false testimony to the grand jury and that he himself had not knowingly testified falsely. [WSPF reply brief, pp. 43–44, transcript citations omitted.]

H. R. Haldeman

The essence of Haldeman's testimony was that he had no prior knowledge of the June 17 break-in or the CRP intelligence gathering process, that he had no intention of curtailing the FBI investigation or of silencing the burglars, and that he had no motive to engage in the criminal acts charged.

As to the question of advance knowledge, Haldeman insisted that he had not read Strachan's report about CRP's political espionage plans and denied having told Strachan to destroy any documents after the break-in. Concerning his tape recorded conversations with President Nixon on June 23, 1972 [the "smoking gun"] and March 21, 1973 ["cancer on the presidency"], Haldeman said that he had only reported information that he had received from others. His meeting with CIA representatives on June 23, he added, was not for the purpose of stifling the FBI's Watergate investigation, but only to keep the FBI out of areas that might be politically embarrassing.

Regarding "hush money," Haldeman admitted having known of payments to the break-in defendants and of Strachan's delivery of the $350,000 fund to LaRue, but claimed that his understanding was that the money was for legal fees and living expenses. [pp. 45–46]

John Ehrlichman

Ehrlichman's basic position was that, far from having conspired or endeavored to obstruct justice, he consistently had advocated full disclosure, but had been deceived by President Nixon, who thereby thwarted Ehrlichman's efforts to get the facts out. He also denied prior knowledge of the Gemstone Plan, having ordered Hunt out of the country, having told Dean to "deep six" materials from Hunt's safe, or having discussed with Dean using the CIA to pay the burglars. Although he—like Haldeman—admitted having contemporaneous knowledge of payments to the burglars, he claimed to have believed that the funds raised by Kalmbach were for legitimate attorneys' fees. He further denied having suggested clemency for the burglars.

Finally, Ehrlichman denied that his connection with the Ellsberg break-in provided him with a motive to engage in the Watergate cover-up. Although he admitted having approved a "covert operation" to secure Ellsberg's psychiatric records from Dr. Fielding's office on the condition that the venture not be traceable to the White House, Ehrlichman claimed that he had not contemplated the break-in which, he contended, was authorized and executed solely by his subordinates. [pp. 46–48]

The trial jury, however, had disagreed with the defendants down the line. Since they had been found guilty on all counts, any contested questions of fact were deemed to have been found in favor of the government. The only arguments available to the defendants on appeal were procedural ones: pretrial publicity prevented a fair trial, material evidence had been improperly admitted or turned away, a critical witness (the former president) was missing, and the judge did not give proper instructions to the jury on the law.

Since the appellate brief for each defendant was limited to 125 pages, the four appellants divided the task of arguing certain issues that applied to all of them. Thus, Haldeman's brief made the lead arguments on prejudicial pretrial publicity, on challenges to the admission of the thirty-three White House tapes, and on Sirica's jury instructions. Mitchell's brief made the case that Sirica should not have presided over the trial and that his voir dire was inadequate. Ehrlichman's brief took the lead on the issues of venue and on the prejudice resulting from the absence of Nixon's testimony.

The defendants' briefs were well argued. I have conveyed the basis for most of the procedural arguments advanced by the defendants on appeal in my earlier discussion of Sirica's conduct of the cover-up trial and will not repeat them here. But the clash of the defendants' points and authorities on these major issues with those of the WSPF reply brief—essentially adopted by in the appeals court's opinion—reads like an exchange at the United Nations between competing factions—they aren't communicating at all, just stating their opposing positions for the record. Besides, the court disregarded the defendants' arguments as though they were unworthy of serious consideration.

Of course, each brief also advanced arguments unique to its particular defendant. Ehrlichman argued that he had been denied the ability to mount an effective defense because of restrictions on access to his own files, which had been retained by the White House upon his departure. Under procedures approved by the special prosecutor, he could review his files only in a small room on the first floor of the Old Executive Office Building, under the watchful eye of a Secret Service agent. He could not photocopy or even make notes. If he wanted to remember something, he had to go into an adjacent room and make notes from memory. His counsel was not allowed to accompany him and was forbidden entry into the White House compound. Ehrlichman (and others) could listen to tape recordings expected to be introduced at trial by WSPF prosecutors only during certain hours at WSPF offices. Even the transcripts prepared by the government were available for review only at WSPF offices, and they became available at all only shortly before trial was to begin. There was apparently no opportunity for any of the defendants to review tape recordings that had not been selected for introduction into evidence by the government.

Both Ehrlichman and Haldeman addressed their inability to call Nixon as a witness in the cover-up trial. When the trial began, the former president was hospitalized for phlebitis. He required surgery at the end of October and almost died from complications. Though he had been subpoenaed as a witness by the prosecution and the defense, his lengthy hospitalization made him unavailable to testify at the trial in Washington.

Ehrlichman claimed prejudice, asserting that Nixon would have testified that Ehrlichman had always been an advocate of full and prompt disclosure. This would have undermined the government's contention that Ehrlichman's motive for joining the conspiracy had been to prevent disclosure of the Plumbers' break-in. Ehrlichman also claimed prejudice because he had been forced to mount his defense on the belief that Nixon would recover enough to appear as a witness or at least to be deposed in California, with his sworn testimony read to the jurors. When Sirica finally concluded that Nixon was not well enough to testify at all,

Ehrlichman had moved for a continuance until he had recovered. Sirica ruled that Nixon's appearance was not critical to the defense, since the defendants could themselves testify as to what Nixon would have said. Ehrlichman countered that this violated his Fifth Amendment right not to testify, since he was being forced to take the stand in his own defense only because it had become clear that Nixon would not appear.

Haldeman claimed that without Nixon's testimony, no proper foundation had been laid for the admission of the thirty-three White House tapes. There was no one to testify that Nixon had consented to be taped (a requirement for their legality) and no one to certify that a particular tape accurately reflected the conversation that had been recorded.

Both Ehrlichman and Haldeman claimed that Sirica's omission to give the standard "missing witness" instruction—and particularly to explain to the jury that the former president was too ill to appear—prejudiced them, since Nixon had been identified at the beginning of the trial as an expected witness, and the jury might take his absence as an indication that his testimony would have been harmful to their case.

Mitchell argued that he was unfairly forced to testify before the Ervin Committee, since his taking the Fifth Amendment would have prejudiced potential jurors in the Vesco case, where he was a "virtual defendant." His case was stronger on this issue, since he had raised it at the time of his committee testimony, but to no avail.

Finally, Mitchell and Ehrlichman objected to the admission of prejudicial evidence. Mitchell argued that it was error to admit into evidence the recorded conversations of others discussing the certainty of his guilt as a result of his knowledge of the Liddy plan, because the prejudicial effect of this testimony far outweighed its probative value concerning the existence of a conspiracy. Ehrlichman argued that it was error to admit into evidence three days of testimony about the Plumbers break-in, supposedly as his motive for joining the cover-up, since he had already been convicted for that offense (although it remained on appeal) and it constituted a sort of double jeopardy. Like Mitchell, he maintained that the prejudicial effect of that testimony far outweighed its probative value as to his possible motive for joining the cover-up.

The prosecution, now led by Henry Ruth, the longtime deputy who had become special prosecutor upon Jaworski's resignation, filed its 280-page reply brief on October 15, 1975. It denied that pretrial publicity had tainted the jury pool. Publicity had been largely factual, it was consistent with defendants' admissions that there had been a cover-up (although each denied being a part of it), and defendants had countered much of it with their own testimony and public denials.

Sirica's voir dire, the prosecution argued, had been properly conducted, and each of the jurors had asserted his belief that he could put aside any advance knowledge of the case and reach a verdict based only on what had been presented during the trial. Because there was no taint or bias in the jury, there was no reason to move the trial outside of the District of Columbia, to postpone the trial, or to grant the defendants more juror challenges.

There was no reason for Sirica to recuse himself, because he had denied any personal bias against the defendants and all his knowledge of Watergate had come from his own judicial involvement—so there was no external evidence before him.

Among the signers of the prosecution brief were both Peter Rient and Judith Denny, the authors of the memorandum of November 15, 1973, discussed in Chapter 7, which recorded the testimony of the original Watergate prosecutors that Dean had not accused Ehrlichman or Haldeman of any wrong-doing in his eight initial meetings with prosecutors in April 1973. The brief assured the court, "Recognizing its obligation under [citations omitted], the prosecution thoroughly reviewed all materials in its possession and voluntarily produced all documents and other materials even remotely relevant to the issues to be tried."

With regard to the defendants' assertion that Sirica should have recused himself, the prosecutors stated (footnotes and citations omitted):

> As he was required to do, the trial judge reviewed the factual allegations in the recusal motions (assuming them to be true) and concluded that "[e]very action, decision and comment of the court cited by defendants arose in the course of official

judicial activity." This conclusion—not controverted on appeal—is dispositive.

One can only wonder, in light of the series of ex parte meetings and communications between the WSPF prosecutors and Judge Sirica, whether they really believed Sirica's assertion or carefully crafted this statement to avoid asserting to the court that they had not met privately with the judge.

THE CIRCUIT COURT'S DECISION

The appeal was argued before the circuit court sitting en banc on January 6, 1975—precisely one year after the defendants had been convicted in the cover-up trial. The oral argument was notable for the paucity of questions from the judges, who acted as though they couldn't wait to get the defendants out of their courtroom.

Ten months later the court handed down its per curiam opinion adopting all the arguments submitted by the prosecution.[13] While the opinion itself was lengthy, it appears that the court was convinced by the WSPF's assertion that the issues raised by defendants were "common and familiar."

The opinion reads as though this were such a routine and run-of-the-mill case that it was hardly worth the court's time. In most cases a single judge writes an opinion for a three-judge appellate court. Sometimes all of the judges sign a key opinion to emphasize its importance. In the Watergate cover-up appeal, none of the judges thought the opinion was worth signing. The implication in such cases is that it is a routine matter, of no precedential value, and deserves no further attention.

APPEAL TO THE SUPREME COURT

In a last attempt to obtain justice, Mitchell, Haldeman, and Ehrlichman, the three remaining defendants, appealed to the U.S. Supreme Court. If the prosecutorial and judicial collusion that had marred the case from its inception had been disclosed, the outcome probably would have been different, but as it was the defendants failed to get the four votes necessary for a writ of certiorari and a place on the high court's docket.

Even that vote was not without controversy. It appears that Chief Justice Warren Burger, a Nixon appointee, undertook a second effort to obtain the necessary fourth vote.[14] Nina Totenberg's disclosure of Burger's effort is described in a 1992 article in *Vanity Fair*:

> Totenberg's critics burst into a chorus of "Foul!" in 1977, when she reported an astonishingly insider item concerning the Court's disposition toward an appeal from former Nixon top dogs and Watergate conspirators, H. R. Haldeman, John Ehrlichman and John Mitchell. Totenberg reported that the Court had voted 5-3 against reviewing the infamous case, and that all three dissenters were Nixon appointees. [The fourth Nixon appointee, Justice Rehnquist, had recused himself.] The report stunned many, because Court votes concerning appeals are held in secret. Moreover, the story claimed that Chief Justice Warren Burger, one of the Nixonians, had postponed announcing the outcome of the vote in hopes of persuading others on the Court to change their minds. Totenberg's story embarrassed the Court and raised potential legal problems concerning the decision, not to mention a few eyebrows. The *New York Post* even ran a gossip item proclaiming that Justice Stewart, "said to be a close friend of Totenberg's," was the "most popular choice" as the story's source and decried the charge as "sexist."[15]

It appears that the Supreme Court may have been as politicized by Watergate as was the D.C. court of appeals, although certainly not as corruptible.

The Supreme Court's denial of certiorari was the end of the line for the defendants. The outrages against due process, we now know, had been plentiful and egregious, and their concerns were raised in timely and specific manners, but to no avail.

PART V

THE VIEW FROM HERE

I think I have made a strong, well-documented case that President Nixon was forced to resign and his senior aides were convicted and imprisoned not only because of false charges but because of the collusion between judges and prosecutors who had convinced themselves that their desired ends justified any means. In the Watergate prosecution, the constitutional protections that are supposed to guarantee individual rights in highly politicized controversies were deliberately swept aside in the rush to judgment.

But all that was forty years ago. Nixon, Haldeman, Ehrlichman, and Mitchell are dead, as are Sirica, Bazelon, Cox, and Jaworski. The only surviving figure who played a central role in the scandal is John Dean. One might ask, then, "So what?" Is Watergate now of only academic interest, with no implications for law and politics today? Or are there lessons here to be learned, for the oppressors and the oppressed alike?

The Watergate prosecutions, I would argue, deserve careful study because of their lasting effects on the defendants, on our understanding of the scandal, on President Nixon and his legacy, and on the rest of us.

CHAPTER 10

SO WHAT?

JUSTICE FOR THE DEFENDANTS AND THEIR HEIRS

The Watergate defendants, particularly Mitchell, Haldeman, and Ehrlichman, were systematically and deliberately denied a fair trial. They faced a hanging judge whose numerous secret ex parte meetings with interested parties and prosecutors should appall anyone acquainted with the standards of judicial conduct and whose temporary sentencing ploy underscores his lack of objectivity. They were pursued by highly partisan prosecutors who favored their friends and punished their enemies. They were tried by jurors drawn from a hopelessly tainted and biased pool, a disadvantage the responsible judges refused to ameliorate. Finally, they had recourse only to a partisan appellate court that had been corrupted by an ex parte meeting between its chief judge and the special prosecutor.

The assault on due process in the Watergate cover-up prosecution is all the more troubling because the key factual contentions of the leading defendants, John Mitchell, H. R. Haldeman, and John Ehrlichman—

nicely summarized by the prosecution's appellate brief quoted in chapter nine—now appear at least plausible enough to raise a reasonable doubt about their guilt.

It is possible that Mitchell, as he consistently contended, did not approve Liddy's campaign intelligence plan at the March 30, 1972, meeting in Miami. Fred LaRue, who was there at the time and was also a government witness at the cover-up trial, concurred in this view. Further, revelations in John Dean's recent book suggest that the idea of Mitchell's alleged approval emerged quite late in the internal taped conversations among the White House staff, who thought that Magruder's approval had inadvertently been triggered either by Colson's phone call or by Strachan's following through on Haldeman's tickler system. If Mitchell didn't approve Liddy's plan—if Magruder just made this up to explain his own wrongdoing—then Mitchell did not have the alleged motive for his tangential involvement in the cover-up.

Haldeman, as he consistently contended, did not intend to limit the FBI investigation. We now know that the "smoking gun" tape, which appeared to suggest the opposite, has been misunderstood and that Haldeman was simply trying to protect the identities of prominent Democratic donors. As in Mitchell's case, the alleged motive for his participation in the cover-up has evaporated.

Ehrlichman, as he consistently contended, turns out to have been an advocate of full disclosure almost from the outset, in spite of the risk that his involvement in the Plumbers break-in (which he felt could be defended on grounds of national security) would be disclosed.

The information that has recently come to light, had it been available to a neutral jury, could have raised sufficient doubt about the defendants' guilt to preclude their convictions. Two similar cases in which exculpatory information emerged after a conviction offer instruction on how these Watergate convictions might be handled.

On American Soil: How Justice Became a Casualty of World War II by Jack Hamann,[1] published in 2005, tells how forty-three black U.S. soldiers were court-martialed for rioting and murdering an Italian prisoner of war at Fort Lawton, near Seattle, in 1944. An initial investigation had concluded there was insufficient evidence to bring charges, but the army became concerned about repercussions regarding treatment of its own prisoners of war in Italy. A sharp young army prosecutor named Leon Jaworski handled the re-investigation and eventually secured twenty-eight convictions. The problem was that there was no direct evidence against these soldiers, some of whom were imprisoned, and all of whom were dishonorably discharged.

The army's initial investigation had indicated that the black soldiers were not at fault for the riot. Jaworski knew about that investigation but kept it from the defendants' lawyers, who could have used prior inconsistent statements to discredit Jaworski's lead witness. The publication of Hamann's book led the army to seek out each of the wrongfully discharged soldiers or his heirs, to correct his record with an honorable discharge, and to restore his back pay. Jaworski's reputation as a fair and objective prosecutor who respected the due-process requirement of disclosing exculpatory evidence was badly tarnished.

Many years later, the prosecution of Senator Ted Stevens of Alaska involved a violation of due process almost exactly parallel to that in the Watergate cover-up prosecution. In the election year of 2008, the Public Integrity Unit of the Department of Justice charged Stevens with not disclosing the value of vacation home renovations on his Senate financial disclosure forms. His conviction cost him his re-election and provided the Democrats with the critical sixtieth vote in the Senate that made them immune to Republican filibusters on Obamacare, on financial regulation, and on confirmations of presidential appointees.

If Senator Stevens had in fact improperly accepted improvements to a home in Alaska, the evidence and all of the witnesses would be in Alaska, and the wrongdoing could better have been prosecuted there. But prosecuting a popular senator on his home turf would be difficult, so the Department of Justice reconfigured the charges as a failure to disclose such improvements on Senate forms—which meant that he could be prosecuted in the District of Columbia, with a jury pool well known for its dislike of Republicans.

Shortly after the trial, an FBI whistle-blower informed the federal district court judge that prosecutors had not told defense counsel of the substantial changes that had occurred in the testimony of the government's primary witness, and that a possibly exculpatory witness had been whisked back to Alaska so that he would be unavailable at trial. The Department of Justice then undertook its own investigation. Concluding that it could no longer support the verdict, it formally requested in April 2009 that the senator's conviction be withdrawn. It was too late to restore Stevens to the Senate seat he had lost the previous November, but a special investigating magistrate, appointed by the judge, ultimately issued a scathing three-hundred-page report documenting the prosecutorial misconduct.[2]

Justice delayed may be justice denied, but these cases show that it is important for the health of our justice system to correct the record, if possible, even many years after a miscarriage of justice. Judge Sirica should not have been allowed to preside at the Watergate cover-up trial. The convictions handed down there should have been reversed and remanded for a new trial. If a fair trial had been held—one in which exculpatory evidence had been disclosed to the defendants, the credibility of prosecution witnesses had not been manipulated with fake prison terms, and the jury was untainted and unbiased—it is quite possible that the jury would have concluded that the prosecutors had not proved their case beyond a reasonable doubt.

So what can be done? After forty years and the deaths of the defendants, retrials are no longer feasible, but there remains a way to challenge these convictions and perhaps to trigger a thorough investigation of the wrongdoing detailed in this book. The defendants' heirs could petition the original trial court, the federal district court for the District of Columbia, for a writ of error coram nobis, a remedy for a judgment that rests on an error of fact which was not known at the time of the judgment and which, if known, would have prevented the judgment.

Maintaining such an action would be expensive, time-consuming, and fraught with uncertainty. The burden of proof would be on the descendants and strictly-enforced rules of evidence might preclude introduction of much of the material revealed in this book. It remains, however, a tantalizing possibility, especially because it would place the issue formally before the district court and could put the petitioners in a position to request that the court undertake its own investigation. After all, it is the reputation of the district court that has been challenged by these disclosures, and the court might conclude that it has an interest in responding. As in Senator Stevens's case, the court could undertake its own investigation, without the necessity of the heirs' seeking public release of relevant grand jury and other restricted documents.

There might even be an evidentiary hearing of the sort requested by the defendants in their effort to preclude Sirica from presiding at their trial. The defendants had hoped to explore the nature and extent of ex parte contacts between Sirica and the Watergate prosecutors. We know of nine such meetings, but persons still living—who worked alongside of Sirica, Cox, or Jaworski—may know of many more. It was the prosecutors who dodged this issue on appeal, never even responding to the defendants' request. It would be instructive to have their associates questioned, under oath, regarding such secret contacts between judge and prosecutor.

If the court were to conclude that due process had been denied to these defendants, it could take corrective measures on its own volition, including vacating the convictions.

The Department of Justice would be a necessary party to any coram nobis action and might be asked to undertake its own internal investigation in response or be instructed to do so by the court. The department might conclude that it simply could not support the verdicts and urge, as it did after the disclosures in Senator Stevens's trial, that they be vacated. If nothing else, the department would have to respond to the petition itself.

Regardless of whether such a petition is filed, the Watergate trials will eventually be studied, not as an example of how our Constitution worked in a time of great stress, but as a case in which fundamental rights of due process were cast aside in a political maelstrom.

WATERGATE IN AMERICAN HISTORY

Any future analysis of the Watergate scandal will have to take into account the disclosures I have detailed, which means starting from scratch. The cover-up convictions have been treated as the capstone, precluding any meaningful review of whether the defendants might have been telling the truth. The mindless conclusion "They stand convicted on all counts, so their individual stories and excuses can be dismissed outright," which historians have never accepted as the last word in other controversial prosecutions, cannot be the last word here.

Chief Judge David Bazelon's own words, quoted in chapter nine, undercut any dismissive argument that the defendants were "guilty anyway." Moreover, guilt can be found only by a court after a constitutionally sound trial.

But removing that capstone, by showing that the cover-up convictions were improperly obtained and are indefensible as a matter of law, would ensure that serious students continue to "wallow in Watergate" (as Nixon put it) for many years to come.

There is no question that the original Watergate break-in and the ensuing cover-up entailed extensive criminal wrongdoing. The essential question, then as now, is whether this criminal activity was confined to the level of Gordon Liddy, Jeb Magruder, and John Dean or whether these men were operating under the direction and control of one or more of John Mitchell, Bob Haldeman, and John Ehrlichman. I strongly suspect that the former view is at least as persuasive as the latter.

There ought to be further investigation into how the judges and prosecutors abused their oaths to uphold the Constitution. Examined in the calmer atmosphere that historical distance affords, their spectacular misdeeds appear more egregious than those of the defendants they persecuted with ruthless abandon.

Any fair analysis of the alleged abuses of power that were the basis for the second article of impeachment brought against Nixon will have to be undertaken in the context of the extensive invasions of privacy stretching back to 1936 that were so well documented by the Church Committee soon after Nixon left office, as well as contemporary assertions of presidential authority by subsequent administrations (particularly Barack Obama's).

THE LEGACY OF RICHARD NIXON

History will be kinder to Richard Nixon than most people now realize or than some liberals would like. His many accomplishments, in foreign and domestic affairs, will receive their due appreciation. Moreover, as the Watergate scandal slowly gives up its secrets, future generations of Americans will come to wonder how his political enemies were able to force Nixon's resignation and undo his landslide re-election by the American people.

One of the most striking historical twists of Watergate is that the effort to bring Nixon down was led by people from the only two political jurisdictions that had voted against his re-election: the Commonwealth of Massachusetts and the District of Columbia. From the former came Senator Edward Kennedy, whose personal investigation evolved into the Ervin Committee and who demanded a special prosecutor as a condition of confirming Elliot Richardson (also of Massachusetts) as attorney general. It was Congressman Tip O'Neill, later to become Speaker of the House, who was the principal behind-the-scenes advocate of impeachment.[3] And it was Archibald Cox and his Harvard cohort who dominated the Watergate Special Prosecution Force and turned Nixon's idea for a special supervising prosecutor into a hundred-man inquisition that investigated every aspect of the Nixon presidency. From the District of Columbia came all of the judges and jurors who tried and convicted the Watergate defendants.

Few today regard the impeachments of Andrew Johnson and Bill Clinton as anything other than partisan excesses spawned by the fevered politics of their respective times. It should come as no surprise when the same conclusion is reached in the future about Nixon's forced resignation and the conviction of his top aides.

Once John Dean's recent revelations have been absorbed, especially the clarification of the meaning of the "smoking gun" tape, and historians have a better understanding of the judicial and prosecutorial treachery that misled the House Judiciary Committee, the entire Nixon presidency can receive the measured and unemotional evaluation that it deserves.

This book is a part of that process, but it will be helped along as more and more scholars realize that the Nixon presidency is by far the most well documented in history. This is not only because of the taping system (with all of its ugliness), but because of the centralization of foreign and domestic policymaking in the executive office of the president (through the revitalization of the National Security Council, the transformation of the Office of Management and Budget and the creation of the Domestic Council), and because Nixon's decision-making process required written documentation.

Indeed, it would not be surprising for Nixon to make yet another comeback, one more spectacular than his election as president in 1968.

WATERGATE AND THE REST OF US

Once we have corrected the record on Watergate, a necessary first step, how do we citizens protect our country from such abuses in the future?

Perhaps Philip Lacovara best described the situation in an interview with Bob Zelnick on NPR's *All Things Considered* on October 17, 1974, some two months after the president had resigned, when he said:

> I wish I could say that I share the unbridled optimism of many people who say that Watergate has shown that the system does work. The system worked in this instance, but only, I'm afraid, because of a unique interplay of events that are unlikely to be repeated [referring to the White House tapes that captured Nixon's own words during key conversations].
>
> These circumstances, I think we can assume, will never again be repeated in history, even if some future President abuses his public trust. So I'm not quite as sanguine as others

about how wonderfully the system has worked. And, frankly, I'm not sure that the mentality that led to a—to the Watergate phenomenon has been erased. I think we've found that other public officials, who are more popular than Mr. Nixon was, more easily are being excused for very, very questionable conduct simply because they are seen as important to the conduct of our international affairs or because they have some personal popularity that makes them less vulnerable targets. I don't think that that is the way our legal or constitutional system should operate, but I'm afraid we're right back to where we were before Watergate.

Lacovara's candor earned him a personal rebuke from Jaworski, whose confidential files contain the copy of a handwritten note, alongside the above paragraph, which has been underlined:

Phil—In all candor I think it is simply unprofessional for you to get into comments of this type—What prosecutions did you recommend that fell into this category? LJ[4]

But history has shown Lacovara's concerns to be well-founded. The Church Committee's detailed disclosures show that abuses of power were a growing, if hidden, scandal well before the Nixon presidency, and the record of abuses by the Obama administration make Nixon's look positively amateurish.

The failure of the Watergate reform legislation merely shows what many have known since time immemorial: morality cannot be legislated. There will always be demagogues, charlatans, and outright criminals in public life, as elsewhere. Power will always corrupt, and the powerful will always be tempted to cut corners to achieve their earnestly desired goals.

Much as I would personally love to see the Obama administration officials who were involved in the Fast and Furious, Benghazi, and IRS cover-ups squirm before grand juries convened by a special prosecutor, I find myself in agreement with Justice Antonin Scalia and D.C. Circuit Court Judge Laurence Silberman that specially selected prosecutors, at least those operating with total independence from the Department of Justice, violate the separation of powers and are unconstitutional.

Even our friend Justice Jackson had little to offer in his 1940 speech with regard to becoming better prosecutors within the Department of Justice. He concluded by saying that it was impossible to define the specific qualities that made a good prosecutor, but it certainly included a sensitivity to fair play and sportsmanship, saying that the best protection against prosecutorial abuse would come from the prosecutor who tempered zeal with kindness, who sought truth and not victims, who served the law and not factional purposes, and who approached his task with humility.

The sad truth is that there is no way to assure those with the power to prosecute will not overreact to alleged wrongdoing in the future. It is so easy to repeat the cliché that those who will not study history are destined to repeat it, but this also does us no real good. As unsatisfying as it sounds, we are left to rely on those characteristics that have proved helpful time and again in our nation's history: an active and informed citizenry with a sense of fair play and a free and vibrant press. And if I may say so, it helps to have independent researchers willing to dig through thousands of pages of archival documents to find what supposedly thorough investigative reporters have somehow overlooked.

As for me, I am content to live in Nixon's shadow—to keep arranging staff reunions and producing Nixon Legacy Forums as long as any of us are left. So much good was accomplished by his administration that the public has yet to appreciate. I carry the burden, with the rest of Nixon's defense team, of having failed the president. We were overwhelmed by his many opponents, but perhaps we could have done more. I felt at the time that a president was being driven from office for lack of an effective legal defense—and I still believe that is what occurred. But I do hope that through this book and my other efforts I have given Richard Nixon a fair return for the extra $250 scholarship he extended to that struggling Whittier College student some fifty years ago.

LIST OF APPENDIXES

APPENDIX A

Key Watergate dates

Discussed at p. 20 in text

1971

February: White House taping system is installed.

October: Dean is assigned responsibility for developing a campaign intelligence plan for the Committee to Re-elect the President (CRP). He soon recruits Liddy for its design and implementation.

December 8: Liddy leaves the WH staff to become CRP general counsel, with added responsibility for the campaign intelligence plan.

1972

January 27: Liddy presents his plan in Attorney General John Mitchell's office. Dean and Jeb Magruder are also present. The one-million-dollar plan includes proposals for "mugging, bugging, kidnapping, and prostitution."

February 4: Liddy presents his scaled-down plan in Mitchell's office, with Dean and Magruder again present. Proposals for mugging, kidnapping, and prostitution are omitted, but the five-hundred-thousand-dollar plan includes specific targets for bugging.

March 1: Mitchell resigns as Attorney General to become head of CRP.

March: Charles Colson calls Magruder to urge proceeding with Liddy's intelligence plan. He later claimed that he knew nothing of its specifics.

May 28: The first illegal entry into Democratic National Committee (DNC) offices at the Watergate office building. Photographs are taken and wiretaps are planted on phones of Larry O'Brien and Spencer Oliver.

June 17: The second illegal entry into DNC offices, supposedly to repair the tap on O'Brien's phone. McCord, CRP's head of security, and four Cubans are arrested on site. Liddy and Hunt are arrested some weeks thereafter.

June 19: Dean meets with Liddy in the morning and learns that it is his operation that has gone bad. Dean also meets with Mitchell, Magruder, and others in Mitchell's apartment that evening to begin orchestrating the cover-up.

June 20: The first recorded Nixon-Haldeman conversation following Watergate arrests. Haldeman notes say "Watergate," but a portion of their conversation is lost (the "eighteen-and-a-half-minute gap").

June 23: In a meeting with Haldeman, Nixon agrees to Dean's recommendation that the WH direct the CIA to ask the FBI to limit their investigation. (This conversation would become known as the "smoking gun.")

July 1: Mitchell resigns as head of CRP, supposedly to tend to his difficult spouse, Martha.

September 15: A grand jury indicts seven men for the Watergate burglary, including Liddy, Hunt, and McCord.

November 7: Nixon is re-elected, beating George McGovern with 61 percent of the popular vote, the second-largest margin in U.S. history.

December: Edward Bennett Williams meets privately with Sirica to handle problems caused by efforts of *Washington Post* reporters to interview Watergate grand jurors.

The reporter Clark Mollenhoff has a series of meetings with Sirica, urging an aggressive role in presiding over the break-in trial. He then writes a column predicting such conduct and praising Sirica for it.

1973

January 30: Liddy and McCord are convicted on all counts in the Watergate burglary trial. Hunt and the Cubans had already pleaded guilty. Sirica, believing that his attempts to uncover the truth have been frustrated, calls for a Senate investigation and produces a list of people to be called before the grand jury.

February 7: The Senate establishes a Select Committee on Presidential Campaign Activities (the Ervin Committee).

March 17: Sam Dash, majority counsel for the Ervin Committee, meets privately with Sirica and urges maximum sentencing, with the possibility of reduction conditioned on the defendants' cooperation with the Senate's investigation.

March 21: 10:00 a.m., Dean's "cancer on the presidency" meeting with Nixon; 10:00 p.m., LaRue makes the final payment to Hunt's lawyer.

March 22: Nixon-Mitchell meeting in which Nixon announces his determination to require all staff to appear before the Ervin Committee without a claim of executive privilege (Nixon's "Stonewall" comments).

March 23: Dean goes to Camp David to prepare a report on the scandal; Sirica releases the McCord letter alleging a cover-up and imposes provisional sentences of up to thirty-five years on the convicted Watergate burglars.

March 28: Dean is recalled from Camp David when he admits he is unable to produce the promised report. He then retains Charles Shaffer as his criminal defense counsel.

April 17: At a news conference, Nixon announces "major new developments" in the Watergate case and states that WH staff members will appear voluntarily before the Ervin Committee, under oath and without claim of executive privilege.

April 22: Dean vacates his WH office over the weekend, boxing up many counsel files for later negotiation with career prosecutors in an attempt to obtain personal immunity.

April 30: Nixon announces the resignations of Haldeman, Ehrlichman, Dean, and Attorney General Richard Kleindienst. He nominates Elliot Richardson as attorney general and gives him the discretion to appoint a special supervising prosecutor.

May 25: Richardson appoints Archibald Cox as Watergate Special Prosecutor. Cox's staff soon grows to almost a hundred positions.

June 25: Dean begins testimony before the Ervin Committee, saying Nixon knew of the cover-up as early as September 15, 1972. He essentially accuses Nixon, Haldeman, and Ehrlichman of knowing participation in the cover-up.

July 16: Alexander Butterfield reveals the existence of the White House taping system.

October 19: Dean pleads guilty to a single felony count, with sentencing postponed indefinitely.

October 20: Special Prosecutor Cox is fired in what becomes known as the Saturday Night Massacre.

November 5: Leon Jaworski is sworn in as special prosecutor.

November 21: WH discloses the existence of the eighteen-and-a-half-minute gap.

December 14: Jaworski and three members of his staff meet privately with Judges Sirica and Gesell.

Late December: WSPF prosecutors establish that the final payment to Hunt's lawyer was made on the evening of March 21, 1973.

1974

January 21: WSPF memorandum urges a private meeting with Sirica to alert him to the intended grand jury report, to be sent to the House Judiciary Committee.

February 11: Sirica meets privately with Jaworski to urge quick action on the Watergate cover-up indictments. Jaworski uses the occasion to discuss their intended grand jury report.

March 1: The grand jury indicts seven people for the Watergate cover-up (Mitchell, Haldeman, Ehrlichman, Colson, Mardian, Strachan, and Parkinson) and names eighteen unindicted co-conspirators (including Nixon). Separately, the grand jury asks Sirica to forward its report (known as the "Road Map") to the House Judiciary Committee. Later that day, Sirica assigns himself as trial judge for the cover-up case.

March 19: Judge Sirica turns seventy and is required to step down as chief judge of the federal district court, thereby losing his ability to assign cases to specific judges (including himself).

April 28: Mitchell and Stans are acquitted on all charges in the Vesco trial in New York City.

May 9: The House Judiciary Committee opens its impeachment hearings.

June 7: The D.C. Circuit denies a writ of mandamus to remove Sirica as judge in the cover-up trial in a one-line, unsigned order, without opportunity for a hearing.

July 24: The Supreme Court rules eight to zero that sixty-four subpoenaed tapes must be turned over to Judge Sirica for review. Eight hours later, the WH announces its intent to comply.

July 27–29: The House Judiciary Committee approves three resolutions recommending that the full House impeach President Nixon.

August 2: Sirica sentences Dean to a prison term of one to four years for his role in the cover-up. Dean's sentence is to begin on September 3, the scheduled date for the first day of the cover-up trial.

August 5: The WH releases transcripts of the remaining tapes, including three Nixon-Haldeman conversations of June 23, 1972 (the "smoking gun").

August 8: In an evening speech to the nation, Nixon announces that he will resign the following day.

August 9: Nixon's resignation becomes effective at noon. Vice President Gerald Ford is sworn in as president.

September 8: Ford grants a full, unconditional pardon to Nixon.

October 1: The cover-up trial begins, having been postponed for one month at the urging of the D.C. Circuit.

1975

January 1: The cover-up trial concludes with guilty verdicts on all counts for Mitchell, Haldeman, and Ehrlichman.

January 8: On his own motion, Sirica reduces the sentences of Dean and Magruder to time served, freeing them after only several months of confinement.

February 21: Sirica sentences Mitchell, Haldeman, and Ehrlichman to terms of two and a half to eight years. Each will serve approximately eighteen months in prison.

1976

October 12: The D.C. Circuit upholds the cover-up convictions of Mitchell, Haldeman, and Ehrlichman.

APPENDIX B

Woodward notes from Jaworski interview of December 5, 1974

Discussed at p. 91 in text

Jawerski I, 2-4 p. m. 12/5; his office.

J started off by saying how strongly he feels about
our book, that it is a piece of history etc. ~~thet~~ which
must be accurate and how he will do anything he can
to make sure that it is. Says there were a lot of
one-on-one conversations that nobody knows about but
him and the other party. Says he has been deluged with
book offers, but--for the present at least--no plans
to do so. After these preliminaries, J. launched into
what he called "my concepts of what led to the downfall,"
which folows. As you will see, much of what follows
in this first interview we already knew and J. thought
he was really opening up.

Most important "focus" in his view was working out
arrangement to get the material to House Judiciary; this
especially crucial because of decision not to indict
RMN (much more on that decision in J. III). HJC was
"very slow" getting started, he sez, and would never
have gotten off the ground without the info provided
- by SPO. It was "a roadmap" he stressed more than a
few times.

Sez HJC "had a very difficult time getting underway,"
that Doar admitted it to him. Doar "an excellent man,
thoro. Still, he had nothing to catch hold of; he was
engulfed by the Watergate Committee material," but it
was badly organized and not nearly definitive enough.

"What we did--the first real step--was to cast the die."
"The grand jury had to make up its mind what to do
(this in latter part of Feburary) mmm..what action to
take regarding the President. The grand jury had determined
that he was guilty of obstruction." This based primarily
on Dean testimony, Magruder testimony and tapes, including
March 21. Importance of tapes (initial ones) was not
just that they had Nixon implicating self. Also verified
Dean's veracity and excellence as a witness.

"But there was no legal precedent for the indictment
of a President and it was my strong judgement that
in all likelihood the Supreme Court would say no. Thus
the proper place (for bringing evidence against the
President and securing his removal from office) was
the impeachment process." Discussed at length with
top staff, particularly Lochavara, who also expressed
"serious question that the President could be indicted."

Knew that he could go ahead and indict RMN and then
have it challenged in the courts but rejected that
strategy. "To me, what was so serious was that if--as
we thought it probably would--the Supreme Court held no,
then we'd be in one hell of a mess; the nation would
have this teriffic wound that just kept getting deeper
and deeper and the process would take longer and longer.
So what was the alternative? Judiciary was setting up
and for the first time in our history the grand jury
would prepare a report which listed step-by-step
the President's involvement in a crime--in the coverup."

APPENDIX C

Jaworski letter to Sirica of December 27, 1973, confirming ex parte meeting with four prosecutors on December 14

Discussed at pp. 7, 52–54 in text

WATERGATE SPECIAL PROSECUTION FORCE
United States Department of Justice
1425 K Street, N.W.
Washington, D.C. 20005
December 27, 1973

PAL:sek

Honorable John J. Sirica
Chief Judge
United States District Court
  for the District of Columbia
Washington, D. C.   20001

Dear Chief Judge Sirica:

When Messrs. Ruth, Lacovara, Ben-Veniste and I met with
you and Judge Gesell at your request on Friday, December 14,
you suggested that it would be helpful if we could provide
you with some sense of the caseload that we would be generat-
ing for the Court over the next several months. I have reviewed the status of the investigations currently under way
with my task force leaders, and have put together what I
believe is a reasonable projection of the scale of indictments that may be returned between the beginning of the new
year and the end of April.

In January and February, I foresee the possibility that
the grand juries may return three multi-defendant indictments
that would take approximately a week each to try. During
that time I can calculate approximately three additional
indictments that might consume two weeks each of trial.
Another case might last for three weeks. I also anticipate
that, should an indictment be voted in another area actively
under investigation at the present, it would take from four
to six weeks to try the case. And finally, I believe that
by the end of January or the beginning of February we may
have an indictment in a case that could well take three
months to try.

Looking ahead to March and April, I have reason to
anticipate two or three indictments that may involve one-
week trials, one involving a two-week trial, and another
possibly leading to a three-week trial. Of course, there
are a number of other matters currently at the preliminary
stages of investigation which might be ready for indictment
during March and April as well. Added to the cases referred

- 2 -

to above are a number of relatively straightforward cases that, if not terminated by an agreed upon plea of guilty, should take no more than a day or two to try.

I am sure you can appreciate that the estimates I have given are extremely rough. It is, of course, possible that the grand jury will elect not to return indictments in some of these areas. In addition, willingness by potential defendants to agree to plead guilty before or after indictment may substantially reduce the number or length of the trials. It is my opinion, however, that the estimates I have given, while perhaps erring on the side of being overly inclusive, will provide you with information that you may find helpful in planning for the assignment of cases during the early part of the new year.

No doubt in making your own assessment of caseload you will consider the time that will be consumed between indictments and trials in these cases by pre-trial motions, particularly motions for continuances or transfers based on pre-trial publicity, including the report of the Ervin Committee which is scheduled to be released in the Spring.

If further information or detail would be helpful, I would be happy to respond to any questions you may have. Let me take this opportunity to express again my deepest appreciation for the extremely careful and responsible way you have been handling these matters and for the courtesies you have extended to me and to my staff.

Sincerely,

/s/

LEON JAWORSKI
Special Prosecutor

cc: Mr. Jaworski
     Mr. Ruth
     Mr. Lacovara
     Task Force Leaders
     Files

APPENDIX D

Lacovara memorandum to Jaworski of January 21, 1974, urging separate ex parte meeting with Sirica to gain his concurrence in the grand jury's sending a report to the House Judiciary Committee

Discussed at pp. 7, 55–56 in text

WATERGATE SPECIAL PROSECUTION FORCE   DEPARTMENT OF JUSTICE

Memorandum

TO   : Leon Jaworski   DATE: January 21, 1974
         Special Prosecutor

FROM : Philip A. Lacovara
         Counsel to the Special
           Prosecutor

SUBJECT: Presentment by Watergate Grand Jury Concerning
          the President

As part of our consideration of the most appropriate way of dealing with evidence tending to implicate the President in the Watergate cover-up, we have discussed the possibility of advising the grand jury that it may return a presentment setting forth its views of the President's complicity even though it might be determined as a matter of law or policy that the President should not be indicted. Peter Kreindler was asked to prepare a memorandum on this subject and he has reached the conclusion, reflected in the attached memorandum, that submission of such a presentment by the grand jury would be constitutional. I have been discussing this subject with him since the beginning of his research and am familiar with the authorities. I agree with his analysis and conclusions in all respects.

If you agree that presentment in lieu of either indictment or non-action is the proper mode to pursue, there remains the question of procedure. Specifically, the relative rarity with which presentments are filed in federal courts makes it desirable to advise Chief Judge Sirica in advance of this proposed course. It would be most unfortunate, for example, for the grand jury to return a presentment without forewarning and then have the judge summarily refuse to receive it because of his lack of awareness of the basis for such a submission. However, it is also questionable whether we should discuss this procedure with the chief judge before the grand jury, whose decision would be involved, has had an opportunity to consider this possible course. Yet there would be some risk in discussing such an approach with the grand jury, and perhaps planting a seed that could not be unsown, before the judge has at least tentatively indicated that he would be prepared to accept such a presentment.

- 2 -

In light of all of the foregoing factors, I recommend the following course:

1. That you decide formally and as quickly as possible what advice you want given to the grand jury in your capacity as its counsel on the questions of (a) the President's indictability as a matter of law, (b) the policy factors concerning indictment of an incumbent President, and (c) the propriety of the grand jury's submission of a presentment naming the President, either in open court or under seal, with a request that it be forwarded to the House Committee on the Judiciary. My own recommendation is that the grand jury be told (a) we believe that the President can constitutionally be indicted for the crime of obstruction of justice but that the question is subject to considerable doubt, and therefore (b), in light of the severe dislocations that would immediately flow from the naming of a sitting President as a criminal defendant, it would be preferable to leave formal proceedings to the House of Representatives. With regard to (c) the grand jury should be advised that it may return a presentment, which states its conclusions based on the evidence it has heard but which does not initiate a criminal proceeding, and I would propose that the presentment be submitted under seal to the chief judge, with a request that it be forwarded to the House Judiciary Committee after counsel for the President have been given an opportunity to submit any objections, either on the law or the facts, that they may have.

2. After you make the foregoing decisions, I recommend that you or I or both appear before the grand jury, at the conclusion of the presentation of the tapes, to advise them of these determinations. They should candidly be told that it is not certain how the court will respond to the submission of a presentment but should be advised that this matter will be discussed with the chief judge if the grand jury is inclined to return a presentment involving the President.

3. If the grand jury indicates its tendency toward returning a presentment, we should schedule a conference with Chief Judge Sirica to apprise him in advance of this possible development. I would be prepared to submit a memorandum of law to him at such a meeting, if he indicated an interest in receiving it.

- 3 -

4. At any such meeting we should recommend to Judge Sirica that the presentment be received by him under seal, with disclosure only of the fact that the grand jury has made a submission to him, and that the White House be given ten days to review the presentment and to make objections to its filing and transmission.

Attachment

cc: Mr. Ruth (w/attachment)
     Mr. Kreindler (w/o attachment)
     Mr. Ben-Veniste (w/o attachment)

APPENDIX E

Jaworski memorandum to confidential Watergate file of February 12, 1974, detailing ex parte meeting with Sirica of the day before

Discussed at pp. 7, 56–59 in text

LJ/flc

Feb ary 12/1974

C O N F I D E N T I A L

        On Monday, February 11, I met with the Judge at which
time several matters were covered as we sat alone in the jury
room. He again indicated that provided the indictments came down
in time he would take the Watergate Case, stating that he had
been urged to do so by any number of Judges from across the
nation the most recent of them being those who were in
attendance with him at a meeting in Atlanta. He expressed the
opinion that these indictments should be returned as soon as
possible. He also stated that henceforth all guilty pleas
would be taken by him. We talked about the Vesco case and he
merely expressed the thought that perhaps a sealed indictment
might be of some help. He mentioned one or two personal
matters such as an effort to smear him because of a completely
fabricated tale relating to him and his son, of which he
wanted me to be aware. Actually the discussion began with
his unburdening himself to me on that particular matter. He
also mentioned that he had been urged to speak at the State
Bar of Texas in San Antonio and indicated that he would
accept this invitation.

2

He sought my reaction and I urged him to do so.

The Judge commented upon the status of matters before the grand jury which led into further comments on the possibility of the grand jury considering some type of special report or presentment. He considered this a very touchy problem and cautioned as to what the public's reaction would be to a grand jury stepping out with something that was beyond its normal bounds. He cautioned that the whole effort could be tainted by something irresponsibly being done by the grand jury. He stated that the public would rightfully conclude that the entire proceeding had not been judicious but simply one of wanting to hurt the President. He further said that it was not the function of the grand jury but that of the House Impeachment Committee to express itself on that point. He then told me that in the event I observed anything along that line being considered by the grand jury that he thought it would be appropriate for him to meet with the grand jury in camera. I expressed the belief that it was appropriate for the grand jury to refer to having in its possession evidence that it believed to be material and relevant to the impeachment proceedings and to suggest to the Court that it be referred to the House Committee for that purpose. He countered by stating that he believed he should be informed of the discretion that he could exercise in matters of that kind and further requested that I have a memorandum prepared for him that covers this subject. I agreed to have this done.

APPENDIX F

Wilson letter to Sirica of March 12, 1974,
asking about private meetings with WSPF

Discussed at p. 59 in text

ROGER J. WHITEFORD 1886-1965
RINGGOLD HART 1886-1965
JOHN J. CARMODY 1901-1972
JOHN J. WILSON
HARRY L. RYAN, JR.
JO V. MORGAN, JR.
FRANK H. STRICKLER
WILLIAM E. ROLLOW
CHARLES J. STEELE
JOHN J. CARMODY, JR.
JAMES EDWARD ABLARD
KEVIN W. CARMODY

COUNSEL
DONALD L. HERSKOVITZ

LAW OFFICES

WHITEFORD, HART, CARMODY & WILSON

815 FIFTEENTH STREET, NORTHWEST

WASHINGTON, D. C. 20005

202-638-0465

CABLE ADDRESS

WHITEHART WASHINGTON

MARYLAND OFFICE
7401 WISCONSIN AVENUE
BETHESDA, MARYLAND 20014
301-656-5700

JO V. MORGAN, JR.
FRANK H. STRICKLER
WILLIAM E. ROLLOW
CHARLES J. STEELE

March 12, 1974

Honorable John J. Sirica
Chief Judge
United States District Court
United States Court House
Washington, D.C. 20001

Dear Chief Judge Sirica:

Would you be willing to inform us whether you
were consulted by or whether you conferred with the
prosecutors, the Grand Jury, or the foreman or other member
thereof, regarding the report which the Grand Jury presented
to you in open court on March 1, 1974, before such report
was actually presented; or that you had notice of the Grand
Jury's intention to present such a report prior to its
actually doing so?

Respectfully,

JOHN J. WILSON

JJW:hie

cc: All Counsel

APPENDIX G

Ruth memorandum to Jaworski of February 19, 1974, discussing timing of the indictment, with handwritten response from Jaworski noting, "Judge Sirica expects it"

Discussed at p. 60 in text

WATERGATE SPECIAL PROSECUTION FORCE

DEPARTMENT OF JUSTICE

Memorandum

TO   :   Leon Jaworski

DATE: Feb. 19, 1974

FROM :   Henry Ruth

SUBJECT: Vesco Trial

Jim Rayhill called this morning at the request of
Judge Gagliardi to determine if we had a date certain
for the Watergate indictment and, if not, whether we
would state that the Watergate indictment would
definitely be returned before the conclusion of the
Vesco trial.

I told Rayhill that we did not now have such a date
certain, but that the indictment would definitely be
returned before the conclusion of the Vesco trial.

I also stated for Rayhill's information that the
indictment would occur within the next 3 weeks at the
most.

Phil Lacovara joined in the phone call as I was replying
to Mr. Rayhill's questions.

cc:
   Mr. Lacovara
   Mr. Ben-Veniste
   Mr. McBride

2/19/74

Hank: I think you phoned contact
Rayhill and be more specific. We knew
that barring unforseen circumstances the
indictment will be in Wed or Thurs of next week, +
Judge S. expects that. In view of our knowledge
of this - the comment that it would occur within 3
weeks, maybe misconstrued, should the indictment
come down next week. - - (more specific inform.
may expedite the jury
selection)

APPENDIX H

Jaworski memorandum to confidential Watergate file about events of March 1, 1974, detailing his ex parte meetings with Sirica that preceded and followed the hearing in which the indictment was announced

Discussed at pp. 7, 60–62 in text

On the eve of Thursday, February 28, with the Mitchell-
Stans jury selected in New York and sequestered, it became apparent that we would move to bring in the Watergate cover-up
indictments on Friday morning. After checking with Judge Sirica,
the hour of 11:00 a.m. was decided upon. ~~I had previously talked
to Judge Sirica about the bringing in of a sealed report by the
grand jury, in addition to the indictment, and this had his
approval.~~ I made known to him in advance that such a report was
forthcoming, ~~so as not to have him startled by this matter.~~

On Thursday evening, February 28, just as I was preparing
to leave the office around 6:45, Alexander Haig called saying that
there were so many rumors afloat that he was concerned - that he
feared unexpected developments, etc. and he wondered if there was
anything I could properly disclose. I told him that there was
nothing I could disclose as to the contents of the indictment or
the report he had heard would be made. I did tell him that if the
grand jury made a report, in addition to returning to an indictment,
he should expect Judge Sirica, as would I, to accept it and act on
it. He stated that he and the White House generally were fully
expecting the grand jury evidence to be made available to the House
Judiciary Committee - that they realized it belonged there. I suggested to him that the evidence may well have serious repercussions
and he stated that he was aware of that. I suggested that he and
the President's counsel take a close look at the March 21 meeting
and the actions that followed, even though the President took no
personal part in the events that followed the March 21 meeting.

/2 - /

Finally, he asked whether there was any indictment contemplated involving present White House aides, inasmuch as he needed to make arrangements to meet the situation. I told him none was contemplated at this time

Twice during the conversation, he said that he really called to tell me that I was a "great American." The second time he mentioned it, I said "Al, I haven't done anything other than what is my duty and I hope to continue to follow that course."

We parted with my again expressing my concern that the President's counsel had not sufficiently and accurately assessed the facts pertaining to the March 21 conference and the events that took place that night. He said it would be again reviewed.

On the morning of March 1, I met with Judge Sirica in chambers at 10:30. We reviewed the agenda consisting of (1) presentation of indictments and sealed special report of the grand jury; (2) unsealing of the special report and reading by Judge Sirica, and the acceptance of the report and its resealing. I told Judge Sirica that I would ask the Court to specially assign the case in view of its length and protracted nature and that I was estimating the case would take three to four months to try. I asked him to tell the grand jury to return in two weeks for further consideration of other matters that had not been disposed of. I had in mind the possibility of perjury indictments. I also asked the Judge for a gag order under Rule 1-27 restraining extra-judicial statements.

Shortly before 11:00, I left Judge Sirica's chambers
and went into the courtroom. As I left Judge Sirica's chambers,
I heard the Judge tell his marshal not to be nervous. But the
Judge showed some signs of nervousness too. He told me that he
had not slept since 3:00 that morning. When court opened, Judge
Sirica's marshall was so nervous he could hardly speak the ritual
followed in opening a court.

After opening, Judge Sirica looked at me, asked if I
had anything to take up with the court. I then rose, went to the
lectern, and said: "May it please Your Honor, the grand jury has
an indictment to return. It also has a sealed report to deliver
to the Court." The rest of the agenda was then followed including
delivery of a briefcase of material, along with the special report
to the Court - also a key to the briefcase. The Judge indicated
that he would have an order on the special report by Monday (he
told me he would transmit to the counsel for the House Judiciary
Committee under rules that would not interfere with the trial of
the. accused). The Judge in open court asked if I had any further
comments, and I stated: "Due to the length of the trial, conceivably three to four months, it is the Prosecution's view that under
Rule 3-3(c), this case should be specially assigned, and we so
recommend." This meant that Judge Sirica could assign the case
to himself, which he did do by order later entered that day.

The Judge then announced his gag rule and then adjourned
court.

We met in the Judge's chambers. I told him I thought all
went smoothly. He in turn thanked me for my help. The Judge was

leaving today to speak at the University of Virginia tomorrow, to be back on Sunday. I told him I was going to Texas and that I would be back on Tuesday. We both agreed we would call each other in the interim, if necessary.

APPENDIX I

Lacovara memorandum to Jaworski, "Criminal Responsibility for Joining Ongoing Conspiracy," January 7, 1974, confirming WSPF's belief that Nixon had ordered Hunt's blackmail demands be met

Discussed at p. 75 in text

WATERGATE SPECIAL PROSECUTION FORCE   DEPARTMENT OF JUSTICE

Memorandum

TO   : Leon Jaworski   DATE: January 7, 1974

FROM : Philip A. Lacovara

SUBJECT: Criminal Responsibility for Joining Ongoing Conspiracy

      Some question has been raised about the criminal liability of a person who learns about a criminal conspiracy that is already in being and then gives some encouragement to it but may not personally perform any subsequent overt act.

      As the attached memorandum from Peter Rient demonstrates, it is hornbook law that a person who attaches himself to a pre-existing conspiracy, has some stake in its continuation, and makes it his own, becomes fully liable as a co-conspirator. To the extent that the advice of the neophyte member of the conspiracy is subsequently followed, his culpability is even more clear.

Attachment

cc: Mr. Ruth
     Mr. Ben-Veniste
     Mr. Rient

WATERGATE SPECIAL PROSECUTION FORCE

DEPARTMENT OF JUSTICE

Memorandum

TO   : Philip A. Lacovara

DATE: January 3, 1974

FROM : Peter F. Rient

SUBJECT: Hypothetical Conspiracy Case

You have asked me to assess the possible criminal liability, under federal conspiracy law, of a person in the following hypothetical situation:

D, the subject of this discussion, is an elected official in charge of a government organization. During an election year, Group A, supporters of D, engage in criminal conduct, believing that they are assisting D's re-election. When Group A is caught, Group B, subordinates and close associates of D, engage in a variety of efforts to prevent the members of Group A from revealing that Group A's criminal activities had been sanctioned by Group B. To this end, the members of Group B, who are motivated by self-protection and by a desire to ensure D's re-election, proceed to make periodic cash payments to the members of Group A to procure their silence in the face of official investigations and a criminal trial.

The conspiracy to obstruct justice proceeds smoothly for a number of months until Al, a knowledgeable member of Group A, threatens to talk unless he receives an additional substantial cash payment. At this point, Bl goes to D, who has been re-elected in the meantime and who is unaware of the existence of the conspiracy. Bl informs D of the existence and nature of the conspiracy and of the roles of the various conspirators. Bl further explains to D that in order for the conspiracy to continue successfully it is necessary to pay a large sum of money to Al who is threatening to talk and who can implicate a number of D's close associates in criminal activities, with consequent embarrassment to D. D commends Al on his efforts to prevent the scandal from affecting the outcome of the election, but agrees that a new plan is needed to deal with the situation in the future so that it does not come to rest on D's doorstep. D also states that he does not want any

- 2 -

criminal liability for his close associates, and agrees with Bl
that the payment should be made to Al to "buy time" until a new
plan can be formulated to meet the desired objectives. Finally,
D directs Bl to meet with D and certain members of Group B for
the purpose of discussing how the situation should be handled.
Shortly thereafter, the payment is made to Al by B2, on instructions from B3, and the meeting ordered by D takes place.

As to whether given this hypothetical scenario D has
knowingly joined a conspiracy to obstruct justice, one starts
from the premise that "once the existence of a conspiracy is
established, slight evidence may be sufficient to connect a
defendant with it." Nye & Nissen v. United States, 168 F.2d
846, 852 (9th Cir. 1948), aff'd, 336 U.S. 613 (1949). Since the
existence of a conspiracy to obstruct justice is undisputed in
our hypothetical situation, the question is whether it can
fairly be concluded that D became a knowing participant. As to
this question, it is obvious that D had knowledge of the nature
and scope of the conspiracy as a result of his conversation with
Bl. This, however, is not sufficient to make D a member of the
conspiracy -- something more is required. United States v.
Potash, 118 F.2d 54 (2d Cir. 1941). The "something more" is
generally described as having "a stake in the success of the
venture." United States v. Peoni, 100 F.2d 401 (2d Cir. 1938);
United States v. Falcone, 109 F.2d 579 (2d Cir.)*, aff'd, 311
U.S. 205 (1940); United States v. DiRe, 159 F.2d 818 (2d Cir.
1947); United States v. Cianchetti, 315 F.2d 584 (2d Cir. 1963).
Although the "stake" need not be financial, United States v.
DeSapio, 435 F.2d 272, 282 (2d Cir. 1970), it must be such as to
demonstrate that the defendant "cast in his lot with the conspirators." United States v. Cianchetti, supra. Finally,
although at least one member of the conspiracy must commit an
overt act in furtherance of the conspiracy, it is not necessary
that the defendant whose participation is in question be the
one to do so. Bannon v. United States, 156 U.S. 464, 468
(1895).

Applying these basic principles of conspiracy law to the
hypothetical facts recited above, there can be precious little
room for doubt that D threw in his lot with the conspirators.
With full knowledge of the conspiracy's essential contours and
awareness of the problems in making it continue to succeed, D

---

*The defendant "must in some sense promote [the] venture
himself, make it his own, have a stake in its outcome." 109
F.2d at 581.

- 3 -

advised one of the conspirators how to proceed, i.e., to "buy time" so that a new plan could be devised to avoid criminal liability for his associates, and ordered a meeting between himself and several of the conspirators to discuss their strategy. Nor was this gratuitous advice by a disinterested by-stander. D's "stake" in the success of the venture, while not monetary, was nonetheless substantial, as both D and B1 recognized during their conversation. If the conspiracy to obstruct justice were to come to light, not only would D's close associates be subject to criminal liability, (a matter of grave concern to D) but D himself would be seriously af- fected since he must shoulder ultimate responsibility (in a moral, if not a legal sense) for their actions. Thus, D could expect that failure of the conspiracy to continue success- fully would jeopardize his ability to continue in office and to discharge his obligations effectively. The course of action he advised and which was, in fact, followed was plainly intended to ensure that the conspiracy did not fall apart. Accordingly, it is only fair to conclude that D knowingly, deliberately, and for his own benefit adopted and promoted the unlawful venture, thereby making it his own.

APPENDIX J

Draft Jaworski memorandum to Ruth of January 21, 1974, criticizing WSPF as believing that "the President must be reached at all cost"

Discussed at p. 77–81 in text

                                    DRAFT
          ⟍   LJ/flc
                                    1/21/74

MEMORANDUM TO HENRY RUTH

        I believed that the written exchange between us on
the subject of dealing with the President in the light of
the evidence adduced and to be adduced would be helpful
because they afforded opportunities for a thorough
consideration of the questions and issues that are presented.
But I am beginning to wonder whether they are not wasted
effort. Some of the comments in your last memorandum
(January 14) almost preclude further discussion. In fact I
deferred replying to it because some of the innuendoes don't
do justice to calm and reasoned judgment.

        I said before and I emphasize again that the mere
conclusion that the President is not indictable or should.
not be named as an unindicted co-conspirator furnishes
no basis for our pursuing still another course beset with
restraints that should not be violated. I meant this: If it
is not sound in law or policy to indict the President; if
it is not sound in law or policy to name him as an
unindicted co-conspirator -- it cannot become so simply
because the efforts of the House to impeach are frustrated.
Differently stated, if the House bogs down in impeachment
because of lack of evidence that cannot be properly and
legally released to it or because of its own failures, the
unindictable President does not, perforce these shortcomings,
become indictable.

- 2 -

It seems to me that your reasoning leads to the
inevitable conclusion that whatever may be normally unsound
in reaching the President becomes a laudable course
to follow if he cannot be reached some other way. Although
our mandate authorizes us to proceed against the President,
it nowhere suggests that we are to do so regardless of
fairness and just procedure. More specifically it does not
authorize us to violate grand jury procedures, something I
observed your memorandum avoids dealing with.

As I have indicated to you verbally, I think we
have another course open to us that will not be violative
of any of our obligations and responsibilities. I will be
working on a possible presentation by the grand jury to Judge
Sirica that will avoid the escape that concerns you.

I have carefully examined Phil's latest memo
(January 16) and the attachments. His conclusion that
the President is indictable is not strongly buttressed.
What convinces me that this route should not be considered
is the long and legal battle that would follow over this
question and, in the end ~~xxxxxx~~ quite likely result in a
negative holding. Therefore, it is my conclusion that
those of us working with the grand jury should advise
against any course other than referring the evidence at an
appropriate time to be determined by the court to the House
Committee.

- 3 -

Now let me address myself to the general tenor of
your memorandum which reflects an attitude I discussed with
you before - the subjective conviction that the President
must be reached at all cost. It is also reflected in your
references to St. Clair's letter. He stated nothing that
you should not have expected in all fairness. Your
intimations that there may have been agreements that you did
not know about are especially insupportable because you
have been kept informed of all discussions. Moreover you
are aware of all of the references to grand jury proceedings
in our letters to the White House in which we sought this
information and I would have assumed that you would want to
respect these assurances, expressed and implied, as much
as I do.

What is of ~~some~~ concern ~~to me are the discussions,~~
~~plans and understandings had and reached between staff~~
~~members prior to any discussions with me.~~ This results
in convictions already ~~formed and frankly, under such~~
~~circumstances, the meetings are of no help to me.~~

Perhaps ~~I should not consider it~~ ~~~~ly
ta~~sk, but~~ ~~inasmuch as I have the chief responsibility,~~
hen~~ceforward the discussions I seek will be with those I~~
de~~signate.~~ The stubborn fact remains that we must be alert
not to give support to the White House charges that have
been leveled against the staff. Perhaps it is too late to

- 4 -

get objective opinions from others so I will do the best
I can in the making of decisions for which I -- and not
the staff -- will be held responsible. It is a simple
thing for you and others to discuss views and convictions
you formed along the way because you do not have the
ultimate responsibility.

I expect to consult a number of the members of
the staff on some of the points on which decisions need to
be made. I can accomplish much more by consulting these
separately than having group gatherings that have not been
particularly helpful. Needless to say the staff will
continue to be kept informed of all matters of significance
to the best of my ability.

The suggestions on page 2 of your memorandum, in
the main, cannot possibly be followed because we still
know nothing about the House Judiciary Committee's procedures.

If you or any member of the staff wishes to furnish
any written comments, suggestions or recommendations to
me on any of the matters mentioned by you, I shall be glad
to receive them. I will then reach a decision on each of
these as well as other matters in due course of time.

APPENDIX K

Partial Chart of the Kennedy/Johnson Department of Justice, showing those who later became key players in Watergate

Discussed at p. 147 in text

Kennedy-Johnson Department of Justice

OFFICE OF THE ATTORNEY GENERAL: Robert F. Kennedy (1961–1964),
Nicholas Katzenbach (1965–1966), Ramsey Clark (1967–1969);
SPECIAL ASSISTANT: James Vorenberg (1964–1967)

CRIMINAL DIVISION

SOLICITOR GENERAL
Archibald Cox (1961–1965)
Philip Heymann (1961–1965)
Philip Lacovara (1967–1969)

U.S. ATTORNEY OFFICES

ORGANIZED CRIME SECTION
Thomas McBride (1961–1965)
Henry Ruth (1961–1964)
Charles Ruff (1967–1972)
Jill Wine Volner (1968–1973)

OFFICE OF CRIMINAL JUSTICE
James Vorenberg (1964–1965)
Henry Ruth (1964–1965)

SOUTHERN DISTRICT OF NY
Robert M. Morgenthau
(1961–1970)
Charles Shaffer (1959–1961)
Bernard Nussbaum (1961–1966)
David Dorsen (1963–1968)
Peter Rient (1965–1973)
Terry Lenzner (1966–1968)
Richard Ben-Veniste (1968–1973)
Jay Horowitz (1969–1973)
Richard J. Davis (1969–1973)

**LABOR & RACKETEERING UNIT
"GET HOFFA SQUAD"**
Carmine Bellino (1961–1964)
William Bittman (1961–1966)
James Neal (1961–1966)
Charles Shaffer (1961–1965)

**CIVIL RIGHTS DIVISION
ASSISTANT AG**
Burke Marshall (1961–1964)
John Doar (1960–1967)
Terry Lenzner (1961–1966)

TENNESSEE
James Neal (1966–1968)

MICHIGAN
William Merrill (1961–1966)

ROLE IN WATERGATE

WSPF PROSECUTORS
Archibald Cox: Harvard Law professor and Kennedy advisor who became original Special Prosecutor

Henry Ruth: Deputy Special Prosecutor, becoming Special Prosecutor upon Jaworski's resignation

Philip Heymann and James Vorenberg: Special Assistant to the Special Prosecutor and fellow Harvard Law professor with Cox

Philip Lacovara: Counsel to the Special Prosecutor and Chief of the Law Research Section

James Neal: Head of the Watergate Task Force

Richard Ben-Veniste: Deputy head of the Watergate Task Force

William Merrill: Head of the Plumbers Task Force

Thomas McBride: Head of the Campaign Contributions Task Force

Richard Davis: Head of the Dirty Tricks Task Force

Charles Ruff: Member of the Campaign Finance Task Force, becoming Special Prosecutor upon Ruth's resignation (and later Counsel to President Clinton)

Jill Wine Volner: Member of the Watergate Task Force

Jay Horowitz: Member of the Plumbers Task Force

Peter Rient: Member of the Law Research Section

ERVIN COMMITTEE STAFF
Carmine Bellino: Longtime Kennedy aide, who was the committee's political liaison

Terry Lenzer (note he appears twice): the Committee's chief investigator

HJC IMPEACHMENT INQUIRY STAFF
John Doar: The Committee's chief of staff

Bernard Nussbaum: Head of the Committee's Watergate investigation (and later Counsel to President Clinton).

OTHER
William Bittman: Howard Hunt's defense counsel

Charles Shaffer: John Dean's defense counsel

Burke Marshall: Yale Law professor and senior advisor to Senator Edward Kennedy, who arranged for his former students to get key positions on the Impeachment Inquiry staff

APPENDIX L

Rient memorandum to Ben-Veniste of February 6, 1974, detailing discrepancies between Dean's Senate testimony and White House tapes, prepared following Jaworski's public assertion that they knew of no reason to question Dean's veracity

Discussed at pp. 149, 165 in text

WATERGATE SPECIAL PROSECUTION FORCE   DEPARTMENT OF JUSTICE

Memorandum

TO   : Richard Ben-Veniste   DATE: 2/6/74

FROM : Peter F. Rient ~~PFR~~

SUBJECT: Material Discrepancies Between the Senate Select
          Committee Testimony of John Dean and the Tapes of
          Dean's Meetings with the President.

        The following are the material discrepancies between
John Dean's Senate Select Committee testimony concerning his
meetings with the President and the facts with respect to
those meetings as reflected in the White House tapes in our
possession:

9/15/72   1. The President told Dean that Haldeman had kept
Meeting   the President posted on Dean's handling of
               Watergate matter. (uncorroborated)

not a quote; — 2. The President said he was pleased that the case
Dean's conclusion   had stopped with Liddy. (uncorroborated)

           3. Dean said he could not take credit because
               others had done much more difficult things
               than Dean had. (uncorroborated)

           4. Dean said there was a long way to go before the
               matter would end and he could give no assurance
               that it would not start to unravel some day.
               [The tape shows that Dean initially said that
               nothing would "come crashing down to our sur-
               prise" (Tr. 8), but later cautioned "the only
               problems. . .we have are the human problems
               and I will keep a close eye on that." (Tr. 10)]

           5. The President asked whether the criminal case
               would come to trial before the election and
               said he certainly hoped it would not.
               (uncorroborated)

6. The conversation included a discussion
    of using IRS to attack White House enemies.
    (uncorroborated) [There was, however, a
    discussion of using the FBI and Justice
    Department for this purpose. (Tr. 11-12)]

2/28/73   1. The President told Dean to report directly,
Meeting   rather than through Ehrlichman and Haldeman,
                on Watergate. [Toward the end of the conver-
                sation, the President said "And now I will
                not talk to you again until you have something
                to report to me" (WH Tr. 28), which indicates
                that the President may have previously told
                Dean to report to him directly, as Dean testi-
                fied the President did on 2/27/73.]

27 th ? —   2. Dean told the President that Dean had been a
                conduit for post-June 17 activities and could
                be involved in an obstruction of justice, but
                the President told Dean not to worry. [This
                conversation occurred on 3/21/73. On 2/28/73,
                in response to the President's comment that
                the Ervin Committee was after somebody in the
                White House -- Haldeman, Colson, Ehrlichman --
                Dean added "Or possibly Dean -- You know, I am
                a small fish."]

3/13/73   [Much of the conversation which Dean describes as
Meeting   taking place on 3/13/73 in fact occurred on 3/21/73.
            However, neither the 3/13 nor 3/21 tape contains the
            following matters which Dean testified were discussed
            on 3/13:]

17 th ? —   1. The President said he had discussed executive
                clemency for Hunt with Ehrlichman. [On 3/21/73
                the President admitted having discussed this
                subject with someone, probably Colson.]

17 th ?   2. The President expressed annoyance that Colson
                had also discussed executive clemency for Hunt
                with the President. (uncorroborated on either
                the 3/13 or 3/21 tape)

3/21/73
a.m.
Meeting

[Taken together, the 3/13 and 3/21 tapes corroborate Dean's account of the 3/21 meeting except in the following respects:]

1. Dean told the President that he had passed Hunt's message along to Haldeman and Ehrlichman, and, pursuant to Ehrlichman's request, to Mitchell. [On 4/16/73 Dean told the President that Dean had informed Ehrlichman about Hunt's threat and that Ehrlichman had asked him to call Mitchell about it.]

2. Dean told the President that if Dean were called to testify before the Grand Jury or the Senate Committee Dean would have to tell the facts the way he knew them. [Dean said this, in substance, on 4/16.]

3. Dean told the President that Dean didn't think he could give the Cabinet a briefing on Watergate, even a tailored down briefing. [Contradicted by the 3/21 tape which shows that Dean expressed confidence in his ability to brief the Cabinet without disclosing all the facts. (Tr. 42)]

3/21/73
p.m.
Meeting

Dean said to the President that Dean thought Ehrlichman, Haldeman and Dean were indictable for obstruction of justice. [Dean said this to the President on the morning of 3/21. (Tr. 18)]

3/22/73
Meeting

1. The President said to Mitchell that Dean had been doing an excellent job on the Watergate matter. (uncorroborated) 21st

4/16/73
a.m.
Meeting

1. Dean told the President that the letters the President had asked him to sign were virtual confessions of anything regarding the Watergate. [Dean did tell the President that the phrasing of the letters was important so that no one would be caused any problems with a fair trial.]

APPENDIX M

Watergate Final Decisions memorandum of February 20, 1974, containing extensive discussions and dissent regarding Jaworski's decision to omit Bittman from the indictment

Discussed at p. 161 in text

Final Decisions

WATERGATE

Ruth
Volner
Goldman
Frampton
Kreindler
PAL

Feb. 20, 1974

1. Ruth has decided to include Parkinson in indictment. LJ said he agrees with it but did not want to make that decision but will sign indictment.

2. On basis of Ben-Veniste's assessment of chances of conviction of Colson on the evidence, LJ has decided that he should be included. White House has decided not to make available the tapes Shapiro has wanted us to hear. Ben-Veniste said evidence shows he is member of conspiracy, and there is 50-50 chance of conviction. Ruth dissents. LJ said he listened to Colson's January 3-4 conversations with President. Colson and Shapiro were eager to learn what LJ had heard and when told he hadn't heard anything about clemency, they said they were "relieved" -- this implies that they knew they were involved and were glad he wasn't tied in by evidence.

3. Mardian is to be included, according to LJ, because of his early involvement in incriminating activities, even though he withdrew later.

4. There are no doubts about inclusion of Mitchell, Ehrlichman, Haldeman and Strachan.

5. Bittman has testified before grand jury on 2/19 -- after getting his warnings. He argued that prosecutors consider grand jury a rubber stamp and he hoped this grand jury would not consider itself bound by prosecutor's recommendations. This may disadvantage Bittman, since LJ has decided not to charge him; he was appearing as defense counsel acting for guilty client, but one he had obligation to do his best for. His conduct was unsavory, but his role is that of defense counsel and his actions are subject to several interpretations, including those consistent with representing his client's interests.

   LJ said his critical factors were: (1) he will provide information about Parkinson that will be more useful than O'Brien's, since O'Brien seems to be too malleable and may not stand up on cross-examination; (2) Bittman never checked with O'Brien to see what Dean did about message Bittman wanted passed along about Hunt's threats, and this shows that Bittman was not acting out of self-interest in his March 16 activities.

   There may be problems with grand jury -- if so, LJ will discuss this personally with them to give his reasons.

   LJ will allow Bittman to be named in indictment as involved in overt acts, or in Bill of Particulars.

   Ben-Veniste said O'Brien's explanation of timing shows that Bittman learned of action taken on the message -- payment of cash -- within a few days of March 16 - March 21. This was similarly coded, under-the-table contact with Bittman.

   Frampton said Bittman had never before asked for direct response -- his answer always came in form of delivery of cash -- as it did here.

Frampton also said point was not that Bittman's motive changed to financial "self-interest" in March, but that Bittman's facilitation of blackmail by Hunt was criminal.

B-V said in fairness it had to be recognized that Bittman never took initiative.

LJ said skilled defense lawyer would show that Bittman only did what his client wanted him to do.

Frampton said Bittman's conduct on behalf of his client went beyond legal limits and thus that such a motove was no excuse.

Volner points out that Bittman's testimony will contradict O'Brien and Dean on clemency -- and thus weaken case against Colson.

PAL said motive here was not excuse -- he knew what con- sequence was of doing what Hunt wanted -- Bittman prosecuted Hoffa and his staff for jury tampering -- doing what client wanted in "his" interests -- he also knew of significance of use of large sums of cash from that experience.

LJ said "defense lawyers all over the country do that and if defense lawyers couldn't follow their client's instructions, the jails would be full of lawyers."

PAL said: we should not sink to "morals of market place," particularly with Bittman who himself knew better and prosecuted that kind of conduct.

Volner said Bittman's conduct shows not just a single bad judgment but a series of improper actions at his client's sug- gestion or direction -- when he knew exactly what consequences were.

LJ said we were just drawing inferences against Bittman when we had to give him "the benefit of the doubt."

PAL asked (1) why shouldn't jury decide which inferences to draw, and (2) why is Parkinson to be included, since he was lawyer too?

LJ said (1) he has to apply higher standards -- if there is reasonable doubt -- he can't indict. I said I'd tend to agree but BV said chances on Colson are no more than 50-50 so I don't see how those are reconcilable, (2) Parkinson was acting only as lawyer in a civil case, which he said is different.

LJ said if Volner ever wanted to be a criminal defense lawyer, she "would starve" if she followed the line of argument she made today.

APPENDIX N

Lacovara memorandum to Jaworski, "Status of Charles Colson in Watergate Case," February 22, 1974, detailing reasons why Lacovara, Ruth, and Kreindler oppose naming Colson in the indictment

Discussed at p. 162 in text

WATERGATE SPECIAL PROSECUTION FORCE   DEPARTMENT OF JUSTICE

Memorandum

TO   : Leon Jaworski   DATE: February 22, 1974
        Special Prosecutor

FROM : Philip A. Lacovara
        Counsel to the Special
        Prosecutor

SUBJECT: Status of Charles Colson in Watergate Case

    In recent discussions concerning whether to recommend
indictment of Charles Colson in the Watergate case, Rick
Ben-Veniste has indicated that he believes we have sufficient
evidence to overcome a motion to dismiss, but that our chances
of obtaining a conviction are no better than 50-50. My understanding is that it has been the consistent policy from the
inception of this office that we would indict an individual
only if we were reasonably certain of obtaining a conviction.
Hank Ruth and I (and I understand, you) have advised David
Shapiro, Colson's attorney, that this policy would be followed
in our recommendation to the grand jury on Colson. Under these
circumstances, I have considerable doubt whether we should
recommend to the grand jury that it indict Colson.

    From the outset of our discussions, you have felt that
Colson was very deliberate in staying on the periphery of any
conspiracy and cautious to limit any overt activity on his
part. According to my notes, on February 9, you indicated
that the recording of Colson's conversation with Hunt in November was not enough to secure a conviction and told the Watergate task force that you would not be prepared to indict Colson
unless there were more evidence of his complicity in the conspiracy. You reaffirmed this position on February 11. To my
knowledge, the Watergate task force has not developed this
additional evidence, despite repeated exploration of the
clemency issue with Bittman; nor have they expressed greater
confidence in being able to obtain a conviction. As recently
as February 20, Rick Ben-Veniste gave his assessment of the
likelihood of conviction as no more than 50-50.

    Although there is no question that the grand jury would
be fully justified in finding probable cause to indict Colson,
I believe that this office should adhere to the high standard
we have set for ourselves. This is particularly important

- 2 -

where an individual who is not part of the core of the conspiracy, either by his actions or motivations, may be swept up
in a large conspiracy case.

Finally, in making your decision, you should be aware
that, despite his brief to us in the Fielding case, which
states that "the Special Prosecutor informed Mr. Colson and
his counsel that no indictment would be brought unless the
Special Prosecution Force was 'confident that it could obtain
a conviction,'" David Shapiro has said that it might not be
"unfair" to indict Colson in that case if, on the facts and the
law, there were a 50-50 chance of conviction. In my view, however, that should not be sufficient.

(I have discussed this memorandum with Peter Kreindler,
who was present at many of the meetings about Colson and with
his attorney, and he asked that I mention that he concurs in
these thoughts.) (Henry Ruth has also recommended that, for
similar reasons, Colson should not be indicted.)

cc: Mr. Ruth
     Mr. Ben-Veniste
     Mr. Kreindler

APPENDIX O

Portions of Rient and Denny memorandum to file of November 15, 1973, noting Glanzer's and Campbell's statements about Dean's comments regarding the involvement of Haldeman, Ehrlichman, and Nixon

Discussed at p. 168 in text

File - Dean

WATERGATE SPECIAL PROSECUTION FORCE   DEPARTMENT OF JUSTICE

Memorandum

TO   :   Files   DATE: Nov. 15, 1973

FROM :   Peter F. Rient
          Judy Denny

SUBJECT: Meetings with Seymour Glanzer and Donald Campbell -
          September 18 and October 10, 1973.

On September 18, and October 10, 1973, Peter F. Rient
and Judy Denny of the Special Prosecutor's Office interviewed
Assistant U. S. Attorneys Seymour Glanzer and Don Campbell
in Glanzer's office, concerning contacts after April 1, 1973,
between the original Watergate prosecutors and John Dean
and/or Dean's attorneys. During and after these interviews,
Glanzer and Campbell provided their handwritten notes taken
at their May 2 and 3 meetings with Dean. Other documents
referred to are Glanzer's May 31 memo to Cox and a September
6 memo to files from Rient and Denny re Silbert interview.

Except as otherwise stated, Glanzer and Campbell
both gave the following information.

1. Glanzer knew both Charles Shaffer and Tom Hogan
(Dean's attorneys). Glanzer and Shaffer are close friends
and have known each other since Shaffer worked in the Department of Justice. Glanzer knew Hogan when Hogan was a
law clerk for Judge Jones. The two attorneys for Dean came
to Glanzer's office on about April 2, 1972, saying they

- 17 -

11. On the evening of April 23, Shaffer met
with Silbert and Glanzer. Glanzer says that by this
time, the discussions had turned into a political game.
Dean was bargaining with the Senate for immunity and the
prosecutor's attempts at agreeing on a plea were in vain.
Shaffer suggested a plea to misprison of a felony (never a
firm offer), but then rejected this when it was determined
that it was a felony and the possible sentence was too long.

12. On April 29, Shaffer called Glanzer at home
to discuss the Vesco case. (It was not unusual for Shaffer
to call Glanzer to discuss things generally.) Shaffer told
Glanzer that Dean would either be a witness in the case or
would not testify. Shaffer also told Glanzer that Colson
would have information about Haldeman and Ehrlichman.

After April 15, the situation was in a state of
flux. The appointment of Cox and the preparation for the
Senate hearings changed the outlook from all sides.

13. By the end of April, Dean had become much more
antagonistic toward Haldeman and Ehrlichman in his discussions with the prosecutors and also in public, issuing
the "scapegoat" statement. Before that, the impression
he gave of Haldeman was of a "great devoted public servant,"
clean and hard working. He had been restrained in his
praise of Ehrlichman.

- 23 -

Segretti's diaries 4/ show violations of § 612 and possibly § 241 and § 242.

Dean says LaRue was working on some deal with Tom Pappas. 5/

b. Procedural matters:

The meeting broke up in the early hours of the 3rd and was resumed again that night.

15. On May 3, Dean began focusing on Presidential involvement, thus changing dramatically from his previous stance. Glanzer and Campbell agree with Silbert's account of Dean's statements about the President. (See Rient and Denny memo to files dated September 6, 1973 re Silbert interview.) Glanzer and Campbell say, however, that Dean told them that Krogh told him about the instructions for the Ellsberg break-in coming from the Oval office at the

_____

4/ Glanzer's notes add that O'Brien was the one who brought the diaries in.

5/ Campbell's notes indicate the following items were also discussed: the August 29, 1972, Presidential announcement of Dean's investigation (Glanzer puts this on May 3rd) and the President's urging on April 17, 1973 that no White House aides receive immunity. Glanzer's notes add that (1) Strachan's testimony was worked on by Haldeman and Higby, (2) Sloan came to Ehrlichman about the pressure being applied to him (Sloan), and (3) that Dean thought Mitchell had already committed perjury. Glanzer's and Campbell's notes both indicate that it was June 21 that Ehrlichman gave Dean the order to "deep six" material from Hunt's safe.

APPENDIX P

Denny handwritten notes of October 10, 1973, noting that Glanzer's and Campbell's statement that Dean had indicated to them that "H was clean and E's involvement was restrained"

Discussed at p. 171 in text

10/10/73 Rient - Denny meeting with Glanzer & Campbell
Glanzer's office
10:00 A.M. - Noon

5/2 - 5/3   Silbert, Glanzer & Campbell meeting with Dean & Shaffer -

Situation in state of flux because of Senate Committee - Cox after 4/15. Dean becomes antagonistic to E + H, whereas before he had given impression that H was clean + was restrained as to E's involvement. This was around time of "scapegoat" statement by Dean.

4/29 - Shaffer called G from NY to say Colson had info on H + E which would corroborate Dean.

5/2 - prosecutors told Dean he wouldn't get immunity. Note-taking by Glanzer + Campbell.

Dean plays Colson- Hunt dictabelt

Discussion of listening to Dean re Pres. involvement, executive privilege, attorney - client privilege. Prosecutors told Dean that was his decision, they would listen to whatever he had to say.

Told of seeing H after 2/4/72 meeting.

Told of WH pressure on his sec'y, Jane Thomas to provide info re Dean.

Told of Operation Sandwedge with overt - covert aspects including electronic surveillance. Said Operation was forwarded to E in written form. Caulfield took files when C left WH, but that copy should be at WH. Sandwedge had a budget.

Colson called Caulfield at one point to do "bag jobs" on Brookings - didn't mention anything about fire at Brookings.

"Tony", a friend of Caulfield, was supposed to price a boat for WH - describing U's discreet errands.

Pre- 6/17/72 Gemstone summaries went to Strachan + that after 6/17 Strachan told him intelligence material in files had been pulled at H's instruction. Said H's files included meeting between H, S, and Kalmbach about financing.

Taped Segretti interview - later played it for E + H at Camp David on 11/15 at meeting re Chapin's future. Also said he played tape

APPENDIX Q

Watergate-Related Appeals, showing that all twelve appeals from Judge Sirica's Watergate trials were heard en banc from the very outset, but not one of Judge Gesell's four Watergate criminal trials was heard in the same manner

Discussed at p. 203 in text

I. APPEALS OF CASES SEEKING ACCESS TO THE NIXON TAPES

1. *Nixon v. Sirica*, 487 F.2d 700 (D.C. Cir. 1973), http://openjurist. org/487/f2d/700/nixon-v-j-sirica-united-states.

Upheld the Watergate grand jury subpoena for the original nine tapes, which Judge Sirica had ordered enforced.

Argued September 11, 1973; decided October 12, 1973. No appeal was sought before the Supreme Court.

Judges Bazelon, Wright, McGowan, Leventhal, Robinson, MacKinnon, and Wilkey, sitting en banc.

Per curiam decision, with separate dissents by MacKinnon and Wilkey.

2. *Senate Select Committee v. Nixon*, 498 F.2d 725 (D.C. Cir. 1974), http://openjurist.org/498/f2d/725/senate-select-committee-on-presidential-campaign-activities-v-m-nixon.

Upheld Judge Gesell's dismissal of the Ervin Committee's subpoena for White House tapes.

Argued April 2, 1974; decided May 23, 1974.

Judges Bazelon, Wright, McGowan, Leventhal, Robinson, MacKinnon, and Wilkey, sitting en banc.

Bazelon opinion; MacKinnon and Wilkey issued separate concurring opinions.

3. *United States v. Nixon*, 418 U.S. 683 (1974), http://caselaw.lp.findlaw. com/scripts/getcase.pl?court=us&vol=418&invol=683.

Upheld the special prosecutor's subpoena duces tecum for sixty-four additional White House tapes. This was heard as a direct appeal from Judge Sirica's ruling upholding the subpoena and ordering enforcement, which was heard by the Supreme Court on an expedited basis.

Argued July 8, 1974; decided July 24, 1974.

Justices Burger, Brennan, Douglas, Stewart, White, Marshall, Blackmun, and Powell. Justice Rehnquist did not participate. NB: The Supreme Court always sits en banc.

Burger opinion.

II. APPEALS FROM CRIMINAL CASES TRIED BEFORE JUDGE SIRICA

1. *Haldeman v. Sirica*, 501 F.2d 714 (D.C. Cir. 1974), *cert. denied*, 418 U.S. 955 (1974), http://openjurist.org/501/f2d/714/haldeman-v-j-sirica-c-strachan.

Upheld Judge Sirica's decision to transmit the Watergate grand jury's "Roadmap" to the House of Representatives.

Argued March 21, 1974; decided March 21, 1974, as amended March 27, 1974.

Judges Bazelon, Wright, McGowan, Leventhal, Robinson, and MacKinnon, sitting en banc.

Unsigned order; dissent filed by MacKinnon.

2. *Mitchell v. Sirica*, 502 F.2d 375 (D.C. Cir. 1974), *cert. denied*, 418 U.S. 955 (1974), https://bulk.resource.org/courts.gov/c/F2/502/502. F2d.375.74-1492.html.

Denial of petition for a writ of mandamus ordering Judge Sirica to disqualify himself from further involvement in the cover-up case.

Single-sentence order issued on June 7, 1974, as amended on July 9, 1974.

Judges Bazelon, Wright, McGowan, Leventhal, Robinson, and MacKinnon, sitting en banc.

One-sentence per curiam order denying petition, without opportunity for oral argument; lengthy dissent filed by MacKinnon on July 9, 1974.

3. *In re Liddy*, 506 F.2d 1293 (D.C. Cir. 1974), https://bulk.resource. org/courts.gov/c/F2/506/506.F2d.1293.73-1562.html.

Upheld Judge Sirica's contempt order against Gordon Liddy for refusing to testify before the grand jury after he had been granted immunity from further prosecution following his conviction in the break-in trial.

Argued June 14, 1974; decided October 10, 1974.

Judges Bazelon, Wright, McGowan, Leventhal, Robinson, MacKinnon, and Wilkey, sitting en banc.

Wilkey opinion.

4. *United States v. Liddy*, 509 F.2d 428 (D.C. Cir. 1974), *cert. denied*, 420 U.S. 980 (1975), http://law.justia.com/cases/federal/appellate-courts/F2/509/428/222697/.

Denied Liddy's appeal of his conviction in the break-in case on the grounds of Sirica's alleged misconduct during the trial.

Argued June 14, 1974; decided November 8, 1974.

Judges Bazelon, Wright, McGowan, Leventhal, Robinson, MacKinnon, and Wilkey, sitting en banc.

Leventhal opinion.

5. *United States v. Liddy*, 510 F.2d 669 (D.C. Cir. 1974), *cert. denied* 420 U.S. 980 (1975), https://bulk.resource.org/courts.gov/c/ F2/510/510.F2d.669.73—1564.html.

Denied Liddy's appeal of a contempt sentence that was added to his existing sentence, which he had already had begun to serve.

Argued June 14, 1974; decided December 12, 1974.

Judges Bazelon, Wright, McGowan, Leventhal, Robinson, MacKinnon, and Wilkey, sitting en banc.

Wilkey opinion, with separate MacKinnon dissent.

6. *United States v. McCord*, 509 F.2d 334 (D.C. Cir. 1974), *cert. denied,* 420 U.S. 911 (1975), http://openjurist.org/509/f2d/334/united-states-v-w-mccord-j-j.

Upheld James McCord's conviction in the break-in case, which McCord was challenging in light of disclosure of the cover-up.

Argued June 14, 1974; decided December 12, 1974.

Judges Bazelon, Wright, McGowan, Leventhal, Robinson, MacKinnon, and Wilkey, sitting en banc.

Bazelon opinion, with MacKinnon filing a separate concurrence.

7. *United States v. Hunt*, 514 F.2d 270 (D.C. Cir. 1974), https://bulk. resource.org/courts.gov/c/F2/514/514.F2d.270.73-2199.html.

Upheld Judge Sirica's denial of Howard Hunt's effort to withdraw his original guilty plea in the break-in case.

Argued June 14, 1974; decided February 25, 1975.

Bazelon, Wright, McGowan, Leventhal, Robinson, MacKinnon, and Wilkey, sitting en banc.

Per curiam decision; MacKinnon and Wilkey filed separate concurrences.

8. *United States v. Barker*, 514 F.2d 508 (D.C. Cir. 1975), *cert. denied,* 421 U.S. 1013 (1975).

Upheld Sirica's denial of the Cubans' effort to withdraw their original guilty pleas in the break-in case.

Argued June 14, 1974; decided February 25, 1975.

Judges Bazelon, Wright, McGowan, Leventhal, Robinson, MacKinnon, and Wilkey, sitting en banc.

Wright opinion, separate concurring opinion by Bazelon. Mackinnon and Wilkey dissented.

9. *Ehrlichman v. Sirica*, [citation not available], *cert denied*, 419 U.S. 1310 (1974), https://bulk.resource.org/courts.gov/c/US/419/419.US.1310.html.

Denied Ehrlichman's application for a stay of the cover-up trial until January 1975 in light of Nixon's resignation and Ford's pardon.

Chief Justice Warren Burger, sitting as circuit justice, issued an opinion on August 28, 1974, denying Ehrlichman's appeal from the circuit court's decision. His opinion states in pertinent part: "That court [D.C. Circuit], sitting *en banc*, did not rule directly on the petition, but instead remanded and recommended that the District Judge consider delaying the trial three or four weeks...." One of Burger's stated reasons for not "second guessing" the circuit court was that it had heard the case en banc.

10. *Haldeman v. Sirica* [citation not available], *cert. denied*, 419 U.S. 997 (1974).

Denied Haldeman's application for a stay of the cover-up trial until a hearing could be held on his claim that his indictment was flawed because the grand jury's term had been improperly extended.

As with the case above, there is no recorded decision at the circuit court level, but certiorari was denied on November 11, 1974. Here there is no express indication of whether the circuit court had sat en banc, but it is safe to assume that it did so.

11. *United States v. Mardian*, 546 F.2d 973 (D.C. Cir. 1976), https://bulk.resource.org/courts.gov/c/F2/546/546.F2d.973.75-1383.html.

Reversed Robert Mardian's conviction in the cover-up case because his case was not severed when his lawyer became ill during trial.

Argued January 6, 1976; decided October 12, 1976.

Judges Bazelon, Wright, McGowan, Robinson, and MacKinnon, sitting en banc.

Wright opinion. NB: This is the only reversal of the twelve appeals from Judge Sirica's Watergate-related criminal cases.

12. *United States v. Haldeman*, 559 F.2d 31 (D.C. Cir. 1976), *cert. denied*, 431 U.S. 933 (1977), https://bulk.resource.org/courts.gov/c/ F2/559/559.F2d.31.6.8.12.23.75-1384.html.

Upheld the cover-up convictions of Haldeman, Ehrlichman, and Mitchell.

Argued January 6, 1976; decided October 12, 1976. Rehearing denied December 8, 1976.

Judges Bazelon, Wright, McGowan, Leventhal, Robinson, and MacKinnon, sitting en banc.

Per curiam decision, with blistering dissent by MacKinnon.

III. APPEALS FROM CRIMINAL CASES TRIED BEFORE JUDGE GESELL

1. *United States v. Chapin*, 515 F.2d 1274 (D.C. Cir. 1975), https:// bulk.resource.org/courts.gov/c/F2/515/515.F2d.1274.74-1648.html.

Denied Dwight Chapin's appeal of his conviction for perjury in trial before Judge Gesell.

Argued February 7, 1975; decided July 14, 1975.

Judges Wright, Leventhal, and Davis (of U.S. Court of Claims, sitting by designation).

Davis opinion.

2. *United States v. Ehrlichman*, 546 F.2d 910 (D.C. Cir. 1976), *cert. denied*, 429 U.S. 1120 (1977), https://bulk.resource.org/courts.gov/c/ F2/546/546.F2d.910.74-1882.html.

Upheld Ehrlichman's conviction on all counts in the Plumbers trial before Judge Gesell.

Argued June 18, 1975; decided May 17, 1976.

Judges Leventhal, Wilkey, and Merhige (U.S. District Judge from the Eastern District of Virginia, sitting by designation).

Wilkey opinion.

3. *United States v. Barker*, 546 F.2d 940 (D.C. Cir. 1975), https://bulk.resource.org/courts.gov/c/F2/546/546.F2d.940.74-1884.74-1883.html.

Reversed the convictions in the Plumbers case on the grounds that the Cuban defendants had not been allowed to raise the defense of good faith reliance on national security.

Argued June 18, 1975; decided May 17, 1976.

Judges Leventhal, Wilkey, and Merhige (U.S. District Judge from the Eastern District of Virginia, sitting by designation).

Wilkey opinion, with Leventhal filing a dissent.

4. *United States v. Liddy*, 542 F.2d 76 (D.C. Cir 1976), http://law.justia.com/cases/federal/appellate-courtsF2/542/76/25255/

Upheld Liddy's conviction in the Plumbers case.

Argued June 18, 1975; decided May 17, 1976.

Judges Leventhal, Wilkey, and Merhige (U.S. District Judge from the Eastern District of Virginia, sitting by designation).

Merhige opinion.

ACKNOWLEDGMENTS

Many thanks are due to my agent, Jane Dystel, who guided me through the trials and tribulations of a budding author, and to John Jenkins, who recommended her. Jane's strict discipline and candid advice has been essential to getting my work into print.

Also essential were the contributions from the fine folks at Regnery Publishing: Alex Novak, my publisher, for his faith in me and in my story; Tom Spence, my editor, who took none of my assertions for granted and greatly helped in clarifying my somewhat dense professional jargon; and Patricia Jackson and Mark Bloomfield, who helped introduce my book to the market.

Wally Johnson, a former colleague, is a trusted friend whose experience as a federal prosecutor, Senate Judiciary staffer, White House aide, and assistant attorney general was a constant resource and extraordinary help in making sense of my archival discoveries. Without his insights and guidance, my narrative would not be nearly as thoughtful or precise.

I'm also grateful for the invaluable comments from my former colleagues on the Nixon White House staff, particularly those who read my manuscript in one of its many drafts: Jim Cavanaugh, Dwight Chapin, Frank Gannon, Tod Hullin, Ken Khachigian, and Bill Kilberg, as well as several members of the federal judiciary, who have asked to remain unidentified.

While I did all of my own research (and thus any errors are mine and mine alone), I do want to recognize the continuing courtesy of the National Archives staff, particularly David Paynter in the Special Access Section, who has responded to my many document requests over the past decade.

Finally, I would like to thank my loving wife and two sons, Saundra, Jon, and Will, who have had to put up with my life-long Watergate obsession and those many times when I would lose myself in the painful memories of that scandal's unfolding.

NOTES

CHAPTER ONE: IDENTIFYING THE REAL WRONGDOING

1. Carl Sagan, *The Demon-Haunted World: Science as a Candle in the Dark* (New York: Random House, 1996).
2. See http://www.napoleon.org/en/essential_napoleon/key_painting/files/ prudhon_vengeance.asp for a copy of the painting. An earlier rendition of this painting hangs in the Getty Museum in Los Angeles.
3. The phrase seems to originate in Pericles's funeral oration, as recorded by Thucydides in his history of the Peloponnesian War: "But our laws secure equal justice for all in their private disputes...."
4. A full accounting of the far-reaching scope of the investigations conducted by its task forces is set forth in the Report of the Watergate Special Prosecution Force, dated October 1975.

CHAPTER TWO: UNDERSTANDING WATERGATE

1. Judge Sirica's papers are at the Library of Congress. All have been opened, except those classified for national security purposes, which do not seem relevant to this book's disclosures.

2. Judge Bazelon's papers are at the Biddle Law Library of the University of Pennsylvania Law School. They were expressly sealed until after his death, but do not seem to contain any dramatic revelations.

3. Professor Cox's papers are at the Harvard Law School Library in the Special Collections section, along with those of fellow professor and WSPF prosecutor James Vorenberg.

4. Leon Jaworski's papers were given to his alma mater, Baylor University. In 2012, the National Archives retrieved from that collection the WSPF papers that were made available to me in mid-2013 in response to a FOIA request.

5. John Dean is still in possession of all of his own papers, but the WSPF files on him are available in the Special Access section of Archives II in College Park, Maryland.

6. John Prodos, *Vietnam: The History of an Unwinnable War (1945–1975)* (Lawrence, KS: University Press of Kansas). An internet search for "Cable 243" will supply the background of the specific cable that Hunt may have been trying to reconstruct.

7. John Dean, *The Nixon Defense: What He Knew and When He Knew It* (New York: Penguin Viking, 2014), Appendix A.

8. Final Report of the Senate Select Committee to Study Governmental Operations with Respect to Intelligence Activities (Church Committee), Book II, *The Growth of Domestic Intelligence, 1936–1976.*

9. Dean, *The Nixon Defense,* footnote at pp. 55–56: "In short, the smoking gun was only firing blanks." See also my two essays on the smoking gun at http://geoffshepard.com/essays.html.

10. William Merrill, *Watergate Prosecutor* (East Lansing, MI: Michigan State University Press, 2008), 7.

11. The president was justifying his decision to send his colleagues before the Ervin Committee without a claim of executive privilege, emphasizing that each man would have to decide how to testify in his own self-interest. They could stonewall, invoke the Fifth Amendment, or cover up if doing

so would save them. This reading is far more consistent with the remainder of their taped conversation.

CHAPTER THREE: WHAT WENT WRONG

1. The Ervin Committee investigatory papers (apart from its public hearings and published report) were sealed for fifty years, a standard practice for investigatory committees, and won't become available until 2024.

2. All of WSPF papers in possession of National Archives are in the Special Access section of Archives II in College Park, Maryland. They are opened only in response to specific requests under the Freedom of Information Act, after review and redacting of names of unindicted people who are still living. Once reviewed, however, such papers are open to all researchers.

3. Richard Ben-Veniste and George Frampton, *Stonewall: The Real Story of the Watergate Prosecution* (New York: Simon and Schuster, 1977), 35.

4. Like those of the Ervin Committee, HJC investigatory papers are sealed until 2024.

5. The study only became public when it was published in book form. See C. Vann Woodward, editor, *Responses of the President to Charges of Misconduct* (New York: Delacorte Press, 1974). Professor Woodward's papers are at the Yale University Library Center.

6. Renata Adler, *Canaries in the Mineshaft* (New York: St. Martin's Press, 2001), 35–36.

7. See Max Holland, *Leak: Why Mark Felt Became Deep Throat* (Lawrence, KS: University Press of Kansas, 2012).

8. See Jeff Himmelman, *Yours in Truth: A Personal Portrait of Ben Bradlee* (New York: Random House, 2012).

9. All papers of special and independent prosecutors in the possession of the National Archives are maintained in the Special Access Section of Archives II in College Park, Maryland, and are accessible under the same restrictions as with WSPF papers.

10. John Dean, *The Nixon Defense: What He Knew and When He Knew It* (New York: Penguin Viking, 2014), 8, 288, and 591.

11. Ibid., footnote at 312.

12.   Ibid., 95, 119, 421 and 593.

13.   Ibid., 193, 203, 267, 282 and 421.

14.   Ibid., 232–36, 270, 280, 286, and 306.

15.   Ibid., 105–6.

16.   Ibid., 209.

17.   Max Holland, "Naftali Reconsidered," *Washington Decoded*, June 11, 2014. http://www.washingtondecoded.com/site/2014/06/naftali.html.

18.   Dean, *The Nixon Defense*, 20.

19.   Ibid., 253.

20.   Ibid., 55–56. Dean's explanation is still incomplete. The effort was to prevent FBI interviews of apparent campaign contributions by Ken Dahlberg and Manuel Ogarrio, who were really acting as conduits for contributions from prominent Democrats, including Dwayne Andreas and a group of Texas oil and gas producers.

21.   A much more detailed review of the background of the smoking gun conversation is on my website, "Smoking Gun Explored," at http://geoffshepard.com/essays.html.

22.   Bradlee's unpublished 1990 interview, as cited in Himmelman, *Yours in Truth*, 212.

23.   *Estes v. Texas*, 381 U.S. 532 (1965).

24.   *Shaughnessy v. United States ex rel Mezei*, 345 U.S. 206, 225 (1953), Jackson, J., dissenting.

25.   Adversary System, the Free Dictionary by Farley, http://legal-dictionary.thefreedictionary.com/Adversary+System.

26.   See Judicial Code of Conduct for United States Judges, as promulgated by the Judicial Conference of the United States, http://www.uscourts.gov/uscourts/RulesAndPolicies/conduct/Vol02A-Ch02.pdf.

27.   Ibid., emphasis added.

28.   Ibid.

29.   See D.C. Bar Association, Code of Professional Ethics. http://www.dcbar.org/for_lawyers/ethics/legal_ethics/rules_of_professional_conduct/amended_rules/index.cfm.

CHAPTER FOUR: THE SECRET MEETINGS BETWEEN JUDGES AND WATERGATE PROSECUTORS

1.   Carr went on to become special assistant to Attorney General Edward Levy in 1975–1976 and, ultimately, a partner in the D.C. office of Morrison & Foerster. He wrote a law review article lauding Levi's tenure: *In Honor of Edward H. Levi, Mr. Levi at Justice*, 52 U. Chicago L. Rev. 300 (1985). In 1991 Carr served on an ABA special committee on amicus curiae briefs that was chaired by Philip Lacovara, former counsel to the Watergate special prosecutor. One can only wonder if they appreciated their earlier connection.

2.   Woodward's papers are at the Harry Ransom Center at the University of Texas at Austin. See File 6, Jaworski I, 2–4 p.m. 12/5; his office. The top page of Woodward's typed notes from his interview is reproduced as Appendix B. In the second paragraph of that page, Woodward records that Jaworski said that the House Judiciary Committee "was 'very slow' getting started…and would never have gotten off the ground without the info provided by [the special prosecutor's office]." In Jaworski's mind, it was the WSPF that got Nixon. Without its help, the Judiciary Committee would have floundered.

3.   See Jaworski and Ben-Veniste in Annotated Bibliography.

4.   See *Senate Select Committee v. Nixon*, 498 F2d 725 (D.C. Cir. 1974).

5.   Leon Jaworski, *The Right and the Power: The Prosecution of Watergate* (New York: Reader's Digest Press, 1977), 103.

6.   William Merrill, *Watergate Prosecutor* (East Lansing: Michigan State University Press, 2008), 69–70.

7.   Leon Jaworski, *Crossroads* (Colorado Springs: David C. Cook Publishing Co., 1981), 206.

CHAPTER FIVE: STAFFING THE NIXON IMPEACHMENT

1.   See Senate Select Committee to Study Government Operations with respect to Intelligence Activities. Book II, *The Growth of Domestic Intelligence: 1936 to 1976*. Government Printing Office (1976). It is also available at http://www.aarclibrary.org/publib/contents/church/contents_church_reports_book2.htm.

2. Leon Jaworski, *The Right and the Power: The Prosecutions of Watergate* (New York: Reader's Digest Press, 1977), 45.

3. Frampton may not have been the ideal choice for someone to author such important documents, since he lacked any prosecutorial experience. According to the dust jacket of his 1977 book with Richard Ben-Veniste, "He was working as a public interest lawyer in June 1973 when his former professor Archibald Cox asked him to join the Watergate prosecution team a few days after it was set up."

4. Memo of January 3, 1974, from Peter Rient to Philip Lacovara, "Hypothetical Conspiracy Case," 3 (included as a part of Appendix I).

5. James S. Doyle, *Not Above the Law* (New York: Morrow, 1977), 284.

6. Ibid., 285.

7. Richard Ben-Veniste and George Frampton, *Stonewall: The Real Story of the Watergate Prosecution* (New York: Simon and Schuster, 1977), 222.

8. Ibid., 241–42, emphasis in original.

9. See Jerry Zeifman, *Without Honor: The Impeachment of Richard Nixon and the Crimes of Camelot* (New York: Thunder's Mouth Press, 1995).

10. Ben-Veniste and Frampton, *Stonewall*, 217, emphasis in original.

11. Jaworski, *The Right and the Power*, 103.

12. *Haldeman v Sirica*, 501 F2d 714 (D.C. Cir. 1974).

13. Doyle, *Not Above the Law*, 290–91.

14. A Brian Lapping Associates Production for The Discovery Channel and BBC (1994), vol. 3: *The Fall of a President*.

15. Ben-Veniste and Frampton, *Stonewall*, 285–87.

16. Ben-Veniste and Frampton, *Stonewall*, 286.

17. The Frampton revision is too long to reproduce in full, but is available upon request from the Special Access section of the National Archives.

18. Ben-Veniste and Frampton, *Stonewall*, 287.

19. Haldeman's telephone records did confirm a nine-minute call to Mitchell's offices shortly after the meeting with Nixon and Dean. Both Haldeman and Mitchell testified the only purpose of the call was to invite Mitchell to meet with the president the following day. Of course, WSPF prosecutors insisted upon another interpretation.

20. "Dean's Anticipated Trial Testimony—From the Beginning Up Until March 21, 1974," dated July 22, 1974, by George Frampton, 69.

21. "John Dean, Sequence of Testimony," undated, at 44.

22. Ervin Committee Hearings, 997–99.

23. Trial Transcript, 2364.

24. Trial Transcript, 6726–28.

25. Trial Transcript, 6785.

CHAPTER SIX: A FAIR AND IMPARTIAL TRIAL JUDGE

1. Renata Adler, *Canaries in the Mineshaft: Essays on Politics and the Media* (New York: St. Martin's Press, 2001), 366–67.

2. A more recent review of the nature and extent of Sirica's due process violations in the Watergate break-in trial was authored by Anthony Gaughan, now a professor at Drake Law School. See *Watergate, Judge Sirica and the Rule of Law*, 42 McGeorge L. Rev. 343, 2010–2011.

3. Williams's papers are in the Library of Congress.

4. Robert Pack, *Edward Bennett Williams for the Defense* (New York: Harper & Row, 1983).

5. Ibid., 126.

6. Evan Thomas, *The Man to See: Edward Bennett Williams, Ultimate Insider, Legendary Trial Lawyer* (New York: Simon and Schuster, 1991), 277.

7. John J. Sirica, *To Set the Record Straight: The Break-in, the Tapes, the Conspirators, the Pardon* (New York: Norton, 1979), 54–55.

8. G. Gordon Liddy, *Will: The Autobiography of G. Gordon Liddy* (New York: St. Martin's, 1980), 282.

9. Pack, *Edward Bennett Williams for the Defense*, 18, citing Bernstein, 225–27.

10. Jeff Himmelman, "The Red Flag in the Flowerpot," *New York Magazine*, http://nymag.com/news/features/ben-bradlee-2012-5/.

11. Jeff Himmelman, *Yours in Truth: A Personal Portrait of Ben Bradlee* (New York: Random House, 2012), 204.

12. The book has an interesting history. Supposedly, the young reporters were waiting for a resolution of the Watergate scandal to write their book. They were approached by Robert Redford, who wanted to do a movie

on their roles, however, and were urged to produce a book rather quickly—focusing on themselves and their roles in ending the cover-up—which Redford felt was needed in advance of his proposed movie. The book, and subsequent movie, created the idea of investigative reporters as individual heroes and changed forever the relative obscurity of the Washington press corps.

13. Himmelman, *Yours in Truth*, 202.

14. Carl Bernstein and Bob Woodward, *All the President's Men* (New York: Simon and Schuster, 1974), 211–13.

15. Ben Bradlee, for example, later admitted in an unpublished interview that he harbored serious doubts about Deep Throat and many of the specifics of Woodward's reporting. Jeff Himmelman devotes two chapters in his book to this, as well as to Woodward's reactions in attempting to prevent Bradlee's doubts from being disclosed. See Doubt (Part One) and Doubt (Part Two), Himmelman, *Yours in Truth*, 211–31.

16. Himmelman, *Yours in Truth*, 210.

17. When Himmelman's story first broke in 2012, the then chief judge of the D.C. District Court, Royce Lamberth, was petitioned to request an investigation into the grand juror interview incident, from which we might have learned even more about the breach of the Watergate grand jury, but that motion ultimately was rejected. See *In Re Petition of Luke Nichter*, Misc. 12-74, particularly Letter of Luke Nichter, filed June 13, 2012, and subsequent Order of Judge Lamberth, dated November 2, 2012.

18. Many of Clark Mollenhoff's papers are in the Special Collections Department of Iowa State University.

19. Clark Mollenhoff, *Game Plan for Disaster: An Ombudsman's Report on the Nixon Years* (New York: Norton, 1976), 349.

20. Ibid., 289–90.

21. Ibid., 249.

22. Ibid., 250.

23. Ibid., 250.

24. Clark Mollenhoff, *Investigative Reporting* (New York: Macmillian, 1981), "Watergate and the Aftermath," 337–38.

25. Mollenhoff, *Game Plan for Disaster*, 251.

26. Ibid., 253.

27. Email of April 24, 2014, to the author from Michel Gardner, former president of the *Des Moines Register*. See also Michael Gartner's memories of the *Des Moines Register*: http://www.dmcityview.com/cover-story/2013/05/29/michael-gartners-memories-of-715-locust-street/.

28. Files from Silbert's Watergate investigations are a part of the Watergate Special Prosecution Force files in the Special Access Section of Archives II in College Park, Maryland.

29. Sirica, *To Set the Record Straight*, 38.

30. Samuel Dash's papers, other than those sealed as a part of the Ervin Committee, are in the Library of Congress.

31. Samuel Dash, *Chief Counsel: Inside the Ervin Committee—The Untold Story of Watergate* (New York: Random House, 1976), 26.

32. Ibid., 26.

33. Ibid., 26.

34. Ibid., 26–27.

35. Ibid., 27.

36. Archibald Cox letter to Charles Shaffer, Dean's criminal defense counsel, dated October 18, 1973.

37. *Watergate: Chronology of a Crisis* (Washington, DC: Congressional Quarterly, 1975), 616, "Transcripts of 46 Tapes (May 4, 1974)."

38. John Dean, *Blind Ambition* (New York: Simon and Schuster, 1976), 358.

39. Sirica, *To Set the Record Straight*, 270–71.

40. Dean, *Blind Ambition*, 355.

41. Ibid., 384–85.

42. Deposition of John Dean, *Dean v. St. Martin's Press*, January 22, 1996, 10.

43. Brian Lamb, January 29, 2004 interview of John Dean. See: http://www.c-spanvideo.org/videoLibrary/transcript/transcript.php?programid=154549.

44. Amy Goodman interview of April 7, 2004, with John Dean. See http://spymaster.tblog.com/post/142297.

45. Chapman University's *Panther* newspaper interview of January 29, 2012. Posted by staff contributor Taylor Johnson. See: http://www.thepantheronline.com/news/q-a-with-former-nixon-counsel-john-dean.

46. Excerpt from Dean's July 24, 1974, financial statement, from his sentencing file among Judge Sirica's papers in the Library of Congress.

The Bantam contract disclosure was an interesting finesse. Earlier, Sirica had banned activities by convicted Watergate defendants that might allow them to cash in on the notoriety stemming from the Watergate scandal, certainly including books. Thus, Dean describes these as "non-Watergate books," but no such books were ever forthcoming in this time frame. Dean's first and only book in the relevant time frame was *Blind Ambition*, published in 1979.

47.   Richard Ben-Veniste and George Frampton, *Stonewall: The Real Story of the Watergate Prosecution* (New York: Simon and Schuster, 1977), 107.

48.   Trial Transcript, 2499–2501.

49.   Ben-Veniste and Frampton, *Stonewall*, 343.

50.   Sirica, *To Set the Record Straight*, 270–71.

CHAPTER SEVEN: EVENHANDED, NONPARTISAN PROSECUTORS

1.   George V. Higgins, *The Friends of Richard Nixon* (Boston: Little, Brown and Co., 1975), 9–67.

2.   Geoff Shepard, *The Secret Plot to Make Ted Kennedy President: Inside the Real Watergate Cover-Up* (New York: Penguin Sentinel, 2008), chapters 11–14, 18–20.

3.   John A. Farrell, *Tip O'Neill and the Democratic Century* (Boston: Little, Brown and Co., 2001), 355.

4.   Judge Silberman was named Deputy Attorney General following the Saturday Night Massacre and served in that capacity through the end of the Nixon administration. He played a key role in holding the Department of Justice together as Watergate wound toward its conclusion.

5.   *In Re Sealed Case*, 838 F.2d 476 (1988). The Circuit Court's decision was reversed by the Supreme Court in *Morrison v Olson*, 487 U.S. 654 (1988), Justice Scalia dissenting, but Silberman's concerns have characterized the actions of a whole series of subsequent special prosecutors.

6.   Shepard, *The Secret Plot to Make Ted Kennedy President*, 138.

7.   Richard Ben-Veniste and George Frampton, *Stonewall: The Real Story of the Watergate Prosecution* (New York: Simon and Schuster, 1977), 107.

8. William J. Campbell, *Eliminate the Grand Jury*, 64 J. CRIM. L.&
    CRIMINOLOGY 174 (1973).

9. See In Re Petition of Geoff Shepard, DC Federal Court, Case 1:11-mc-
    00044 (RCL).

10. This analysis that follows is primarily taken from a loose leaf legal trea-
    tise by Professor Paul Marcus, first published by Mathew Bender in 1978
    and revised seven times since then.

11. 65 Geo. L. J. 970 (1976–1977). The article is also available online as a
    part of the Faculty Publications by William and Mary Law School, where
    professor Marcus presently teaches.

12. Richard Harris, Reflections, "The Watergate Prosecutions," *The New
    Yorker*, June 10, 1974, 60.

13. John Mitchell, H. R. Haldeman, John Ehrlichman, Charles Colson,
    Robert Mardian, Kenneth Parkinson, and Gordon Strachan.

14. Gray had secretly accepted possession of documents retrieved from
    Howard Hunt's safe, which he did not share with his agents and later
    destroyed. He also had lied about this on two occasions to Henry
    Petersen, the head of the Criminal Division. His actions came to light
    only when John Dean began his meetings with prosecutors to work out
    his own plea bargain. His exclusion was a judgment call by the Special
    Prosecutor. With the notable exceptions of John Mitchell and Robert
    Mardian, no one who had served in the Department of Justice was
    included in the cover-up indictment.

15. Of those not ultimately indicted, William Bittman was Howard Hunt's
    defense attorney, and Herbert Kalmbach was Nixon's personal attorney.
    Bittman was never charged; Kalmbach pleaded guilty to a campaign
    finance violation and became a witness for the government at the cover-
    up trial.

16. Bittman was quite a hero in Democratic circles, since he had obtained a
    conviction against Jimmy Hoffa in the Test Fleet pension-abuse case in
    Chicago in 1964 and had prosecuted Bobby Baker, Lyndon Johnson's
    secretary when he was majority leader of the Senate, without implicating
    Johnson himself.

17. It was learned later that Bittman had secreted a memo from Howard
    Hunt containing disclosure threats if money was not forthcoming, and

he again came under threat of indictment. Henry Ruth, having been named special prosecutor upon Jaworski's resignation, decided on July 3, 1975, not to indict, and Bittman again walked free.

18. Lacovara memo to Jaworski, "Status of Charles Colson in Watergate Case," February 22, 1974.

19. *Giglio v. United States*, 405 U.S. 150 (1972).

20. *United States v. Agurs*, 427 U.S. 97 (1976), 112–14.

21. *Agurs v United States*, 510 F2d 1249 (1975). Interestingly, Silbert was on the brief for the U.S. attorney's office and Chief Judge Bazelon was one of judges voting to overturn the murder conviction. He did not, however, write the opinion itself.

22. Ben-Veniste and Frampton, *Stonewall*, 106.

23. See "2 Sides Warned on Dean Debate," *Washington Star News*, February 15, 1974, A-4. Copy obtained from Jaworski's confidential Watergate files.

24. These files concerned what Mitchell later referred to as the White House Horrors and contained information regarding the Huston Plan, the Plumbers break-in, the NSC wiretaps, the Dairy Producers campaign contributions, and the Townhouse Project.

25. John Dean, *Blind Ambition* (New York: Simon and Schuster, 1976), 253.

26. This twenty-six-page memo was reproduced in full at Appendix U of Shepard's *The Secret Plot*; it is reproduced in part in Appendix O of this book.

27. Dean later claimed to have sought Haldeman out after his February 4, 1972, meeting in Attorney General Mitchell's office, where Liddy was describing his scaled-down campaign intelligence plan. The difficulty for WSPF prosecutors was that Dean did not make this assertion until May 2, after a full month of meetings with the career prosecutors. WSPF prosecutors later maintained that this meeting was when Dean had dropped out of the conspiracy to undertake the break-in.

28. Had Nixon ever been prosecuted, one can only imagine the devastating effect this notation (had it become public) would have had on Dean's witness credibility.

29. This is an apparent reference to the files Dean had taken from the counsel's office when he jumped ship.

30. James Neal memo to Larry Lason, "John Dean's Contacts and Information Imparted to the Original Prosecutors," October 2, 1974.

31. Trial Transcript, 2398–2399.

32. Trial Transcript, 2404.

33. *United States v Haldeman*, Brief for the Respondent, 251.

34. In 2003, Magruder suddenly, and for the first time, recalled overhearing a telephone call between Mitchell and President Nixon at this very meeting, wherein the president ordered Mitchell to approve Liddy's plan. *Salina Journal*, July 27, 2003, 1.

35. Among the many challenges faced by prosecutors was that Magruder's book, *An American Life: One Man's Road to Watergate*, had been published in 1974, well before the cover-up trial. It was thus important that his testimony not seriously contradict his published story. In his book, at page 210, Magruder denied that he had ordered Liddy's team back into the Watergate office building. Instead, Liddy had admitted that one of the bugs was not working and had stated that he would "get everything straightened out right away." Liddy's own book, published in 1980, strenuously contradicted Magruder's version.

36. Buzhardt repeated this conversation to me shortly after it occurred.

37. Dean, *Blind Ambition*, 359.

38. Lawyers cannot lead their witnesses on direct testimony. They are supposed to introduce general topics and let their witness respond accordingly. It is only on cross-examination that opposing counsel can ask leading or direct questions.

39. The abusive prosecutions of Perry and Walker are continuing as this book goes to press.

CHAPTER EIGHT: AN UNTAINTED AND UNBIASED JURY

1. John Dean, *Blind Ambition* (New York: Simon and Schuster, 1976), 377–78.

2. Bob Woodward and Scott Armstrong, *The Brethren: Inside the Supreme Court* (New York: Simon and Schuster, 1979), 234.

3. With more potential jurors dismissed for hardship than were in the pool to be further examined, the defense maintained on appeal—albeit in

vain—that the remaining jury pool was not representative of the community. See Mitchell appellate brief, 69.

4.   In fact, juror No. 6 admitted after her selection to having written several letters—one of which went to the Ervin Committee—decrying the moral tone of the United States and offering "Watergate" as an example of what was wrong with the country. Judge Sirica found her to be an interested student of Watergate, but refused to dismiss her from the jury. See Ehrlichman appellate brief, 74.

5.   Mitchell appellate brief, 116.

6.   The combination of the first and last procedural rules would have allowed the government to remove a neutral juror and replace him with what the defendants' felt was a decidedly pro-prosecution juror, so they did not exercise their final two challenges. See Mitchell appellate brief, 116–18.

7.   Richard Ben-Veniste and George Frampton, *Stonewall: The Real Story of the Watergate Prosecution* (New York: Simon and Schuster, 1977), 327.

8.   *United States v. Haldeman*, 559 F.2d 31 (1976), MacKinnon dissenting.

CHAPTER NINE: THE AUTOMATIC RIGHT TO AN APPEAL

1.   Kim Isaac Eisler, *A Justice for All: William J. Brennan and the Decisions that Transformed America* (New York: Simon and Schuster, 1982), 202–4.

2.   David Bazelon, *Questioning Authority: Justice and Criminal Law* (New York: Alfred A. Knopf, 1988), 139.

3.   The definitive article on the en banc procedure and the extreme rarity of its use was written by D.C. Circuit Court Judge Douglas Ginsburg, who went on to become that circuit's chief judge. See Douglas H. Ginsburg and Donald Falk, *The Court En Banc: 1981–1990*, 59 GEO. WASH. L. REV. 1008 (1991). Interestingly, Ginsburg's law school roommate was Ronald Carr.

4.   The one case that was reversed, *United States v. Mardian*, 546 F.2d 973 (1976), seems perfectly understandable. Mardian's lawyer fell ill less than two weeks into the trial, but Judge Sirica had demanded he continue to stand trial with the rest of the defendants. This was too much even for the liberal bloc, who reversed his conviction and remanded for a new trial.

But Mardian was small beer. A senior official at CRP, he was in on the cover-up from its outset but went home to California after only a month. The special prosecutor ultimately decided not to retry him at all.

5. The author believes this was the most critical effort by the defendants to assert their due process rights, not only because of the issues that were raised at the time, but because they clearly suspected there had been collusion between Judge Sirica and WSPF prosecutors. As such, the circumstances are worth close and careful examination.

6. George V. Higgins, *The Friends of Richard Nixon* (Boston: Little, Brown and Co., 1975), 255.

7. *Mitchell v. Sirica*, MacKinnon dissent.

8. *United States v. Liddy*, 509 F.2d 428 (D.C. Cir. 1974).

9. *United States v. Hunt*, 514 F.2d 270 (D.C. Cir. 1974).

10. *United States v. Barker*, 514 F.2d 508 (D.C. Cir. 1975).

11. *United States v. McCord*, 509 F.2d 334 (D.C. Cir. 1974).

12. I again refer readers to the excellent law review article by Professor Anthony Gaughan, cited in Chapter 6, that details the series of due process violations in the burglary trial: "Watergate, Judge Sirica and the Rule of Law," 42 McGeorge L. Rev. 343, 2010–2011.

13. *United States v. Haldeman*, 559 F.2d 31 (D.C. Cir. 1976).

14. *United States v. Haldeman*, cert. denied, 431 U.S. 933 (1977).

15. *Vanity Fair*, January 1992, http://www.bardachreports.com/articles/v_19920100.html.

CHAPTER TEN: SO WHAT?

1. Hamann, Jack, *On American Soil, How Justice Became a Casualty of World War II* (Chapel Hill, NC: Algonquin Books of Chapel Hill, 2005).

2. The district court's order that the special prosecutor's report be made public can be read at http://www.emptywheel.net/wp-content/uploads/2012/02/120208-Sullivan-Stevens-Order.pdf.

3. John A. Farrell, *Tip O'Neill and the Democratic Century* (Boston: Little, Brown and Company, 2001), chapter 14, "Watergate."

4. Taken from copy of NPR transcript contained in Jaworski's confidential Watergate files at Archives II.

ANNOTATED BIBLIOGRAPHY

FOR SERIOUS STUDENTS OF WATERGATE

There are hundreds of books about Watergate, but nothing published to date can be called objective. The intensity of the scandal's political nature prevents that—and new disclosures undermine previous analysis.

The full list of books that I own and consulted during the course of my research are listed on my website: http://geoffshepard.com/bibliography.html.

The following are the works that I found most helpful in filling out my own understanding of the Watergate scandal.

CHRONOLOGY OF PUBLIC DISCLOSURE

Watergate: Chronology of a Crisis. Congressional Quarterly (1975). Beginning with the Ervin Committee's formation, CQ issued a weekly compilation of Watergate's public developments, which continued through the cover-up verdicts. A true chronology, it is an ideal source for researching the unfolding of the scandal in real time. It thoroughly answers the question, "What did the public know and when did it know it?" The master index is an invaluable resource.

THE *REAL* HORROR STORY

Senate Select Committee to Study Government Operations with respect to Intelligence Activities. *Book II: The Growth of Domestic Intelligence, 1936 to 1976.* Government Printing Office (1976). One of the Watergate reform initiatives, the committee chaired by Senator Frank Church (D-Idaho), investigated governmental invasions of privacy stretching back four decades. If someone was labeled a "subversive"— whether a suspected German or Communist sympathizer, a civil rights agitator, or an opponent of the Vietnam War—his basic rights were shredded in the name of national security. The Church Committee's report, written by Democrats trying desperately to down play their own misdeeds, demonstrates the hypocrisy behind the prosecution of Ehrlichman for the Plumbers' break-in and of the Watergate prosecution as a whole. Here is a link to the electronic version: http://www.intelligence.senate.gov/pdfs94th/94755_II.pdf.

My own analysis of the committee's sworn testimony concerning FBI conduct in the Kennedy and Johnson administrations, as well as that testimony itself, is available at my website: http://geoffshepard.com/churchcommittee.html.

THE VICTORS

The victors and their progeny have had a field day writing self-congratulatory books. They also contain the most tantalizing admissions against interest, if read with a critical eye. (Arranged by date of publication).

Bernstein, Carl, and Bob Woodward. *All the President's Men.* New

York: Simon and Schuster, 1974.

Supposedly, Robert Redford approached these authors with the idea for a movie and urged them to do a book first about their roles as reporters. Interestingly, there is no indication in their book of where "Deep Throat" might be employed.

Sussman, Barry. *The Great Cover-up: Nixon and the Scandal of Watergate: The First Complete Account from Break-in to Resignation*. New York: Thomas Y. Crowell Company, 1974.

Sussman was Woodward and Bernstein's editor at the *Post* and played a huge role in the paper's Watergate coverage, but he was written out of *All the President's Men*. Fame can be fickle.

Bernstein, Carl, and Bob Woodward. *The Final Days*. New York: Simon and Schuster, 1976.

As became their habit, the authors tend to favor and protect their sources and punish those who decline to cooperate. As such, their rendition of the collapse of the Nixon presidency is rather biased and surprisingly uninformed.

Dean, John. *Blind Ambition*. New York: Simon and Schuster, 1976.

As the lead prosecution witness, Dean has been classified with the victors. In later depositions, Dean disowned much of this book's narrative and swore that it was an invention of his ghostwriter, Taylor Branch.

Dash, Samuel. *Chief Counsel: Inside the Ervin Committee—The Untold Story of Watergate*. New York: Random House, 1976.

Contains a lot of behind-the-scenes material on how the committee investigations were conducted. In later interviews, Dash bragged about having orchestrated the hearings and supplying questions to individual senators. In essence, the hearings were scripted for their TV audience.

Mollenhoff, Clark R. *Game Plan for Disaster: An Ombudsman's Report on the Nixon Years*. New York: Norton and Company, 1976.

Mollenhoff was ombudsman for ten months in the Nixon White House but left in frustration and became Nixon's fiercest journalistic critic. This is his dance on Nixon's grave.

All the President's Men: The Movie. Burbank, CA: Warner Bros., 1976.

Unlike the book, the movie strongly (and erroneously) indicates that "Deep Throat" was a member of Nixon's White House staff.

Ben-Veniste, Richard, and George Frampton Jr. *Stonewall: The Real Story of the Watergate Prosecution*. New York: Simon and Schuster, 1977.

The authors were members of the Watergate Task Force, who prosecuted the cover-up trial.

Doyle, James. *Not above the Law: The Battles of Watergate Prosecutors Cox and Jaworski*. New York: William Morrow and Company, 1977.

Doyle was director of media relations for the special prosecutor. Not being a lawyer, he makes a number of interesting disclosures, especially regarding how they worked the media—and used the media to work Jaworski.

Jaworski, Leon. *The Right and the Power: The Prosecutions of Watergate*. New York: Reader's Digest Press, 1977.

Jaworski replaced Cox as special prosecutor. One suspects the revealing memos in his confidential files were prepared in anticipation of writing this book.

Sirica, John J. *To Set the Record Straight: The Break-in, the Tapes, the Conspirators, the Pardon.* New York: W. W. Norton and Company, 1979.

Judge Sirica presided over both the burglary and the cover-up trials. His early drafts are a part of his papers at the Library of Congress.

Ervin Jr., Sam. *The Whole Truth: The Watergate Conspiracy.* New York: Random House, 1980.

Ervin chaired the Senate Watergate Committee but was eighty-four when this book was published. One can question whether he did much of its actual drafting.

Mollenhoff, Clark R. *Investigative Reporting.* New York: Macmilllan Publishing Co., 1981.

One can get a more complete picture of the role that Mollenhoff played in Watergate by combining this book's disclosures with those of his prior book. It also is instructive to compare his chapter on Nixon with the preceding one on Lyndon Johnson. One wonders just who was the bigger crook.

Eisler, Kim Isaac. *A Justice for All: William J. Brennan and the Decisions That Transformed America.* New York: Simon and Schuster, 1993.

A biased but interesting insider's view of Brennan's influence on Judge Bazelon and on the writing of the Supreme Court opinion in *United States v. Nixon.*

Brian Lapping Associates. *Watergate.* Volume One: *A Third-Rate Burglary*; Volume Two: *The Conspiracy Crumbles*; Volume Three: *The Fall of a President.*

Video series aired on the Discovery Channel and BBC (1994). Their interview of Dean's lawyer, Charles Shaffer, reveals his brilliant tactics in preparing his client for the Ervin Committee hearings.

Merrill, William H. *Watergate Prosecutor*. East Lansing, MI: Michigan State University Press, 2008.

The author headed the Plumbers Task Force. This slim volume, published posthumously, gushes with patriotic observations but also contains a whole series of admissions against interest that show how due process was denied in Ehrlichman's separate prosecution in the Plumbers trial.

Dean, John. *The Nixon Defense: What He Knew and When He Knew It*. New York: Penguin Viking, 2014.

This most recent of Dean's Watergate books is commented upon in Chapter 3.

THE VANQUISHED

Most of the major defendants, with the notable exception of John Mitchell, wrote their side of the Watergate story. In the intervening years, much of what they said has turned out to be true. (Arranged by date of publication.)

Magruder, Jeb Stuart. *An American Life: One Man's Road to Watergate*. New York: Athenaeum, 1974.

Since this book was published prior to the cover-up trial, it restricted Magruder's ability to alter his recollection of events to conform to some aspects of the government's case.

McCord Jr., James W. *A Piece of Tape: The Watergate Story: Fact and Fiction*. Rockville, MD: Washington Media Services, Ltd., 1974.

McCord remains an enigma. His actions and motivations figure prominently in the series of doubter books described in the next section.

Colson, Charles W. *Born Again.* Old Tappan, NJ: Chosen Books, 1976.

Colson was a controversial Nixon political operative. He was only tangentially involved in Watergate and yet was indicted in both the Plumbers and the cover-up cases. He may have been among the most wronged of the Watergate defendants. Prudently, he reached an early plea bargain and spared himself the terrors of actual trials.

Haldeman, H. R., with Joseph DiMona. *The Ends of Power.* New York: Times Books, 1978.

Haldeman insisted to the end that he had done nothing more than serve his president as chief of staff. One of the few non-lawyers involved in Watergate, he may never have realized the risks from his actions.

Nixon, Richard M. *The Memoirs of Richard Nixon.* New York: Grosset and Dunlap, 1978.

The former president's section on Watergate comes as close as could be to an admission of deliberate inattention, if not of actual wrongdoing.

Stans, Maurice H. *The Terrors of Justice.* New York: Everest House, 1978.

When the onslaught was over and the multitude of accusations against him turned out to be baseless, Stans asked (rhetorically) where he should go to get his reputation back.

Liddy, G. Gordon. *Will: The Autobiography of G. Gordon Liddy.* New York: St. Martin's Press, 1980.

While the moving party in most of the wrongdoing, Liddy refused to break his silence, becoming known as the Ironman of Watergate and serving the longest jail term of any defendant (over five years) before his sentence was commuted by President Carter.

Ehrlichman, John. *Witness to Power: The Nixon Years.* New York: Simon and Schuster, 1982.

Of the major Watergate defendants, Ehrlichman was the least involved and received the shabbiest treatment at the hands of the prosecutors. Although Nixon's counsel, the taping system was kept secret from him, for which he never forgave Haldeman or the president.

Haig Jr., Alexander M. *Inner Circles: How America Changed the World.* New York: Warner Books, 1992.

Haig replaced Haldeman as Nixon's chief of staff largely out of a sense of duty but was overwhelmed by the political onslaught the scandal had become.

Haldeman, H. R. *The Haldeman Diaries: Inside the Nixon White House.* New York: G. P. Putnam's Sons, 1994.

The posthumous publication of his secret diaries was criticized as the ultimate act of disloyalty at the time, but they show a candor and lack of criminal intent with regard to his Watergate involvement.

Gray III, L. Patrick, with Ed Gray. *In Nixon's Web: A Year in the Crosshairs of Watergate.* New York: Times Books, 2008.

This was also published posthumously but shows how Gray was totally out of his element as acting FBI director, never realizing that his deputy, Mark Felt ("Deep Throat"), was secretly undermining him at every opportunity.

Bork, Robert H. *Saving Justice: Watergate, the Saturday Night*

Massacre, and Other Adventures of a Solicitor General. New York: Encounter Books, 2013.

Bork lost any chance of being confirmed for the Supreme Court when he agreed to stop the carnage at the Department of Justice by firing Archibald Cox. He did it out of the most patriotic of motives but got "borked" for his good deed.

WATERGATE DOUBTERS

This series of books raises doubts about the accuracy of the conventional wisdom regarding the Watergate scandal. Interestingly, most were not written by Republican stalwarts but by authors and journalists who identified disturbing discrepancies. (Arranged by date of publication.)

Higgins, George V. *The Friends of Richard Nixon.* Boston: Little, Brown and Company, 1975.

Higgins is a former federal prosecutor who first wrote about the complete lack of due process at the Watergate trials.

Thompson, Fred D. *At That Point in Time: The Inside Story of the Senate Watergate Committee.* New York: Quadrangle/The New York Times Book Company, 1975.

Thompson was minority counsel to the Ervin Committee. His book is replete with stories of how Republican efforts to pursue alternative investigations were thwarted by the Democratic majority.

Hougan, Jim. *Secret Agenda: Watergate, Deep Throat and the CIA.* New York: Random House, 1984.

Hougan did the early and seminal work on highlighting all of the discrepancies in the stories of how the break-in occurred and was investigated in such a strange manner.

Colodny, Leonard, and R. Gettlin. *Silent Coup: The Removal of a President*. New York: St. Martin's Press, 1991.

Their book is really two separate stories. The first is how the military so distrusted Nixon and Kissinger that they set up a spy ring within the White House and may have conspired to facilitate Nixon's downfall. The second, the "Golden Boy" section, focuses on John Dean and his disturbing role in instigating Watergate events. Colodny's extensive research files, including taped interviews with dozens of key figures, recently have been donated to Texas A&M.

Zeifman, Jerry. *Without Honor: The Impeachment of Richard Nixon and the Crimes of Camelot*. New York: Thunder's Mouth Press, 1995.

Zeifman was majority counsel to the House Judiciary Committee and describes how the impeachment inquiry staff was taking secret direction from Kennedy administration stalwarts.

Rochvarg, Arnold. *Watergate Victory: Mardian's Appeal*. Lanham, MD: University Press of America, 1995.

Rochvarg was a summer law clerk for the law firm handling Robert Mardian's appeal from the cover-up trial. His description of how they argued and won a reversal of his conviction contains lots of good insights into the unfairness of Sirica's actions in the trial itself.

Adler, Renata. *Canaries in the Mineshaft: Essays on Politics and the Media*. New York: St. Martin's Press, 2001.

Adler was a member of the impeachment inquiry staff but is a contrarian and thus included in this section. Her first and last essays are of significant interest. "Searching for the Real Nixon Scandal," published in *The Atlantic* in 1976, questions the work of the House impeachment inquiry (of which she was a part). "A Court of No Appeal," published in *Harper's* in 2000, harshly criticizes Judge Sirica and his conduct of the Watergate trials.

Rosen, James. *The Strong Man: John Mitchell and the Secrets of Watergate*. New York: Doubleday, 2008.

Rosen spent seventeen years researching this excellent book about John Mitchell and defending his role in the Watergate scandal.

Shepard, Geoff. *The Secret Plot to Make Ted Kennedy President: Inside the Real Watergate Cover-up*. New York: Penguin Sentinel, 2008.

This is my first Watergate book and details how the scandal was so successfully exploited for political gain by Democrats who had served in the Kennedy administration and longed for a return to power.

Colodny, Leonard, and Tom Shachtman. *The Forty Years War*. New York: HarperCollins, 2009.

A sequel to *Silent Coup*, this book describes the continuing foreign affairs battles between the neocons and the realists.

Merritt, Robert, as told to Douglas Caddy. *Watergate Exposed: How the President of the United States and the Watergate Burglars Were Set Up*. Chicago: Trine Day LLC, 2011.

The author claims to have been a police informant and in possession of inside information with regard to the circumstances surrounding the Watergate burglary arrests. His co-author was their initial counsel. Much of the book strains credulity, but if even 10 percent of it is correct, it will dramatically affect views of the origins of the Watergate scandal.

Holland, Max. *Leak: Why Mark Felt Became Deep Throat*. Lawrence, KS: University Press of Kansas, 2012.

The author argues that Deputy FBI Director Mark Felt leaked information about the Watergate investigation to Bob Woodward not out of disinterested patriotism but in the hope of displacing the acting director of the FBI, Pat Gray. Felt's credibility should be evaluated in that context.

Himmelman, Jeff. *Yours in Truth: A Personal Portrait of Ben Bradlee.* New York: Random House, 2012.

In the course of researching a book about the *Washington Post*'s former executive editor, Himmelman came across evidence that documented Bernstein's grand juror interview, an infraction denied for the prior four decades. His courage in revealing these long-held secrets was denounced by his former friends and colleagues.

Stanford, Phil. *White House Call Girl.* Port Townsend, WA: Feral House, 2014.

This is a sequel to Colodny's "Golden Boy" section on John Dean. Stanford, an Oregon journalist, delightfully describes embarrassing associations of Dean and his wife and then documents his disclosures with the thoroughness of an academic paper.

Stone, Roger, and Mike Colapietro. *Nixon's Secrets: The Rise, Fall, and Untold Truth about the President, Watergate, and the Pardon.* New York: Skyhorse Publishing, 2014.

Stone, who worked at CRP and was close to Nixon in his later years, recaptures the good, the bad, and the ugly about what we now know (or suspect) about Nixon and Watergate.

INDEX